ENGLISH COUNTRY HOUSES

CAROLINE

1625-1685

Wilton House, Wiltshire. The Double Cube Room, by Inigo Jones and John Webb, c. 1650, *looking East.*

ENGLISH COUNTRY HOUSES

CAROLINE

1625-1685

OLIVER HILL
AND
JOHN CORNFORTH

ANTIQUE COLLECTORS' CLUB

© Country Life 1966
an imprint of Newnes Books
a division of Hamlyn Publishing Group Ltd.

World copyright reserved
ISBN 0 907462 78 2

First published in 1966 by Country Life Ltd.
This reprint published in 1985 for
the Antique Collectors' Club by
the Antique Collectors' Club Ltd.

British Library CIP Data

Hill, Oliver
English country houses: Caroline 1625-1685
1. Country homes — England — History
2. Architecture, Domestic — England — History
I. Title II. Cornforth, John   III. Hussey, Christopher
728.8'3'0942 NA7620

Printed in England by Antique Collectors' Club Ltd.,
Church Street, Woodbridge, Suffolk.

PREFACE

The volumes of *English Country Houses* so far published, surveying the years 1715–1840 (*Early*, *Mid* and *Late Georgian*), were written by Christopher Hussey, who is the editor of the series. A volume devoted to the Baroque period, 1685–1715, is projected.

The present volume covers the reign of Charles I, the Commonwealth, and the reign of Charles II. Although it was one of the most disrupted epochs of English history, the notable developments in domestic architecture produced perhaps the most characteristic type of English house. The evolution of this type, the Caroline house, gives the period a unity in the field of domestic architecture transcending its disruption on the political plane. Its beginning is marked by Inigo Jones's introduction of the Italian classical idiom, with his design for the Queen's House, Greenwich, in 1615. The consequences were revolutionary, but were limited by political events.

Had the ensuing catastrophe of Civil War not occurred, it can be supposed that the Caroline epoch would have produced an English classical architecture parallel to the contemporary French. The eclipse of Court and aristocracy substituted a specifically domestic basis for design, derived from the Protestant and republican Netherlands in place of the Catholic aristocracies, which was to persist for a generation. It was the fusion of these influences and requirements that produced the outstandingly satisfying synthesis definable as the Restoration, or Caroline, house.

Thus the Caroline period, although divided by events into three well-marked phases, constitutes a no less distinct unity. The rarity of references in this survey of its domestic architecture to Sir Christopher Wren may seem surprising, but is in accordance with the facts and draws attention to the reasons that led to the Caroline house being superseded. The outstanding figure of the period's final phase was almost exclusively a court and public architect. But it was the training in Wren's great undertakings of a school of adept executants that made possible the Whig aristocracy's realisation of the large-scale baroque projects which distinguish the ensuing period.

Acknowledgment by the authors is due in the first place to H. Avray Tipping's *English Homes*, Periods III (1558–1649) and IV (1649–1714), published half a century ago by *Country Life* and long out of print. Much new light has since been thrown on the age, notably in *The Life of Inigo Jones*, by J. A. Gotch; in R. T. Gunther's *The Architecture of Sir Roger Pratt*; H. M. Colvin's *Biographical Dictionary of English Architects*; Sir John Summerson's *Architecture in Britain*; Margaret Whinney and Oliver Millar's *English Art 1625–1714* and James Lees-Milne's *Age of Inigo Jones*. To these and to the descriptions of houses that have appeared in *Country Life* (by Christopher Hussey, Arthur Oswald, Mark Girouard and the late Gordon Nares) the authors are considerably indebted.

Thanks are specially due to the owners of houses that have been re-photographed, whose help has been indispensable. The photography for *Country Life* during the last few years has been undertaken by Mr Alex Starkey and Mr Jonathan Gibson.

Above all, we would like to express our great indebtedness to Christopher Hussey, the editor of the series, who has generously given us the benefit of his great experience and devoted much time and thought to the book's improvement.

CONTENTS

ACKNOWLEDGMENTS

The authors are indebted to the following owners of paintings, drawings, engravings and works of art for permission to reproduce them. This list does not include pictures, drawings or objects at the principal houses illustrated in the book.

The Duke of Norfolk, Fig. 2; R.I.B.A. Drawings Collection, Figs 3, 5, 6, 18, 48, 51, 65–8, 96, 135, 369; The Provost and Fellows of Worcester College, Oxford, Figs 9, 95, 118–21; The British Museum, Figs 29, 72, 151; Col E. R. Pratt, Figs 24, 416; Mr H. J. R. Bankes, Fig. 27; Nottingham Castle Museum, Fig. 32; Lord Sandys, Fig. 33; Marguerite, Lady Hastings, Fig. 34; The Metropolitan Museum of Art, Fig. 35; City of Norwich Museums, Fig. 41; The Marchioness of Cholmondeley, Fig. 40; The Duke of Beaufort, Fig. 50; The National Portrait Gallery, Figs 208, 417, 418; The Trustees of the Earl of Craven, Figs 224, 225; The Bodleian Library, Oxford, Figs 226–34, 236, 241–243, 245, 308, 310; Earl Spencer, Fig. 370; Miss Elizabeth Cartwright, Fig. 37a; Mr and Mrs Paul Mellon, Fig. 375; The Duke of Grafton, Fig. 386; R. W. Ketton-Cremer, Fig. 390; The Hon. R. W. Morgan-Grenville, Fig. 406; Mr J. C. F. Prideaux-Brune, Fig. 407; The Duke of Northumberland, Fig. 415.

Most of the photographs in the book are the copyright of *Country Life*, but the authors would like to acknowledge the following for additional photographs: Victoria and Albert Museum, Figs 1, 77–80, 82, 84–9, 115, 116; The Ministry of Public Building and Works (Crown Copyright), Figs 4, 53; The Courtauld Institute of Art, Figs 9, 99, 118–21; The National Monuments Record, Figs 14, 15, 220, 368, 381, 394, 412, 413; A. F. Kersting, Figs 17, 62, 64, 67, 404; Hallam Ashley, Figs 34, 390; The Survey of London, Fig. 60; Sydney Sabin, Fig. 375; Herbert Felton, Fig. 406. Fig. 132 is based on the plan in R. T. Gunther's *The Architecture of Sir Roger Pratt* (Oxford University Press); Fig. 152 on the plan in Nathaniel Lloyd's *A History of the English House* (Architectural Press); Fig. 197 on the plan in Belcher and Macartney's *Later Renaissance Architecture in England* (Batsford); Fig. 211 on the plan in Vernon J. Watney's *Cornbury and the Forest of Wychwood*.

1. *Bust of Charles II by Honoré Pelle, 1684.* (*Victoria and Albert Museum.*)

INTRODUCTION

I. CAROLINE SOCIETY AND THE COUNTRY HOUSE

'Everymans proper *Mansion* House and *Home*, being the *Theatre* of His *hospitality*, the Seate of *Selfe-fruition*, the *Comfortablest* of his owne *Life*; the *noblest* of his sonnes *Inheritance*, a kinde of private *Princedome* . . .'

Sir Henry Wotton,
The Elements of Architecture, 1624

Significantly, the broad sweep of Sir Henry Wotton's interpretation of the place held by the country house in the pattern of Caroline society transcends niceties of architectural style and ornament. The fundamental aspect of 'everyman's proper mansion house and home' was indeed to bear heavily on the aesthetic and technical, throughout the turmoils, transitions and disasters of the period covered by this volume. Yet Wotton was fully conscious that he wrote in the first years of an aesthetic revolution; a revolution that during the ensuing sixty years transformed the character of mansion and home. Initially the transformation reflected the standards of the European High Renaissance. But it was almost immediately complicated, and would soon be dominated by political, social and economic stresses which, exploding into civil war, were not wholly resolved until the second, bloodless, revolution of 1688. It is this interaction of political and aesthetic influences which is specifically characteristic of the period and gives it historical unity.

Wotton could not have foreseen this in the early 1620s, when the age of the prodigy-house was scarcely over. Such splendid mansions as Longleat, Burghley, Kirby and Hardwick were scarcely a generation old, and their great Jacobean successors, Theobalds, Audley End and Hatfield, no less dazzling and even larger, were hardly completed. To appreciate the social cause of the transformation it is necessary to recall the purpose of these fantastic mansions. Display and an intention to impress lay behind their conception, but even more important was the strong desire to honour the sovereign who might pay a visit. Elizabeth, and to a lesser extent James I and Charles I, expected during their spectacular progresses each summer to receive lavish entertainment from the aristocracy and gentry who lived along the route. Underlying this hospitality was the hope of receiving some benefit, perhaps a title, a grant of land, an office or pension, or at least the continuation of royal favour. In 1579, when the walls of Burghley and Holdenby were rising, Lord Burghley wrote to Hatton: 'God give us long life to enjoy her for whom we both meant to exceed our purses in these.' Royal favour was essential to advancement and to the maintenance of position — or as Francis Bacon put it: 'The rising into place is laborious; and by pains men come to greater pains . . . By indignities men come to dignities. The standing is slippery, and the regress is either a downfall, or at least an eclipse, which is a melancholy thing.'[1]

[1] Quoted in *The First Duke and Duchess of Newcastle-upon-Tyne* (1910), p. 33.

The remarks of Burghley and Bacon go a long way to explain the attitude to country house building in the early years of the 17th century, but it was one that was soon to change. The old aristocratic families were increasingly hard hit by the substantial rise in prices that had continued throughout the 16th century; and many had already spent heavily on building. James I, equally pinched by the economic situation, had proportionately less to offer them and tended to favour a different circle than the one that had benefited so richly from former church property at the Tudor court. Yet he was certainly more lavish with honours than Queen Elizabeth and created seven times as many peerages as she did.

The result of the changing scene at court was to convince courtiers that large-scale building was fast becoming a poor

2. *'The Father of Virtu in England'* — *Thomas Howard, Earl of Arundel, by Mytens,* c. 1615.

investment, so that in the 1620s and 30s ambitious schemes became increasingly rare. As the courtiers' attitude changed to the defensive, the support they would otherwise have given to the new architecture of the court prodigy Inigo Jones was limited or withheld. The outstanding exception was the rebuilding of Wilton House, Wiltshire, in the 1630s (p. 75), which, Aubrey records, was undertaken at the suggestion of Charles I. Yet it is not cynical to relate this to the fact of the Earl of Pembroke's income having been almost doubled by the profits and fees from his official appointments. In 1634 the Duke of Newcastle (as William Cavendish became in 1665) entertained the King and Queen at Bolsover Castle, in Derbyshire, adding the terrace range in anticipation of their visit. His ambition was to be awarded the guardianship of the young Prince of Wales, and it was to this that he referred in a much-quoted letter to Strafford: 'I have bent my estate with the hope of it.' To John Ford, the dramatist, this Court life was one of 'range, range on/ And roll about the world to gather moss,/The moss of honour, gay reports, gay clothes,/Gay Wives, huge empty buildings, whose proud roofs/Shall with their pinnacles even reach the stars'.[1]

Society, on the other hand, was in a state of flux, continually receiving new blood supported by the new fortunes gained from trade, and occasionally from more efficient management of land. The new families were anxious to invest in land, and the old-established ones more than ready

to marry heiresses whose dowries or expectations outweighed their lack of quarterings. Except in the most troubled years of the middle of the century, estates that came on the market appear to have been eagerly bought up. This social mobility had a two-fold effect on country house architecture: firstly, the new families were not concerned with life on the Burghley-Newcastle scale, or to take the gamble of a court preferment; they would have agreed with Fuller that 'a house had better be too little for a day than too great for a year.' Secondly, they were more prepared to accept architectural innovation and were more eager to adopt the latest London fashions, even if they were not always those of Inigo Jones. Consequently, these new men, rather than the older circle of courtiers, became the vital patrons of architecture for most of the period 1615–85.

Yet within this bracket there is noticeable from the beginning of the period until the Restoration, and even after, a division in the progression of country house architecture. The old vernacular style survived in remote districts, side by side with the court style of Inigo Jones, and the artisan style of London. A small circle at court patronised one group of craftsmen and the rich City merchants another; both schools are more fully discussed later in the Introduction.

Deep as the social and architectural cleavages in the 1620s and 30s became, the links were just as important, for social divisions were never absolute, and connections between families went up and down the social scale as well as across. Elaborate series of marriage alliances can be traced that

---

[1] *The Dramatic Works of John Ford*, 1811. Vol. I, p. 157. From *The Lovers Melancholy*, 1628.

3. *The Queen's House, Greenwich. Design for a chimneypiece by Inigo Jones*, c. 1635.

reveal illuminating and otherwise unsuspected connections between houses. There are many links, for instance, between both Inigo Jones and John Webb and the Herberts; the first appears to be that of the widow of the 2nd Earl of Pembroke and Inigo Jones at Houghton Conquest, Bedfordshire, which was revived by her son, the 4th Earl at Wilton, in the 1630s and 40s. His eldest son, Lord (Charles) Herbert, married Lady Mary Villiers (a daughter of the 1st Duke of Buckingham), who, after his early death, married the 1st Duke of Lennox. For the Lennoxes Webb made designs for Cobham Hall, Kent, in 1654. It is also possible that he may have advised James Herbert, the Earl's sixth son, who married a Spiller of Tythrop, Oxfordshire.

The ardent desire to build was present in other families; the Duke of Newcastle, who extended Bolsover, altered Welbeck Abbey and built Nottingham Castle, was a grandson of Bess of Hardwick. The Montagus shared this enthusiasm; the Earls of Manchester and Sandwich and the Duke of Montagu, all considerable builders, were kinsmen, the Duke also being the step-father of the Duke of Somerset, the creator of Petworth. In the architectural field Hugh May was a kinsman of the Earl of Essex, the head of a new and widely connected family, and William Winde was related to Sir John Bridgeman, of Castle Bromwich. Similar relationships re-occur time and again and play a fascinating role in the pattern of country house building.

Alliance by marriage was one of the great bonds of society, and membership of the House of Commons another; it is exceptional to come across a house that was not built by a peer or a Member of Parliament. Such evidence of standing in a county brought the families into closer touch with the metropolis and its fashions. There are one or two small groups of houses, however, whose owners held no political office, and of these the most interesting are those associated with successive Lord Mayors of London: they include Forty Hall and Swakeleys, both in Middlesex. The daughters of several Lord Mayors married into the aristocracy, or their sons obtained peerages: Lord Craven's father had been a Lord Mayor, and the 1st Earl of Northampton married the daughter of Sir John Spencer, Lord Mayor of London in 1594–5.

Before the early 17th century, direct contact with the cities of Italy, other than Venice, had not been easy, so that Renaissance influence was generally indirect. The first translation of Serlio's *Regole generali di architettura* into English, which was published by Robert Peake in 1611, was made from a Dutch edition, and not directly from the Italian. The situation was changing, however, and in 1605 Sir Henry Wotton, James I's Ambassador to Venice, wrote to Cecil that it was much safer for a Protestant to be in Rome. In this more relaxed atmosphere regular links became more common, and the first generation of Grand Tourists set out on their travels. From the beginning the Veneto was the most favoured rendezvous for Englishmen, and John Evelyn was as much struck by the Brenta as were later generations of Georgian travellers: 'The countryside on both sides,' he wrote, 'is deliciously adorned with country villas and gentleman's retirements.'[1]

To a small circle of connoisseurs the accessibility of Italy meant much and to none was it more welcome than to the Earl of Arundel (Fig. 2). He made two visits, the second being a long tour in 1613, when he was accompanied by Inigo Jones, his senior by twelve years. Arundel was a passionate and discerning collector, but we are concerned here only with his architectural activities. Although nominally head of the Howard family, he was not a rich man in his own right, for the family property and honours confiscated from his grandfather, the attainted Duke of Norfolk, had not been restored in full. He was married to Alathea, Countess of Shrewsbury, and it was on her wealth that he was able to draw for his collecting activities. His somewhat uncertain position at court, and in affairs of State, is the probable reason for his not building any significant country house. He had a house, however, at Greenwich, another in the Strand, and one, called Tart Hall, on a site close to the present Buckingham Palace. The only records of them are some designs by Jones for Arundel House in the Strand, some drawings of details by John Smythson and some views of it by Hollar. As a result Arundel appears as a rather shadowy figure in the background of architectural history, but to his contemporaries he was a figure of importance, quite apart from his patronage of Jones. While making due allowance for flattery there is an illuminating passage in James Howell's *Instructions for Forreine Travell*, published in 1642, in which he says that Arundel, 'observing the uniforme and regular way of stone structure up and down Italy, hath introduced that forme of building to London and Westminster, and elsewhere, which though distastfull at first, as all innovations are, For they seeme like Bug-beares, or Gorgons heads, to the vulgar; yet they find now the commodity, firmenesse and beauty thereof, the three maine principles of Architecture.'

[1] *Diary*. June, 1645 (Everyman, Vol. I, p. 203).

II. THE COURT STYLE OF INIGO JONES

In the range of his interests and the quality of his achievements, Inigo Jones was a figure of European stature, fulfilling in a rare degree the Renaissance ideal of the universal man. The only son of a Smithfield cloth-worker, he was born in 1573, nine years after Shakespeare and in the same year as Ben Jonson, but of his early years we know little. He had already been to Italy when he produced his first Royal masque at Whitehall, in 1605, and had developed his remarkable powers as a draughtsman (Fig. 3). His great delight in drawing made the world of the masque particularly attractive to him, giving him scope for working out the fanciful ideas that packed his imagination; many of them based on memories of what he had seen in Europe, or ideas culled from prints. His style of drawing was influenced by the study of Italian draughtsmanship of the 16th and early 17th centuries, particularly that of Parmigianino and the Bolognese school.

His first visit to Italy may have been as early as 1597; he was certainly there in 1601, and again about 1605 and in 1613. While in Venice in 1601 he purchased a copy of Palladio's *I Quattro Libri dell' Architettura*, which he subsequently carried on all his travels and annotated with comments and memoranda. It is easy to imagine the impact, on so receptive a mind, of the Italy of his day and its great achievements in painting, sculpture and architecture: here he had the chance to study the art of the High Renaissance, and the succeeding Mannerist period. His interest in Renaissance classicism has long been recognised, but there seems to be an unwillingness, perhaps fostered by the Burlingtonians in the first place, to accept his interest in Italian architecture later than 1530. Yet Palladio, who meant more to him than any other architect, was, in some degree, a Mannerist, notwithstanding his intense admiration for Bramante and his generation, developing their style along anti-orthodox lines, using the old architectural vocabulary to achieve new effects of mass, decoration and movement. Palladio died in 1580, and, on his Italian visit in 1614, Jones made a point of meeting Scamozzi, his former pupil and the author of *Dell' Idea dell' Architettura Universale*. He studied the master's buildings in Vicenza, proof of which is to be seen in the design of the Banqueting House in Whitehall (Fig. 4), which is influenced by Palazzo Iseppo de'Porti, Palazzo Thiene and Palazzo Porto Barbaro.

One of the most revealing notes in his sketch book is an entry on 20th January, 1614: 'And to saie trew all thes composed ornaments the wch Proceed out of ye aboundance of dessigners and wear brought in by Michill Angell and his followers in my oppignion do not well in sollid Architecture and ye fasciati of houses, but in gardens loggis stucco or ornaments of chimnies peeces or in the inner parts of houses thos compositiones are of necessety to be yoused. For as outwarly every wyse ma carrieth a graviti in Publicke Places, whear ther is nothing els looked for, yet inwardly hath his immaginacy set on fire, and sumtimes licenciously flying out, as nature hir self doeth often tymes stravagantly, to dellight, amase us sumtimes moufe us to laughter, sumtimes to contemplation and horror, so in architecture ye outward ornaments oft (ought) to be sollid, proporsionable according to the rulles, masculine and unaffected'.[1] Proof of these principles is evident in the buildings he was shortly to design and which were in no way inferior to those of Sansovino or Palladio. He absorbed as no other contemporary Northerner the theories of Renaissance architecture, and its system of mathematical proportion controlling both plan and elevation and continuing throughout every detail of a building.

It is not clear when Jones first turned to architecture, but he was certainly consulted in the building of Hatfield House about 1610,[2] probably on account of his being a travelled man with a knowledge of architecture. As early as 1606 Edward Bolton inscribed a book: 'To his own Inigo Jones though there is hope that sculpture, modelling and architecture, painting acting and all that is praise-worthy in the elegant arts of the Ancients may one day find their way across the Alps into our England.' The mention of architecture, following sculpture and modelling, may be significant, because his drawings are full of feeling for sculptural detail (Fig. 3), and as late as the Chatsworth sketch book, which he used on his last journey to Italy, there are more studies of sculpted and painted heads than references to architecture.

His earliest complete surviving building is the Banqueting House (Fig. 4), built between 1619 and 1622. As has been said, he was indebted to Palladio for its design, but it is by no means a pastiche; it is an original composition on a theme attempted by all the great 16th-century Italians — the application of an order to a palace façade. Its proportions comprise a double cube two storeys high, pilasters being used for the outer bays of both with half-columns occupying the central bays, their entablatures breaking forward sufficiently to emphasise the centre. The patterning of the lightly rusticated walling between the pilasters, and the positioning of the carved festoons and heads linking the capitals, show an astonishing sensibility in a man who could have had little experience in the handling of classical detail.

The Banqueting House was begun only four years after Jones succeeded Simon Basill as Surveyor-General of the King's Works and Buildings. His faculty for design was developing fast at the time, as can be seen from a comparison of the Whitehall drawings with the drawing of a frontispiece to a house dated 1616 (Fig. 5), a design lacking confidence and showing no sign of his future Palladianism. Close in date to the early Whitehall drawings are those for the Prince's Lodging at Newmarket (Fig. 6), which have only recently been identified by Mr John Harris.[3] In these essays in the manner of Serlio and Scamozzi, applying the triumphal arch motif as a centrepiece, Jones provided a 'proto-type for the red-brick stone-quoined and hipped-roof house, so prevalent from the mid-century onward.'[4]

---

[1] Sir John Summerson, *Architecture in Britain*, 1530–1830, p. 67 (1963 edition).
[2] *The Building of Hatfield House*, by L. Stone, *Archaeological Journal*, 1955, Vol. 112, p. 100.
[3] *The Prince's Lodging at Newmarket*. John Harris. *Architectural History*, Vol. 2, 1959, p. 26.
[4] Harris, *op. cit.*, p. 40.

4. The Banqueting House, Whitehall. Inigo Jones, 1619–22.

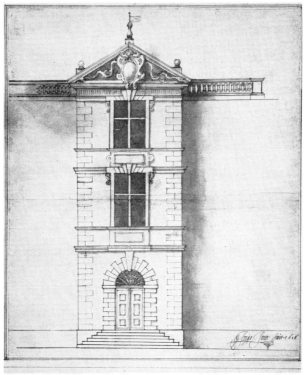

5. Design for the frontispiece of a house, by Inigo Jones, 1616.

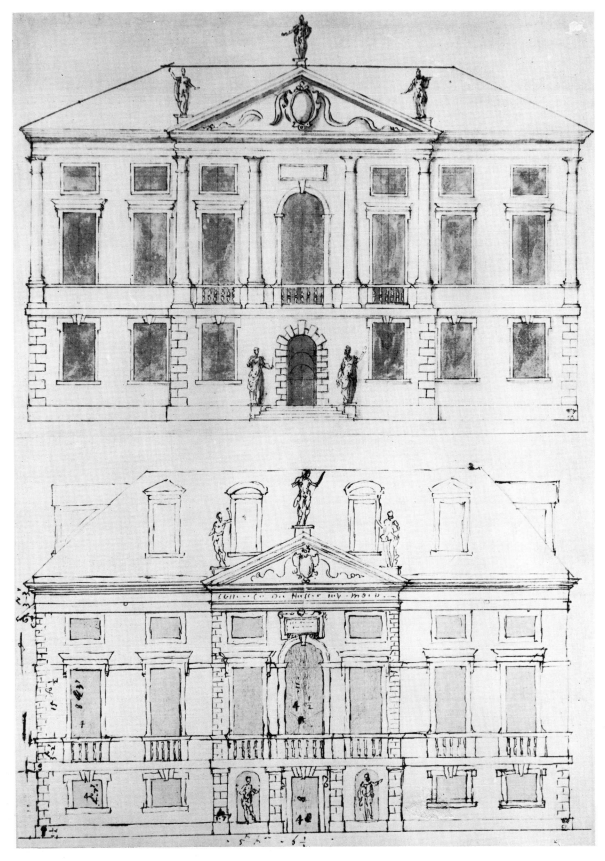

6. *The Prince's Lodging, Newmarket. Designs for the front elevation by Inigo Jones, c. 1618.*

The year before he undertook these two important commissions, work was begun on the first stage of the Queen's House, but it was halted after eighteen months (p. 51) and only completed in the 1630s.

The earliest interior possibly by Inigo Jones is the Haynes Grange Room (Fig. 8, now in the Victoria and Albert Museum), which is supposed to have come from Houghton Conquest House in Bedfordshire, built between 1615 and 1621 by Mary, Countess of Pembroke, mother of the 3rd and 4th Earls, and sister of Philip Sidney. According to Aubrey: 'The architects were sent for from Italie. It is built according to the description of Basilius's house in the first book of the Arcadia',[1] which Sidney dedicated to his sister. Horace Walpole, with commendable caution, noted that some say 'that the two best fronts were improved by Inigo Jones'.[2] Building began soon after he returned from his last Italian tour. It was a characteristic late Jacobean house, and Jones probably contributed the Italianate two-storeyed loggia in the centre of the entrance front, the outline of which recalls one of his early drawings for the west front of Old St Paul's. The room is the earliest known to be completely panelled in pinewood; the boards are butt-joined and set vertically from floor to cornice, without a skirting. The dominant features are the Corinthian pilasters dividing the plain wall surfaces and the surrounds of the window embrasures and niches. The general conception was derived from Serlio's woodcuts showing the interior of the Pantheon. It has been suggested that the formalised pigeons covering the ceiling were inspired by an actual flight seen crossing the uncovered opening in the Pantheon's dome, an image not out of keeping with Jones's sensitivity as a designer. The whole room, as a literal quotation of a classical idea, demonstrates the difficulty that faced English designers of finding suitable models in the classical manner on which to base their own work.

Inigo Jones tended to look to France for models of decorative detail and interiors, to the style of Louis XIII. For instance, Mr John Harris has shown that both he and John Webb used engravings by Jean Barbet for the chimneypieces at Wilton.[3] The carved pendants and drops that they used there and elsewhere were also copied from French designs. Apart from these few identified examples, English designers of the day appear to have been considerably influenced by French decoration: interiors at the Château de Cheverny, and the Château de Tanlay, have much in common with their English equivalents, particularly in the forms of chimneypieces and panelling.

Although Jones was prepared to introduce sumptuous detail into his interiors, it always conformed to his fundamental principle of reason and had little in common with the overcharged grandeur of contemporary Roman Baroque. At Wilton the ornament is plentiful and magnificent, but discreetly marshalled. The east doorway of the Double Cube Room (Fig. 110) shows abundant yet disciplined richness, and the recumbent figures are not 'gesticulating, the masks grimacing or the scrolls contortioning'; they are harmonised

to a decorative convention. 'Masculinity', he said, 'should be at the basis of all ornament.'

Besides being the first Englishman to build in a convincing classical idiom, Inigo Jones produced the prototypes of the main forms of house built in the 17th century. His designs for the projected Palace of Whitehall constituted an ideal from which many subsequent schemes derived, beginning with those of Webb, who inherited all Jones's drawings. At Newmarket, Jones introduced the type of hip-roofed cube which became the basic form of house from 1660 to 1730, of which more will be said. At Stoke Park, Northamptonshire (p. 61), he built the first house in England to consist of a central block linked to flanking wings by curved colonnades. But this Palladian layout, with its sense of movement, appears to have had little influence on contemporary building, and it was not used again until the building of Hackwood, Hampshire, probably designed about 1683 by William Talman.

The problem of the medium-sized house also interested Jones and Webb, who both gave considerable attention to houses with a façade of five to seven bays. Their first thoughts seem to have occurred at the time of the early Whitehall and Newmarket designs, but there are a number of drawings, presumably made rather later, all of which are indebted to Palladian and Serlian inspiration. Few of them are dated, but there is one inscribed 1638, intended for Lord Maltravers, Lord Arundel's son and heir (Fig. 9). This shows a modest two-storeyed house with a hipped roof, but with no centrepiece or embellishment. Some have centrepieces and others not, but their link with the type of house that Pratt and May were to establish after 1660 is clear enough. Masculine and unaffected, as Jones noted, these had none of 'thes composed ornaments the wch Proceed out

7. *Kirby Hall, Northamptonshire. A garden gateway,*
c. 1638–40.

[1] *Brief Lives* (ed. Powell, 1949), p. 34.
[2] *Walpole Society*, Vol. XVI, p. 69.
[3] *Inigo Jones and his French Sources* (Metropolitan Museum Bulletin, May, 1961).

8A *and* B (*opposite*). *The Haynes Grange Room, supposedly from Houghton Conquest, Bedford-shire, and now in the Victoria and Albert Museum. Perhaps de-signed by Inigo Jones,* c. 1615.

of ye aboundance of dessigners and wear brought in by Michill Angell and his followers in my oppignion do not well in sollid Architecture and ye fasciati of houses.'[1]

It would be wrong, however, to suppose that Jones was a classical Puritan. He was above all a man of the theatre, and well versed in Italian architecture of the 16th century, as may be seen in his garden gateways and arches. Nowhere, per-haps, is this more apparent than in the garden gateway on the north side of the green court at Kirby Hall, Northampton-shire (Fig. 7), which, as Mr Sacheverell Sitwell has said,

bears 'in its rustication the breath of the Italy of Vignola . . . Only a blank doorway in a garden wall, but it recalls Capra-rola or Villa d'Este, adapted to this green land . . . It is an Italian doorway; but, at the same time, like a painted doorway in the scenery of a masque'.[1] The Kirby gate exemplifies a form of fantasy that specially appealed to Jones. Fantasy was no new thing in English garden ornament, but he gave it a new direction and a distinction that it retained until the end of the 18th century. It is likely that Jones was summoned to Kirby about 1638–9 by Christopher Hatton III, who wanted

[1] Summerson, *op. cit.*, p. 67.

[1] *British Architects and Craftsmen*, p. 23.

to remodel the north side of the Elizabethan quadrangle. The pilasters and the arcading of the lower storey on the inner face of the range form part of the Elizabethan building; Jones's work appears to have been limited to the design of the fenestration on the upper floors. On the outer side his remodelling was more drastic, and he capped his work with a balustraded parapet and swept gables.

Kirby came almost at the end of Inigo Jones's working life, for the outbreak of war in 1642 and the break-up of the court meant the end of his career. He was a staunch Royalist totally out of sympathy with the regime that deposed the

King. Only one more commission came his way and that was the redecoration of Wilton, after the fire of 1647–48. It is impossible to disentangle his contribution from that of Webb, and it should be remembered that probably he had little sympathy with Lord Pembroke at the time and so might well have been content to leave most of the job to Webb.

In 1652 he died at Somerset House, having survived the sack of Basing House. Two hundred and fifty years later Sir Reginald Blomfield[1] wrote an eloquent obituary that it

[1] *A History of Renaissance Architecture in England* (1897), Vol. I, pp. 121–22.

would be hard to better: 'Inigo Jones was on the whole the greatest architect and one of the most accomplished artists that this country has ever produced. No man has mastered more completely the scholarship of his art; but to this range of knowledge he added a power of design and a quality of imagination which place him, as an artist, higher even than his great successor Wren. . . . His especial strength lay in his thorough mastery of proportion, his contempt for mere prettiness, and the rare distinction of his style . . . No man has ever more completely realised his own ideal of his art.'

III. JONES'S CONTEMPORARIES AT COURT

Like the King he served, Inigo Jones was a curiously isolated figure, for he practised an architecture unfamiliar to an aristocracy who had already invested in the rich Jacobean manner of Hatfield and Audley End. Moreover, so onerous were the demands made on him at Court that he had little time to undertake work for those outside the Court circle. On the other hand, the King himself was never sufficiently affluent to carry out his grandiose schemes. Jones had little chance, therefore, to express his architectural ideas. To Strafford and Laud, for instance, the Jonesian manner made little appeal, nor did it to the owners of Castle Ashby, Rushton, Temple Newsam or Apethorpe. The effect of this limitation of his practice was serious, for it meant that the younger craftsmen in the building trade were not trained in the exacting standards of his classicism. Consequently, it took a long time for Inigo Jones's ideas to be absorbed into the English tradition. This was in marked contrast with the situation after March, 1668/69, when Wren began his long period as Surveyor of the Royal Works. The latter had unlimited opportunities of building and, as a result, the Office of Works became a superb training ground, producing designers, masons and craftsmen of the greatest distinction.

Apart from John Webb, of whom more will be said, the most prominent native figure to emerge during Jones's lifetime was Nicholas Stone, master mason at Whitehall. Stone's principal occupation was the making of sepulchral monuments, which sprang from his apprentice years (1606–1612) in Amsterdam with Hendrik de Keyser, the leading statuary of that city during the first two decades of the century, and one of the formulators of the Dutch mannerist style. His only country house commission was for the wing he added at Cornbury Park, Oxfordshire (p. 131), for the Earl of Danby, who also commissioned him to design the Oxford Physic Garden gateways.

Two other important figures of the time, Isaac de Caus and Balthasar Gerbier, were foreigners. De Caus is now best known for his part in the rebuilding of Wilton, in the 1630s, which Inigo Jones himself was too busy to carry out. He also worked for the 4th Earl of Bedford on the development project for Covent Garden, and was probably responsible for the grotto at the Earl's country seat, Woburn Abbey, Bedfordshire (Fig. 10). Apart from engravings of the grotto at Wilton, this is the only surviving example of a curious court fashion of the day, a stone and shell counterpart to a masque, and reflects the romantic streak in Stuart taste that is so evident in Van Dyck's portraits and in Jones's entertainments for the Court. For John Evelyn 'Cave, Grots, Mounts, and irregular ornaments do contribute to contemplative and philosophical enthousiasm.'[1]

Gerbier was a figure of a different colour. He came to England in 1616 at the age of twenty-five in the suite of the Dutch ambassador. He entered the service of the Duke of Buckingham, whom he assisted in the formation of his collections, and in his entertainments and buildings, particularly at New Hall, Essex, and York House, London. In 1623 he accompanied his master on his visit with Prince Charles to Spain, and in 1626 designed for him the York House Water-Gate on the Embankment. This is based on the Medici fountain in the gardens of the Luxembourg Palace in Paris, which Gerbier had seen the previous year, but the detail is rather coarse and lacks the refinement of Jones's work. After Buckingham's assassination Gerbier entered the King's service in the role of diplomat-cum-picture-dealer, but on neither counts appears as a figure of much integrity. However, with what Walpole called his 'supple and intriguing nature' he managed to survive the changes of regime.

Apart from his work at New Hall, we know of no further country house commissions coming his way until after the Restoration, when he designed Hamstead Marshall, Berkshire, for the Earl of Craven (p. 137). Charles II suspended him from his office of Master of Ceremonies in 1660, but nevertheless he designed the triumphal arches for the Coronation in the following year. In 1662 he published *A Brief Discourse concerning the three chief principles of Magnificent Building*, followed in 1663 by *Counsel and Advice to all Builders*.

9. *Design of a house for Lord Maltravers by Inigo Jones,* 1638.

[1] Letter to Sir Thomas Browne, 28.1.1657, quoted by E. V. Carritt, *A Calendar of British Taste,* p. 56.

10. *Woburn Abbey, Bedfordshire. The Grotto, probably by Isaac de Caus*, c. 1635.

IV. BUILDING OUTSIDE THE COURT CIRCLE

It might be inferred from Colin Campbell's *Vitruvius Britannicus* that Inigo Jones's style was characteristic of the early Caroline period, but that would be far from the truth. Roger Pratt noticed, on his return from Italy in 1649, 'Architecture here has not received those advantages which it has in other parts, it continuing almost still as rude here as it was at the very first.'[1] In his view, Inigo Jones was the one and only English architect and he considered the only worthy buildings were those for which Jones had been responsible, the Queen's House at Greenwich, the Banqueting Hall at Whitehall and the portico of Old St Paul's.

Building was almost entirely in the hands of the master masons, some of whose work was of the type that Sir John Summerson has aptly labelled 'artisan mannerism'.[2] In his view this was 'essentially the manner of the best London craftsmen-joiners, carpenters, masons, bricklayers. . . .', not the Mannerism of Michelangelo, Giulio Romano or Peruzzi, or the writers of architectural treatises such as Palladio or Serlio: it was closer to the style of the Low Countries, especially that of Hendrik de Keyser of Amsterdam. In the hands of the Italians it was a highly charged, intellectual and emotional style; transported north at the beginning of the 17th century, it became a debased vocabulary of ornament. Miss Katharine Fremantle[3] quoted a translated passage from van Mander's account of the life of Michelangelo, which throws a light on contemporary opinion of Flemish mannerism: 'In architecture beside the old common manner of the ancients and Vitruvius, he (Michelangelo) has brought forth other new orders of cornices, capitals, bases, tabernacles, sepulchres and other ornaments, wherefore all architects that

follow after him owe him thanks for his having freed them from the old bonds and knots, and given them free rein, and licence to invent something beside the Antique. Yet to tell the truth this rein is so free, and this licence so misused by our Netherlanders, that in the course of time in Building a great Heresy has arisen among them, with a heap of craziness of decorations and breaking of the pilasters in the middle, and adding, on the pedestals, their usual coarse points of diamonds and such lameness, very disgusting to see.'

In the orgy of mannerist ornament that followed this transportation, Wendel Dietterlin's *Architectura* played a part. This book, published in Nuremburg in 1598, consists of a series of plates based on Serlio's orders and gateways, but embellished with strange and outlandish ornament which approaches the fantasies of German gothic (Fig. 11).

The influence of Dutch and Flemish mannerism made its appearance in England about the time Nicholas Stone returned from his Amsterdam apprenticeship and Inigo Jones from his last Italian visit. The earliest records are among the Smythson drawings, which include sketches of 'My Lady Cook's house' and Sir Fulke Greville's house in Holborn, drawn by John Smythson on his visit to London in 1618. In both these houses the most prominent features were the concave-sided gables, voluted at their lower ends, in the manner of classical consoles, and surmounted by pediments. Mr John Harris[1] has suggested that Jones may have designed Sir Fulke's house, an attribution supported by his presence on the Commission in charge of building the Whitehall Banqueting House, as Under Treasurer of the Exchequer. Gables of the kind have a long history and probably spring from early Renaissance attempts to link

[1] Gunther, *Architecture of Sir Roger Pratt*, p. 60.
[2] Summerson, *op. cit.*, 1963 edition, p. 89.
[3] *The Baroque Town Hall of Amsterdam*, p. 88.

[1] *Archaeological Journal*, 1961, p. 184.

11. *A design by Wendel Dietterlin. (Plate 85 from his* Architectura, 1598.)

the disparate elements of the pitched roof and the aisles of a gothic church to a classical façade. The front of St Maria Novella, Florence, by Alberti, is among one of these early examples. The device was revived in the 16th century and used with boldness by Vignola on the Gesu, in Rome. Inigo Jones employed it in his portico for Old St Paul's.

Several artisan houses of the 1620s and 30s, to be found in the villages that have been absorbed by the expansion of London, or in surrounding districts within reach of the capital, illustrate the taste of the more prosperous citizens. The Dutch House at Kew (Fig. 12), one of the earliest, was built in 1631 for Samuel Fortrey, a Flemish merchant. It consists of a block two ranges deep divided by a cross corridor, with a spine wall carrying the prominent chimneys. Its gables and shafted stacks give it a misleadingly old-fashioned air, but the compactness of the plan was a new development. Boston Manor, Brentford; Forty Hall, Enfield (Fig. 15); St Clere, Kent, and the Old House at Mickleham, Surrey, all date from about this period, and their plans have a similar compression.

It is difficult to determine when this form of rectangular 'double-pile' was evolved; it was occasionally used from the middle of Elizabeth's reign and an early example is Whitehall, Shrewsbury, built in about 1578–82. From then on variants were adopted on a number of occasions, but it was not until the late 1620s and the 30s that a definable group of houses can be recognised. They were of considerable importance in preparing the way for the much more articulate architecture of Roger Pratt and Hugh May, a

12. *The Dutch House, Kew,* 1631. *The Entrance Front.*

13. *Broome Park, Kent, 1635–38. The Entrance Front.*

14. *Swakeleys, Middlesex,* c. 1630.

15. *Forty Hall, Middlesex.*

combination of European experience with English tradition.

In their ornament and decoration the artisan craftsmen rarely displayed the same restraint and sense that is found in the plans of these middling houses. Two of the more ambitious houses of the 1630s, Swakeleys, Middlesex (Fig. 14), and Broome Park, Kent (Fig. 13), are conservative in plan, but rich in external detail. In the former the windows retain traces of elaborate strapwork frames combined with ornate gables decorated with niches. At Broome, which is built on an H plan, emphasis is given to elaborate gables rising above a bold brick cornice. On the ends of the wings three pediments of different design rise, one through another, and in the recessed centre a run of 'Holborn gables' is employed as decorative features.

In other houses of more moderate extent this coarseness of style was not so apparent, albeit the effects were often awkward. At West Horsley Place, Surrey, the early Caroline front of thirteen bays, which is a refacing of an older house, displays in the centre an elaborate gable totally unrelated to the order of pilasters and cornice on the first floor; their 'capitals', however, are an engaging heresy, perhaps a misreading of an indifferent woodcut. Balls Park, Hertfordshire, built immediately before the Civil War, contains many such mannerisms. The pilasters at the corners of the façade are flanked by inward and outward-looking quoins; Ionic capitals on the upper pilasters support carved consoles, while brackets are placed in pairs between the windows. The chief interest of Balls lies in its brickwork. The unknown bricklayer clearly enjoyed building in his medium and demonstrated his exuberance in the brick framing of the windows, the boldly cut string-course, and the quoins and pilasters.

Technical excellence in brick-building is one of the best qualities of the style. A soft, fine-textured brick was introduced about this time, capable of being rubbed and cut to any desired shape. Flemish bond, i.e. headers (short ends) and stretchers (long sides) laid in the same course, with rather thinner joints than previously customary, replaced English bond, which consists of headers and stretchers laid in alternate courses with comparatively wide joints. The Dutch House at Kew, Broome Park and parts of Raynham, Norfolk, are built in Flemish bond. The development of brick-building at this time was of lasting benefit and led to the great feats achieved in brick by Wren and his school later in the century.

V. THE CIVIL WAR AND COUNTRY HOUSES OF THE COMMONWEALTH

When King Charles hoisted his standard at Nottingham, in 1642, Civil War became a reality instead of a threat. It probably took most of the land-owning class by surprise. Looking back after three centuries to events that led to the outbreak of hostilities, war appears as the inevitable end to the story, but to contemporaries this was by no means apparent. Indeed, the pace of country house building in the late 1630s, particularly in the London area, does not seem to have abated. Sir John Harrison, for instance, began building Balls Park, Hertfordshire, only about 1640. A wily farmer of sugar customs, he must have had his eye on the trend of events and would not be likely to have embarked on building so costly a house had he foreseen trouble ahead.

From 1642 until the end of the decade, there was little building activity, though probably some owners continued work already in hand. However, occasionally one comes across men like Arthur Pulter, who 'shortly after the breaking forth of the late Civil War declin'd all publick Imployment, liv'd a retir'd Life, and thro' the importunity of his Wife began to build a very fair house of Brick' at Broadfield in Hertfordshire.[1]

The Civil War failed to interrupt the general pattern of life, but, for landowners, it was a period of marked instability and, frequently, of distress, as may be gathered from the Verney Papers, the diary of Richard Symonds, or the Proceedings of the Committees for Compounding and the Advance of Money. Sir Ralph Verney's father was killed fighting for King Charles at Edgehill, but his property suffered from the depredations of the Royalist troops; Sir Ralph himself had to go abroad and remained out of the country until 1653. While in exile, he had thought of selling Claydon, Buckinghamshire, but decided not to because of the glut on the property market and the lowness of prices. In June, 1655, he was imprisoned, and in the same year wrote: 'I confess I love Old England very well, but as things are carried heere the gentry cannot joy much to bee in it'.[1] On another occasion he says: 'Of all my acquaintance, there is scarce an honest man that is not in a borrowing condition.'[2]

Death, exile and imprisonment, accompanied by loss of office, sequestration of property, and compounding for it at the rate $\frac{2}{3}$ to $\frac{1}{10}$ of the value of the property (this was supposed to be two years rental in pre-war terms), were the

[1] Chauncey, *History of Hertfordshire*, p. 72.

[1] *Memoirs of the Verney Family*, Vol. II, p. 1.
[2] *op. cit.*, Vol. II, p. 27.

16. *Wisbech Castle, Cambridgeshire. Probably designed by Peter Mills, c. 1658. (Demolished.)*

order of the day; 119 peers and 178 baronets tried to compound.[1] There was sequestration for delinquency (i.e. support of the Royal cause), and for recusancy, and, in addition, there were the high demands of the Committee for the Advance of Money, the Parliamentary equivalent to the loans raised by the King, which went unrepaid. Sir John Harrison, the builder of Balls Park, being a customs farmer, was a particular target for the Parliamentary side. In 1646 he compounded for delinquency and was outlawed for debt; in the following year he was fined over £10,000 or half the value of his property; his wife pleaded for the use of Balls, which had been sequestrated, on the grounds that 'she is altogether destitute of habitation and means to provide for herself and her children'.[2] But such prominent Royalist profiteers were not the only sufferers. John Cartwright of Aynhoe was assessed at £1,000 by the Committee for the Advance of Money in 1643, but managed to get a discharge the next year, because he had contributed over £800 in property and had 'suffered much by the King's forces'.

The examples of suffering that could be quoted are numerous (a number will be found in the Appendix), but there are also a number of cases where a family claimed to be over-burdened by the demands of the regime one year and undertook considerable building work the next. This makes it difficult to arrive at any but general conclusions of the effect of Civil War on house building. Sir Ralph Verney returned from exile in 1653 and promptly set about restora-

tion at Claydon. While in prison, in 1655, he met Sir Justinian Isham, then in the process of adding a new wing to Lamport, Northamptonshire (p. 97). Sir Justinian had already been before the Committee for the Advance of Money between 1645 and 1649, but got a discharge, having paid £60 and pleaded he was in debt and his estate encumbered: in 1648 and 1649 he was in trouble with the Committee for Compounding, who demanded $\frac{1}{10}$. Sir George Sondes, of Lees Court, Kent, had a somewhat similar story: he spent two years in prison and his debts mounted to £7,000, while his estate fell to half its old value; then he agreed to hand over half and in 1644 he was fined £3,500; in 1650 his property was sequestered and the woods cut down, but he still paid half his fine. Despite these inroads on his fortune, he was soon to set about the building of his thirteen-bay front at Lees Court.

To dilate on the uncertainties of the Royalists, and their effect on the country house, is to paint but half the picture, for, as D. C. Coleman has shown in his study of Sir John Banks,[1] 'the recall of Parliament in 1640, the onset of Civil War, and the final collapse of royal power, combined with the continuing expansion of these newer branches of English trade to give to these groups of "new men" their chance to exercise power and influence in the 1640s and 50s. The earlier generation of customs farmers were dead or in disgrace, the big businessmen of that age in voluntary or involuntary retirement. The new authority needed new financiers, new business advisers; it was an opportunity

---

[1] Klotz and Davis, *Economic History Review*, Vol. 58, 1943, p. 219.
[2] *Country Life*, XXXI, p. 581.

[1] *Sir John Banks, Baronet and Businessman*, p. 6.

17. *The Vyne, Hampshire. The portico by John Webb, 1655.*

seized by a generation which included many who had gained experience in a new world of English overseas endeavour.' They introduced new blood to the ranks of country house builders, who lost no time, during the 1650s, to invest in land and building. As might be expected, their circle included leaders of the Commonwealth regime. On the whole this new generation, thanks to the Act of Indemnity and Oblivion, survived the change of regime in 1660.

Of the prominent Parliamentarians' houses the finest is undoubtedly Thorpe Hall, Peterborough, Northamptonshire (p. 102), built for Oliver St John by Peter Mills. Mr Howard Colvin's[1] discovery of the contract in the British Museum, which revealed Mills as the designer, is of the first importance; it brings to light a hitherto obscure figure, and removes from Webb's *œuvre* a work that falsified the character of his style. Although the character of Thorpe is rooted in the artisan manner, it has a sense of order and sophistication that raises it high above other houses of the school. Among Mill's other designs was a terrace of houses in

[1] *Country Life*, CXI, p. 1732.

Great Queen Street, London, faced with a giant order of pilasters above a rusticated lower storey, built in 1639.

Thorpe's resemblance to Wisbech Castle, Cambridgeshire (Fig. 16), (now destroyed) and also the political ties between St John and its builder, Thurloe, Cromwell's Secretary of State, make it not unlikely that Wisbech was also designed by Mills. Another member of the Protector's regime to build in a grand manner was Edmund Prideaux, the Attorney-General, who remodelled the monastic buildings at Forde Abbey, Dorset (p. 111).

One of the surprising aspects of the decade 1650–60 is the extent of John Webb's practice. After twenty-two years service as Jones's assistant, he now came into his own, producing designs in the manner of the Master. Among his drawings are several projects comparable in splendour to the Burlington ideal, showing how deeply he was imbued with the Palladio-Scamozzi creed, although he had not seen their buildings at first hand. Some of his projects were purely theoretical, perhaps intended for publication, but he must have expected tangible results from the schemes he produced

18. *Belvoir Castle, Leicestershire. An unexecuted design by John Webb, 1654.*

for Durham House, London, the Earl of Pembroke's town house, or Cobham Hall, Kent, for the Duke of Richmond and Lennox. Neither of them materialised, but the fire at Wilton provided the occasion for redecorating, in partnership with Inigo Jones, the State Rooms. A few years later, in 1654, he produced a grand scheme for the rebuilding of Belvoir Castle, Leicestershire (Fig. 18), for the Earl of Rutland. This was not carried out, but was engraved in the early 18th century and had influence on the Palladians.

Webb, who never shared Inigo Jones's intractable attitude to the Commonwealth regime, received a number of commissions from the leaders, including Chaloner Chute, for whom he altered The Vyne, near Basingstoke, Hampshire (Fig. 17), 1655, adding the portico on the garden front, the first of its kind applied to the façade of an English house. He also altered the entrance, introducing a beautifully detailed doorway, and supplied a number of chimneypieces for the interior. In 1658 he designed Gunnersbury Park, Middlesex, for Sir John Maynard, a Commonwealth judge. It was a literal imitation of an Italian villa and earned the sharp criticism of Roger Pratt: [We must] 'by no means to proceede to a rash and foolish imitation [of Italian models] without first maturely weighing the condition of the severall climes, the different manners of living, etc., and the exact dimensions and other circumstances of the building, especially the lights, etc., in all which things the Hall and Portico at Gunnersberry are verry faulty'.[1]

About the time he was altering The Vyne, Webb was engaged at Chevening in Kent, but the extent of his work there is uncertain. The traditional view of the history of the house derives from Colin Campbell in *Vitruvius Britannicus*, where he said the house had been built by the 13th Lord Dacre. As Lord Dacre died in 1630, this made Chevening a surprisingly early example of the tall, block-like house

[1] Gunther, *op. cit.*, p. 37.

19. *Chevening, Kent, c. 1630. A sketch on an estate map showing the house in 1679.*

usually associated with the 1650s. Doubts, strengthened by Webb's known connection with the house in the 1650s, have been cast on the attribution to the 13th Lord Dacre, and an alternative date in the early 1650s has been proposed. The careful spacing and diminution of the windows, together with the balustraded roof, only known through a drawing on an estate map dated 1679 (Fig. 19), all seem consistent with the later date.

Recently, however, Sir John Summerson[1] has written in support of the traditional date and among other reasons

[1] *Country Life*, CXXXVI, p. 776.

20. *Chevening, the Saloon. Panelling designed by John Webb, 1655.*

points out that the cornice shown in the drawing (which was not that shown by Campbell) was consistent with the work of the Jonesian circle before 1630. It may well have been that Chevening was not finished internally in 1630, and that Webb was only called in to decorate rooms, among them the Saloon, with its handsome wainscot (Fig. 20). This is of most accomplished design and shows the great advances made in interior decoration since the rather conscious classicism of the Houghton Conquest room. Webb may have got the commission in 1655, the year mentioned in the Lamport letters, through his work at The Vyne, because Chaloner Chute had married the widow of the 13th Lord Dacre in 1649.

Chevening stands close in date to Webb's work at Lamport (p. 97) and Drayton, where the Earl of Peterborough was beginning his slow renovation of the medieval and Elizabethan house, after a series of heavy fines. Webb's only surviving work there is the chimneypiece and overmantel in the State Bedroom: his design, dated 1653, is shown in Fig. 48.

Apart from these houses, there are a number of others of considerable interest, dating from the same decade. Of them the most outstanding was Coleshill, Berkshire (p. 90), designed by Pratt about 1649. Of houses in the London area Tyttenhanger, Hertfordshire (p. 119), is a large brick house having a certain affinity to Thorpe; Lees Court, Kent (Fig. 21), had a fine Hall (Fig. 22), subsequently destroyed by fire, a London craftsman's restatement of the hall at the Queen's House, Greenwich. It constituted one of the few examples of an imitation of a Jonesian design before the Restoration. St Giles's House, Dorset, built in 1650, marks the arrival of the new classicism in the west.

With the exception of Wilton, none of these Commonwealth houses corresponds to what has been referred to as the Courtier type. The defeat of the King was a victory for the gentry and the city merchants and it was this victory that was expressed in the field of country house building. For that reason, a form of London artisan-mannerism survived alongside the Palladianism of Jones and Webb until the Restoration.

VI. THE RESTORATION COUNTRY HOUSE: PRATT AND MAY'S CONTRIBUTION

The Restoration was not only a political and social settlement between King, aristocracy and gentry, but one of architecture as well. There had been much experiment during the previous four decades; English architecture had possessed a rare and stimulating excitement, but its full potential, particularly in the field of the country house, had not been realised. In the 1660s and 70s a distinctive type that found widespread acceptance was evolved so that it is possible to refer to a Restoration house in the same way as to an Elizabethan or Georgian house: no such image springs to mind in connection with houses built during the reign of Charles I and scarcely to those of the Commonwealth. This well-marked type of house, as contrasted to a series of individual achievements, was produced by synthesis or fusing together of a variety of current influences of which the aesthetic was only one.

Its architectural character was influenced by the long term effects of Civil War; the losses of the aristocracy prevented their embarking immediately on ambitious programmes. Among the noblemen worst hit were the Duke of Newcastle, who lost, it has been calculated, over £900,000, and the Marquess of Worcester, later Duke of Beaufort, who lost little less. The latter soon recovered and, after the Restoration, began his transformation of Badminton, Gloucestershire, in imitation of Webb's river front of Somerset House. The Duke's accounts show payments made between 1665 and 1676, and these suggest that the slow progress of the work was due to lack of more funds at the outset. Evidence of Newcastle's activities comes from his wife's biography, published in 1667, in which she wrote: 'Nor is it possible for him to repair all the ruines of the Estate that is left him, in so short a time, they being so great, and his losses so considerable.'[1] In fact, the Duke undertook no considerable building work until 1674, when he acquired the site of Nottingham Castle, which he was able to pay for only by the sale of property in Derbyshire.

Such sums made severe inroads on estates, and when owners who had withdrawn abroad returned in 1660, they were rarely in a position to contemplate building new houses, so had to satisfy themselves with patching their old mansions. The losses of these two noblemen were exceptional, but they were luckily both exceptionally affluent. For comparison, according to Klotz and Davies,[1] the estates of forty-one peers were worth £1,241,906, averaging £30,290 each.

There were, accordingly, a number of building projects of the 1660s and 70s that have little connection with the Restoration type of house, but employ the full range of Restoration decoration. Sir John Pakington added diagonal wings at the corners of Westwood Park, Worcestershire, his Elizabethan hunting lodge, and carried out elaborate internal decorations. He had lost about £20,000 during the War and his Buckinghamshire house had been completely destroyed. Both Powis and Chirk Castles, in North Wales, were sacked, the former by Sir Thomas Myddleton, of Chirk, and the latter by both sides. Both places were handsomely restored and redecorated during Charles II's reign, as were the castles at Warwick and Dunster.

The form of the Restoration house was based on the 'oblong square' house depicted in Jones's and Webb's drawings, which was also adopted on occasion by artisan builders between the 1630s and 50s. However, they did not perfect the type, and the credit for this belongs to Pratt and May.

Roger Pratt was essentially an amateur architect, particularly interested in the problem of housing men of his own class in comfort, elegance and convenience. His notes[2] are markedly practical; they give the impression that he was an adapter of others' ideas, both native and foreign,

---

[1] *The Life of the Thrice Noble, High and Puissant Prince, William Cavendish*, by Margaret Cavendish, 1667, p. 93.

[1] *The Wealth of Royalist Peers and Baronets During the Puritan Revolution, English Historical Review*, 1943, p. 217.
[2] Gunther, *op. cit.*

21. *Lees Court, Kent, c. 1655.*

22. *Lees Court. The Hall. (Destroyed by fire in 1910.)*

rather than a formulator of original ones. Mr Michael Kitson[1] has commented that: 'With him the chief instruments of design were the reason and the sensitive, experienced eye, not philosophical humanism and the harmonic scale, as they were with Jones'.

He was born in 1620. At the age of nineteen he entered the Inner Temple and on the outbreak of Civil War went abroad where he became absorbed in the study of architecture. He spent some time in Rome and lodged in the same house as another amateur, John Evelyn. While in Italy he must have seen many of the buildings that had so deeply impressed Inigo Jones. On returning home, in 1649, he was invited by his cousin, Sir George Pratt, to give an opinion on the new house the latter was building at Coleshill in Berkshire. In this matter Pratt seems to have consulted Inigo Jones, and Sir George was persuaded to start anew, on another site, to a fresh design which Pratt drew up, but on which he consulted Inigo Jones. The latter's contribution is uncertain, but it probably amounted to little more than criticisms of the general design.

Coleshill appears to have aroused but slight interest at the time, probably because it took twelve years to complete, and it was not until after the Restoration that further commissions

[1] *Burlington Magazine*, Vol. 99, 1957, p. 315.

came Pratt's way. In 1663, he designed Horseheath Hall, Cambridgeshire (now destroyed), for Lord Alington; a large brick house of eleven bays flanked by stable and kitchen courts which extended the composition in the Palladian manner. The house was an 'oblong square' with a hipped roof and a projecting three-bay pedimented centrepiece crowned by a lantern. In the same year, he designed Kingston Lacy, in Dorset (Fig. 27), for Sir Ralph Bankes, to replace that owner's Corfe Castle, which had been slighted in the War. This was smaller than Horseheath, being of nine bays, and was also of brick with stone dressings. Between 1835 and 1839 the façades were encased in Caen stone and received further embellishments from the hand of Sir Charles Barry: the interior was remodelled at the same time.

Pratt's best known work was Lord Clarendon's town house, in Piccadilly, at the top of St James's Street (Fig. 23). Clarendon House was the first large classical house in London and, according to John Evelyn, 'without hyperbole, the best contrived, the most useful, graceful, and magnificent house in England'.[1] Although it had but a short life, it exercised a wide influence, particularly through its principal façade. Of several houses of the time indebted to it, the most distinguished is Belton House, Lincolnshire (p. 193). The

[1] Letter to Lord Cornbury, 20th January, 1665/66.

23. Clarendon House, London. Designed by Sir Roger Pratt, 1665. (Demolished.)

24. *Ryston Hall, Norfolk. Sir Roger Pratt, 1668–72. (Remodelled.)*

25. *Elevation of a house, a woodcut from Serlio's* Architettura *Book VII, page* 103.

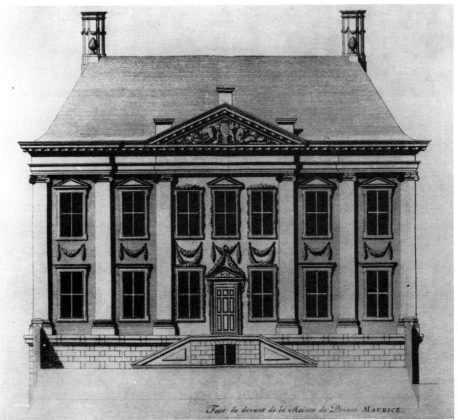

26. *The Mauritshuis, The Hague. Peter Post, 1635. An engraving from Post's* Description . . . (1715).

elements of the entrance front of Clarendon House — flanking wings, hipped roof, pedimented centrepiece and balustraded roof-platform and lantern — were not, of course, new ideas; with the exception of the wings all had appeared in Pratt's earlier work. But intending patrons could not fail to notice and be impressed by this prominent house, which became the model to which they aspired.

While it was nearing completion, in 1666, Hugh May began the new wing to Lord Clarendon's country house, Cornbury Park, Oxfordshire, previously the home of Lord Danby (p. 131). In the following year Pratt inherited Ryston Hall in Norfolk, where he proceeded to build himself a new house (Fig. 24). According to a contemporary painting it consisted of a central pavilion with a large segmental pediment and lower flanking wings, a design more Francophile in character than that of other houses of the day. Here he lived in retirement with his books until his death in 1684.

Hugh May's background is not so clear; he seems to have been a member of the circle that included Lely and Evelyn, and had learnt his architecture in the Low Countries, where he was in the service of the 2nd Duke of Buckingham during the Court's exile. There are records of his being in Holland in 1650–54, and again in 1656, when he went as assistant to Lely, with whom he had lived in Covent Garden. Among the new Dutch houses he would have seen were the Mauritshuis (Fig. 26) and the Huygens House at the Hague, which had been built by Jacob Van Campen about 1635. Constantign Huygens had visited England sometime after 1618 and come in contact with the circle of Inigo Jones. He had been impressed by the new trend in English architecture and had his own house designed in the light of the Jonesian experiments.

These two Dutch houses evidently impressed May and are the source of the design for his first house, Eltham Lodge (p. 150), built in 1664 for Sir John Shaw, a financier and Paymaster General. In its design May was therefore picking up the threads of the earlier Jonesian innovations.

Eltham was followed by Berkeley House, Piccadilly, in 1665, and the new wing at Cornbury a year later. May and Pratt, working side by side on Lord Clarendon's two houses, clearly shared the same opinions.

Pratt made a distinction between houses suitable for noblemen, and those for the gentry, but it was the latter that concerned him most. He recommended the 'double-pile', or 'oblong square' house, that is to say, a house consisting of two ranges of rooms, back to back. 'As to the double-pile', he wrote, 'it seems of all others to be the most useful, first for that we have there much room in a little compass, next that the chambers may there be so laid out, as to be only of use to each other, but nothing of restraint, item great conveniences there for backstairs, item that it is warm, and affords variety of places to be made use of both according to the diverse times of the day, and year also, as shall be most requisite, besides that herein a little ground is sufficient to build upon and there may be a great spare of walling, and of other materials for the roof.'[1]

He made no claim to have invented this particular form and several examples that ante-date Coleshill have already been referred to. Early signs of it may be observed in the wings at Hatfield, dating from about 1611, while the idea was more clearly stated in the 1630s at Kew, St Clere, and in the terrace range at Bolsover. During the 1660s, 70s and 80s Pratt's ideas appear to have been shared by others of his class, and houses such as Ramsbury, Wiltshire (p. 178) and Longnor, Shropshire (p. 155) correspond closely with the conceptions expressed in his notes.

The Restoration house, as may be seen in the examples illustrated, makes a strong claim to be considered the beau-ideal of country houses, essentially comfortable and convenient to live in, satisfying in proportion and scale, and sympathetic in material.

They have hitherto been frequently referred to as Wren houses, but quite erroneously, for he came to the forefront of the architectural scene only after the fire of London, by which time Pratt and May had already built their major houses. Like Inigo Jones, Wren had few opportunities for private house building and, during the whole period covered by this book, he designed only one house, the Manor House at Tring, which is recorded by Oliver's engraving in Chauncey's *History of Hertfordshire*, a rather awkward variant of the characteristic type of the period. Wren's main influence on country houses came later and was felt through his organisation of the Office of Works; under his direction this became the central school for both designers and craftsmen. It was a slow process and its full potential was hardly noticeable before 1685. Prominent architects of the next generation, Talman, Hawksmoor, John James, and Vanbrugh and, of course, the army of craftsmen they employed, were all in debt to Wren, but the assessment of his contribution is a matter for the historian concerned with the 1690s and the early 18th century.

One of the features of the period 1660–85 is the steady increase in building activity; the promise of the 1630s and 50s was now realised. The year 1659 witnessed an economic depression which extended throughout Europe, and the spate started but slowly. However, the new type soon asserted itself throughout the country, at Melton Constable in Norfolk (Fig. 34); at Bell Hall in Yorkshire; at Longnor in Shropshire and Dunsland in Devon (p. 187).

Only in the most northerly and outlandish districts was there apparent resistance. Thomas Fuller wrote of Cumberland: 'This country pretendeth not to the mode of reformed architecture, the vicinity of the Scots causing them to build rather for strength than state,'[1] and similarly of Northumberland: 'One cannot rationally expect fair fabricks here, where the vicinity of the Scots made them build not for state but strength'.[2] However even here there were signs of change, and in the late 1660s and 1670s a number of houses were given a classical dress. In the west Thomas Machell, an antiquary, and Edward Addison, a mason designer, seem to have been the key figures: according to Machell, they were 'the first introducers of Regular building into these parts: Hutton Hall in the County of Cumberland was altered by Addison; Rose Castle in Cumberland, Caesar's Tower (that is, Appleby), Howgill Castle and Crackenthorp Hall in the County of Westmorland by Mr Machell'. The Hutton he refers to is Hutton-in-the-Forest (Fig. 397), where, about 1675, Sir George Fletcher added a new front in a style that recalls London work of the early 1640s. Another interesting façade of about that date is at Moresby Hall, a house belonging to another branch of the Fletchers; there the influence of architectural engraving is marked. In Northumberland a figure equivalent to Machell and Addison appears to have been Robert Trollope, a mason designer from Newcastle. He was responsible for Capheaton Hall, a house with a richly, but rather crudely decorated façade completed in 1668, and also a number of other buildings in the district.[3]

It is tempting to search for considerable foreign influences in English houses of this period, but most patrons were more interested in the London fashion than the types that were being built in France, Holland or Italy; the Pratt-May type

---

[1] Gunther, *op. cit.*, p. 24.

[1] *Worthies of England* (ed. by John Freeman, 1952), p. 99.
[2] *op. cit.*, p. 443.   [3] *Country Life*, CXXXVIII, p. 390.

27. Kingston Lacy, Dorset. Sir Roger Pratt, 1663. Drawing for the elevation.

was English and that, they contended, was sufficient. There were, of course, exceptions to this attitude and the adventures of more enlightened builders will be discussed shortly. For most people, however, the attitudes of William Ashburnham and Lord Scudamore may be taken as typical. The former wrote to his godson, about the house he was building in Sussex: 'Remember I care not a pin how it looks from the top of the hill, whether botcht or uniform',[1] while, in 1673–1674, Scudamore wrote to Anthony Deane, the Holme Lacy mason, that he wanted the principal windows and chimney-stacks 'be done as Sir John Duncombe's are at Battlesden.'[2] Such attitudes represent an untheoretical approach to architecture and help to explain something of the wayward and unaffected charm of Caroline houses.

Pratt had recognised the limitations of the Restoration synthesis from the onset. In his notes he was careful to distinguish between the needs of princes, noblemen and gentlemen, considering that 'building about a court . . . is without all doubt fit only for a large family, and a great purse . . .'[3] An increasing desire for architectural grandeur, matching the tendency to luxury noted by Evelyn, was rendered the more inevitable by the development of the Baroque abroad.

The re-establishment of the cavaliers on their estates, at Court, or in Office, was accompanied by the increasing dominance of France in political power and social fashion. This naturally affected all those who had spent the years of the Civil War in exile there. The Royal Family, moreover,

had close ties with the Bourbons; the King's mother, Queen Henrietta Maria, was French; his sister was married to the Duke of Orleans, while his own alliance with King Louis had, at one moment, brought him almost to the point of unpopularity. In the sphere of architecture French influence was no new phenomenon; Inigo Jones had drawn on French sources for interior decoration, and Le Muet, at the end of his life, had produced a second and influential edition of his *Manière de Bien Bâtir*, a book well known in England.

Wren followed Jones's example. In 1665 he went to Paris, his visit coinciding with that of Bernini. His account of what he saw includes a number of country houses that impressed him: 'After the incomparable Villas of *Vaux* and *Maisons*, I shall but name *Ruel, Courances, Chilly, Essoane, St Maur, St Mande, Issy, Meudon, Rincy, Chantilly, Verneuil, Lioncour*, all which and I might add many others, I have survey'd . . . .' He added: 'I have purchas'd a great deal of *Taille douce* (copper-plate engraving), that I might give our *Country-men* Examples of Ornaments and Grotesks, in which the *Italians* themselves confess the French to excel'.[1]

This pro-French tendency formed the background of a group of notable houses built from the mid-1660s onwards, which revived the tradition of the Courtier type. They were, in fact, built for prominent Courtiers, who, as a group, do not appear to have been particularly active during the first few years. Among the earliest were the remodelling of Euston Hall, Suffolk, and Althorp, Northamptonshire. The former was begun by Lord Arlington, the Secretary of State, in 1666–70. Its designer is unknown, but Evelyn records that the house was 'a very noble pile, consisting of four pavilions after the French, beside a large house.' The roofs of these

---

[1] *Country Life*, CXIII, p. 1246.
[2] H. M. Colvin, *Biographical Dictionary of English Architects, 1660–1830*, p. 384.
[3] Gunther, *op. cit.*, p. 25.

[1] *Parentalia* (1740 edition), pp. 261–62.

28. *Boughton, Northamptonshire,* c. 1683. *The North Front.*

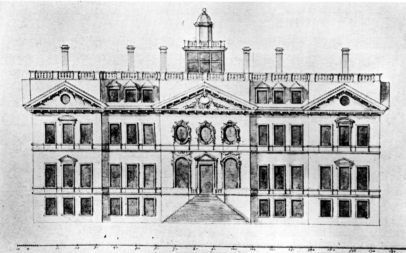

29. *Ragley Hall, Warwickshire. Design by Robert Hooke,* c. 1678.

pavilions were derived from Salomon de Brosse's Chateau de Blerancourt, which Arlington most probably had seen. The medieval and Tudor house at Althorp, which belonged to the 2nd Earl of Sunderland, was transformed into an Italianate palace in the twenty years after 1665–66. It was one of the few houses to win the Grand Duke Cosimo's approval, but the name of the architect has not yet been uncovered. After Henry Holland's alterations all that remains of the Sunderland interior is the layout of the rooms and the noble staircase and picture gallery.

Euston was followed, in 1669, by the building of Montagu House in London, designed by Robert Hooke for Ralph Montagu, the Ambassador to France. Although primarily a scientist, Hooke enjoyed a considerable architectural practice and, like his friend Wren, greatly admired contemporary French architecture. In 1677, he assisted Lord Conway in the building of Ragley Hall, Warwickshire (Fig. 29), a massive block with four corner pavilions; its plan also appears to have derived from Blerancourt. Like others of his family, Montagu was an ardent builder. Soon after he had inherited Boughton, in Northamptonshire (Fig. 28), in 1683, he began its transformation, masking the older house with two new ranges, of which neither the date nor the identity of

the architect is known. Sir Anthony Blunt has shown that the design of the entrance front was taken from an engraving of *Profil d'une maison particulier de Paris* in the *Petit Marot*.

Details in many houses were derived from France; the notion of a screen across a forecourt, for instance, was one more favoured in France than here, and may be the origin of the celebrated screen at Castle Ashby, Northamptonshire (Fig. 379), long attributed to Inigo Jones, but now thought to have been built after the Restoration. There are drawings by Gerbier and Winde for Hamstead Marshall, Berkshire, proposing a similar feature. The use of the segmental pediment crowning a bay, porch or wing, also stems from France; it occurs on houses such as Sudbury and could well have been culled from French books and engravings familiar to their owners.

Apart from introducing a greater magnificence and enlarging the vocabulary of ornament, French architecture doubtless influenced the English handling of space. While Inigo Jones had created an English classical idiom, he had not gone beyond exploring the potentialities of the square, cube or rectangle, and lesser designers were prejudiced against the possibilities of spatial variety; Wotton, for instance, wrote: 'Now the exact Circle is in truth a Figure,

30. *Ashburnham House, Westminster. The Staircase,* c. 1660.

31. *Windsor Castle. King Charles Dining Room,* c. 1674.

which for our Purpose hath many fit and eminent properties. . . . But notwithstanding these Attributes, it is in truth a very unprofitable figure in private Fabriques, as being of all other the most chargeable, and much roome lost in the bending of the walls. . . . The Ovals and other imperfect and circular formes have the same exceptions, and less so benefite of capacity.'[1] This was reasonable argument where gentry houses were concerned, but for princely splendour it was a limiting attitude. The only sign of experiment in Jones and Webb's work appears in a plan of Wilton, drawn in the 18th century, showing the vestibule with a curved wall.

Staircases were perhaps the most likely places to expect signs of spatial experiment, and the earliest example is that at Ashburnham House, Westminster (Fig. 30), a house that may have been built soon after the Restoration by William Samwell for William Ashburnham, who has already been

[1] Wotton, *op. cit.,* p. 17.

mentioned for his easy approach to country house design. This staircase is a marvellous piece of joiner's baroque in which the bottom flight invites one to ascend from an indirectly illuminated space; one passes between Ionic columns to the brilliantly lit main flight, mounting by three stages to the level of the first floor, passing between a second pair of columns adjoining a darker landing, and so to the principal rooms. The main area of the staircase is covered by a ceiling from the centre of which rises a dome supported on four groups of slim columns, linked by a balustrade, suggesting the gallery of another storey. The idea of this dome may have derived from Mansart, who used a rectangular opening over the staircase at Blois in about 1635–38, or from an upper room at the Mauritshuis. The strong sense of theatre in this remarkable staircase was a new element in English domestic architecture.

A decade later Hugh May provided an oval vestibule

32. *Nottingham Castle. Model of the castle, built 1674–9.*

behind his Palladian frontispiece at Cassiobury, Hertfordshire, which he remodelled for his kinsman, the Earl of Essex. So daring an innovation shows the extent to which May developed, in the course of ten to fifteen years, and suggests that he may have been studying the work of Le Vaux as well as Van Campen. The Cassiobury vestibule had a painted ceiling by Antonio Verrio, who had been brought over from France by Ralph Montagu in 1672.

In 1674, the King commissioned May to restore the interior of Windsor Castle and install a new range of State Apartments. The work took eleven years, and the cost was prodigious, but a decorative unity of the greatest magnificence was achieved that provided a new image for the wealthier of the King's subjects. In the next decade the redecoration of Burghley and the rebuilding of Chatsworth were executed in emulation of Windsor; they both survive more or less unaltered, but, unfortunately, most of the Windsor decoration was swept away by George IV's innovations, and only two or three of the rooms survive. The painted ceiling, carved swags and fine panelling in the King Charles Dining Room (Fig. 31) give some idea of the original effect, one that had only been attempted before at Euston

and Cassiobury, on much smaller scale. The plans of May's staircase suggest a striving for spatial effect and provide a fitting approach to the State Apartments. Charles II was, of course, emulating his cousin, King Louis, who understood and appreciated the value of a spectacular approach in the elaborate ritual of court life.

The Duke of Newcastle was an outstanding figure among the aristocrats of the day, although he belonged to an older generation who had served under Charles I. Having devoted the first years of the Restoration to repairing his estates, in 1674 he acquired the site of Nottingham Castle (Fig. 32) and started a new house to a design as novel as May's new State Apartments. The designer was Samuel Marsh, but the idea was the Duke's. The building consisted of a massive cube, two storeys high, rising from a heavily rusticated base composed of a giant order of Corinthian half-columns. The flat roof of the building was hidden behind a balustrade. Such a silhouette was quite new to this country and is the earliest of a series of imposing façades ranging in time from Thoresby to Stoneleigh. The stonework, elaborately worked and enriched with details copied from Rubens's *Palazzi di Genova*, must have looked oddly archaic at the time. The

33. *Chatsworth, Derbyshire. Part of a painting by Knyff, c. 1707.*

present castle is a reconstruction, following a fire during riots of 1831.

Nottingham leads to Thoresby, in the same county, begun by the Duke of Kingston about 1683 to William Talman's design. The outline of its entrance front was similar, but it was a larger house ranged around a courtyard. As at Windsor, great care was taken to create a spatial excitement in the staircase by means of a series of contrasting areas of varying dimension. From Thoresby Talman went on to Chatsworth (Fig. 33), perhaps by way of Burghley, and there created a more palatial example of a courtier's country house; it lies outside the theme of this volume, however, and will be described in the succeeding one.

The image of the Restoration country house is clearly fixed and many fine examples survive, but for the Charles II houses that do not correspond to the type, or contain features of advanced character, the situation is less happy. Euston has since been remodelled and reduced in size after a fire; Ragley was decorated only in the 18th century; Montagu House was rebuilt and destroyed, and Thoresby altered after a fire during building and subsequently twice rebuilt.

With the re-establishment of the Courtier house a basic split in country house design reappeared, for the gentry continued to build for several decades in the Pratt-May manner, until the Palladian villa type became fashionable in the 1720s. To illustrate this continuity two late 17th-century houses, Denham Place, Buckinghamshire (p. 203), and Nether Lypiatt, Gloucestershire (p. 211), are included here. Although in date they belong to the period of the succeeding volume, in idea and execution they are part of the Caroline tradition.

VII. PATRONS AND ARCHITECTURE

The profession of architecture during the 17th century was by no means organised, for many of the ablest exponents were amateurs without formal training. The upheaval of Civil War forced many Englishmen to travel abroad, where they were brought into touch with contemporary European building. Thenceforth foreign travel, the study of architecture and the arts, and the collecting of architectural books, became a recognised part of a gentleman's education, and was reflected, in due course, by the establishment of a classical form of country house.

Inigo Jones had not been trained originally as an architect, but turned to architecture comparatively late in life, having acquired much of his knowledge from his last journey to Italy with Lord Arundel in 1613. Pratt, May, Wren, Samwell and Talman, who came of a different background, seem never to have been entirely dependent for subsistence on their architectural activities, and it was characteristic of the time that Charles II should have appointed a poet, Sir John Denham, to the Surveyorship of the Works, in 1660. Denham, as might be expected, proved himself incompetent

34. *Melton Constable, Norfolk. Model for the house,* c. 1660.

in the job. John Webb, disappointed at having been passed over, remarked that 'he may have, as most gentry, some knowledge of the theory of architecture, he can have none of the practice', whereas Webb had been 'brought up under Inigo Jones, in the study of architecture, and [was] appointed his deputy, till thrust out for loyalty in 1643 . . .'[1] Although Webb was no innovator, as were Pratt, May or Talman, he undoubtedly has claims to be considered the first professional architect of the period.

Pratt, writing in the 1660s, did not recommend intending patrons to go to a professional designer: 'If you be not able handsomely to contrive it yourself, get some ingenious gentleman who has seen much of that kind abroad and been somewhat versed in the best authors of Architecture to do it for you, and to give you a design of it on paper'.[2] As to the provision of materials he thought 'much the better way for gentlemen themselves to agree with the owners . . . for the sending in at such a price such qualified materials, and to bargain with the others only for the working of them. . . .'[3] He continued: 'But because that men of estates have for the most part either not skill, time, or patience for so long and nice an employment, I think it would do best for such to find some honest surveyor of a long experience, and to propose a good reward to him for a faithful discharge of so considerable a trust, who performing his duty, it might very well seem to be the best money laid out.'[4]

These views correspond with the building history of several houses of the period. Sir Roger Townshend, of Raynham, Norfolk, obviously found building 'a nice employment', and, as Mr John Harris has suggested, treated it as 'a spare time occupation.'[5] He seems to have personally directed his mason, William Edge, and developed the design of his house as it progressed. George Vernon was a similar figure, devoting almost fifty years to the completion and decoration of Sudbury, Derbyshire, where among all the accounts, there is only one small payment to a surveyor. Lady Wilbraham of Weston, Staffordshire, possessed several architectural books and, with her husband, probably designed Weston in about 1670. About twenty years later, when the Wilbrahams were building Woodhey in Cheshire, Lady Wilbraham noted the comparative costs of employing various local craftsmen and Londoners, and also the prices of materials. Like John Evelyn, she enjoyed giving advice and seems to have helped her family and friends, including her son-in-law, Sir Thomas Myddleton, of Chirk. There is an entry in the Chirk accounts in 1677 for a 'trip to Weston to get my Lady Wilbraham's directions about the wainscott in the great room in the bell tower', and a number of the craftsmen seem to have gone on from Weston to Chirk, probably armed with Lady Wilbraham's recommendation. Roger North preferred to make his own designs, because 'a profest architect is proud, opiniative and troublesome, seldome at hand, and a head workman pretending to ye designing part, is full of paultry vulgar contrivances; therefore be your owne architect, or sitt still.'[6] That many people shared this view

possibly accounts for the scarcity of houses of the time whose architects are known.

Throughout his notes Pratt inserted warnings about the costs of building. There are many isolated details about the prices of bricks, woodwork and panelling, and a few examples where the total cost of a house is known. References will be made to them, either in the descriptions of the individual houses, or in the list at the end of the book, but it is impossible to sift sufficient evidence to work out the comparative costs of house building and its relation to the resources of patrons. Pratt gives a guide, but, unfortunately, not expressed in financial terms: 'I cannot but touch upon two faults of builders which are but too common, the one is, that their designs are generally too big for their purse so that in the end they are either forced to leave them imperfect, or whilst they strive to finish them they ruin themselves. My advice therefore is that by all means they would endeavour not to exceed this proportion. Let them consider well what the strength of their present stock is, and the superfluity of their income, and according to the sufficiency of these, let their undertaking be no more than what they can buy materials for the first year, build the second, finish the third, and at most finish the fourth one, all which things will very well fall out in the most proper season.'[1]

One of the limitations confronting prospective patrons, before the Restoration, was the undistinguished state of architectural draughtsmanship. John Smythson's drawings are characteristic of his time. A comparison of the drawings he made of Inigo Jones detail at Arundel House, and Jones's own drawings, is revealing; it explains much of the coarseness of detail at Bolsover Castle, which followed from Smythson's London visit, and is an interesting comparison, since his patron, Sir Charles Cavendish, was a kinsman of Lord Arundel. It emphasises the gulf between London and provincial work. The draughtsmanship of Gerbier, judging by his post-Restoration designs for Hamstead Marshall, was hardly more accomplished, and the standard of his contemporaries' work makes Inigo Jones's draughtsmanship the more remarkable. That of Webb was sound, but he never possessed the fire that inspired his master's work (Fig. 18).

There was a marked improvement during the Restoration period, particularly among the more skilled of the craftsmen. The few known drawings of Edward Pierce, the sculptor and carver (Fig. 236), and Edward Goudge (Fig. 231), the leading plasterer of the day, are exceptional in their informed accomplishment. Winde wrote a recommendation for Edward Goudge to his patron, Lady Bridgman, of Castle Bromwich, in June, 1688: 'I will assure yr Ladyp no man in England has a better Tallent in ye way of plastering than himselfe. Hee has bine imployed by mee this 6 or 7 yeares, is an excelent drauftesman and mackes all his desines himselfe. . . .'[2]

One reason for the improvement was the advance made in book illustration and the engraving of ornament. In the first years of the century the key reference book was Serlio's *Regole generali di architettura*, which had appeared between 1540 and 1575. It had first been translated into English in

[1] C.S.P.D. 1660–61, p. 76.   [2] Gunther, *op. cit.*, p. 60.
[3] Gunther, *op. cit.*, p. 48.   [4] Gunther, *op. cit.*, p. 48.
[5] *Archaeological Journal*, 1961, p. 180.
[6] H. M. Colvin, *Architectural Review*, Vol. 110, October, 1951, p. 259.

[1] Gunther, *op. cit.*, p. 54.
[2] *A Renaissance Plasterer*, G. W. Beard, *Country Life*, CX, p. 1157.

1611. As Dr Peter Murray has said, 'it was the first really practical hand-book on the art of architecture',[1] illustrated with small wood engravings of the type shown in Figs. 25 and 125; Palladio's *I Quattro Libri* was also illustrated with wood blocks. Rubens's *Palazzi di Genova* first appeared in 1622, and from the first achieved considerable success, chiefly on account of the fine quality of its illustrations which were printed from engraved copper-plates: this was the first time detailed elevations were readily available (Fig. 154).

Details of interior decoration lagged behind, but advances here had been made in France, notably by Barbet and Le Muet, whose second and more important edition of *Manière de Bien Bâtir* with the *Augmentations de Nouveaux Bâtiment* was published in 1647. The superb engravings of ornament by Jean Marot and Le Pautre began to appear in the next decade.

Books and prints must have poured into England, since native designers had little to offer, and, although there were many print-sellers, there were few publishers at the time. Of the few English prints, the best were those published by Edward Pierce the elder, in 1640, and some etched '*designs For Friezes with Boyes, Beasts and Fruits, usefull for Painters, Goldsmiths, Carvers, etc.*' by Francis Clein. The choice of architectural books was large; by 1670 it included translations of the better known ones. The Serlio of 1611 was followed in 1642 by an English edition of Vignola, by a Palladio in 1663, a Vitruvius and a Scamozzi in 1669, and in 1664 Evelyn published his translation of Freart. All these exerted a powerful influence not only on English taste generally, but on draughtsmanship as well. However, it is difficult to point out many examples of direct quotation, because few contemporary libraries survive in houses of the period, and it is difficult to prove whether or not a patron had access to a particular book. Here, as in so much else, Lamport is a

revealing exception, but it is not always possible to be sure whether books were acquired by Sir Justinian, Webb's patron, or his son. In these circumstances the survival of Lyndon Hall, Rutlandshire (p. 174) and of the papers of its builder, Sir Abel Barker, is of special interest: here it is possible to compare Barker's notes from Palladio, Gerbier and the Act for the Rebuilding of the City of London, with the specification for the house built in the 1670s and with the house as it stands today.

Pratt was aware of the deficiencies of architectural engravings and woodcuts: 'Yet never having seen anything in its full proportions, it is not to be thought that he can conceive of them as he ought, and as for the most part of other delineations, they are rather certain adumbrations, than any perfect descriptions of those fabrics by which they made.'[1] Hence he, like other writers, insisted on the importance of models. Wotton warned: 'Let no man that intendeth to build, setle his Fancie upon a draught of the *Worke* in *paper* ... without a *Modell* or *Type* of the whole *Structure*, and of every parcell and Partition in *Pastboord* or *Wood*.'[2] There are several references to models in building accounts of the time, from Raynham onwards, but few contemporary ones have survived. Perhaps the earliest is that made by Samwell for the King's House at Newmarket, dating from the 1660s. The fine example at Melton Constable, Norfolk (Fig. 34), dates from a year or two later.

There is an element of caution in Pratt's writing that not only corresponds with his social background, but with his awareness of the unfamiliarity of his class and the craftsmen with classical architecture. His own buildings showed no lack of confidence, but a lack of it seems to have played a part in the relationship between patrons and their architects, which probably contributed to the tardy acceptance of Inigo Jones's ideas.

[1] *Architecture of the Italian Renaissance*, p. 197.

[1] Gunther, *op. cit.*, p. 24.   [2] Wotton, *op. cit.*, p. 65.

VIII. CRAFTSMANSHIP AND INTERIOR DECORATION

The evolution of the Caroline house had been a lengthy process hampered by political events, an innate conservatism and a scarcity, until the 1660s, of skilled craftsmen. After the Restoration, however, new skills and techniques were mastered so that the last three decades of the century became the golden age of English craftsmanship. During these years the virtuoso performances of certain outstanding carvers and plasterers dominate the scene, and the interest of the Restoration house shifts from form to decoration.

Inigo Jones's sense of the spatial elements in architecture is apparent in the Queen's House, Greenwich, where the rooms are related, one to another, by contrast of proportion. His control was attained through his complete direction, so that he was able to achieve passable classical detail with only inexperienced and untutored craftsmen. The artisan builders never exercised similar control over their craftsmen, the latter being free to express themselves occasionally in un-learned and ill-executed detail.

Until the Restoration synthesis was established, the chief interest of a house generally rested on the degree of success or failure by which it came to terms with the classical idiom.

In the more ambitious houses, built before 1660, there had been a sense of experiment and conflict that sometimes adds to their effectiveness, but the quality of the decoration was often of a low standard. After the erection of Eltham and Clarendon House there was less need to experiment, because the problems of elevation and plan in relation to needs and taste had been solved, and succeeding examples of the period became variations on the synthesis.

In such a situation the decorative element became the more important, with plasterers, carvers, painters, furniture-makers and upholsterers playing the flutes and trumpets accompanying the organ operated by the masons, joiners and other artificers. Great vitality is evidenced in every aspect of craftsmanship which, contemporaneously with the airs of Purcell and the verse of Dryden, reached its finest flowering.

An extraordinary unity pervaded the whole field of decorative art, a synthesis or common language of style, not only in interior design, but in furniture, metalwork and textiles, all of which bear strong generic influences.

Although a few of the craftsmen were foreigners, there were Englishmen of great, or even greater, ability and a

35. *The staircase by Grinling Gibbons, 1674, formerly at Cassiobury Park, Hertfordshire, now in the Metropolitan Museum, New York.*

tradition developed which, in Evelyn's estimation, became 'equal to any we meet abroad.' The situation contrasts forcibly with that in the 1650s when Webb wrote to his client at Lamport, Sir Justinian Isham: 'As for yor ffrench workeman I desire alwaies to employ our own countriemen, for by emploiment those grow insolent and these for want thereof are dejected, supposing they are not accompted able to perform when indeed it is only want of encouragement makes them negligent to study because a better conceite of foreigners as had they of themselves.'[1]

The standard of competence became such that an architect, when once the main features of a design had been agreed by his client, could turn the matter over to his craftsmen, who submitted their own 'draughts' for the parts they were prepared to execute, which were then signed to show that they had been 'allowed'. Plasterers of the calibre of Goudge and carvers such as Grinling Gibbons and Pierce invariably designed their own work which they submitted to the architect. Winde's letters to Lady Bridgman provide an example; when writing to her in 1688 about the hall doors at Castle Bromwich he said 'if Mr Ayscough (the joiner) will make designes for them & send them to London if they come to my hands I shall readily give my opinion of them.'

WOODWORK

Before the innovations of Inigo Jones the panelling of rooms had usually been divided into small units, but occasionally subdivided into bays by the application of pilasters, as in the room from Bromley Palace, now in the Victoria and Albert

[1] R.I.B.A. Journal, 3rd Series, XXVIII, p. 565.

Museum. Later, an 'order' was applied to the wall surface, dividing it into dado, filling and cornice. The Haynes Grange Room (Fig. 8) is an exceptionally architectural example of this kind of design. The final step as far as the Caroline period was concerned was the disappearance of the order, as at Wilton, where the pilaster is implied by the elaborately carved pendants (Fig. 109). Later large raised and fielded panels, three, four or even six feet wide, framed by bolection mouldings, were made to take the gilt-framed portraits then being turned out from the studio of Lely, while smaller panels filled the spaces above the doors and fireplaces. Oak was the most frequently used for these panels and was carefully cut to display as much of the figure as possible. Mouldings were left plain, but richness was introduced in the carving of architraves, overdoors and overmantels, while the cornice was often embellished with carved acanthus-leaf decoration.

The early Caroline staircase relied for effect on its balustrade, which originated in the richly decorated runs of strapwork set between the massive newels of the Jacobean houses. In the early 1630s, however, strapwork was replaced by pierced panels of naturalistic carving, generally based on great waves of acanthus foliage rolling upwards. Bold in their main lines, yet sometimes crude in rendering, these panels in which fanciful animals, birds and figures disport themselves, represent a high achievement in woodcarving. There is a transitional balustrade at Blithfield in Staffordshire, dating from the 1630s, which has panels of acanthus and other decoration, and newels topped by baskets of fruit. The martial tone of the panels at Ham, Surrey, constructed in the late 1630s, is exceptional (Fig. 81). The acanthus type was

36. *Christchurch Mansion, Ipswich. Woodwork in the Great Hall*, c. 1675.

used at Thorpe (Fig. 160) and Forde (Fig. 179), in the 1650s, at Eltham (Fig. 253), in the early 1660s, and at both Cassiobury (Fig. 35) and Sudbury (Fig. 280) in the 1670s. The staircase at Cassiobury, now in the Metropolitan Museum, New York, consists of runs of superb acanthus carving between massive newels. It is constructed of various woods, pine for the handrail and the oak-leaf and acorn string, ash for the balustrades and finials, and oak for the steps and landings. At Hinchingbrooke, Huntingdonshire, the staircase was made soon after the Restoration by Kinnaird, the King's master joiner, and is unusual in that the acanthus is carved in relief, but not pierced. The execution is not very fluid and shows how undistinguished such work could be at the time when the Monarchy was restored. When it is compared with the stairs at Cassiobury and Sudbury of fifteen years later, the rapid improvement in the standard of craftsmanship is remarkable.

The baluster form of balustrade was an alternative. The best example of this type was the noble staircase at Coleshill, Berkshire, which was one of the few where the spatial possibilities of a staircase were explored. Another of the kind is at Thorpe, Northamptonshire, where the acanthus balustrade of the main staircase gives way, at the second

floor, to balusters in the circular flight leading up to the roof platform. The staircase at Ashburnham House, Westminster, dating from the early 1660s, has already been discussed (p. 34). Among the finer Charles II staircases with balusters as opposed to pierced panels are those at Powis Castle, Montgomeryshire, and Longnor Hall, Shropshire, probably by the same man, and at Wolseley Hall, Staffordshire, possibly by Pierce, where the balusters have spiral turning.

During the last quarter of the century wrought iron balustrades, combined with stone stairs, became usual in the grandest houses, especially after Tijou, the French smith, had published his book of designs. After the long interval from the time of Jones's 'tulip' staircase in the Queen's House, stone and iron, in the French manner, were employed in grand houses like Chatsworth and Drayton.

During the Inigo Jones-Webb period, fireplaces were usually of the continued, or two-storeyed type, but the Restoration architects reverted to the simple Dutch form in which the chimney-breast was panelled similarly to the walls, and the fire-opening emphasised by a bold bolection moulding of coloured marble.

Before the arrival of Grinling Gibbons from Holland, woodcarving had been of the bold, solid and close type, such as we see at Wilton, where heavy swags and drops of fruit form the motifs, without under-cutting or disengaged detail.

In the 1650s, great advances were made in the Low Countries, particularly by Artus Quellin I, who was responsible for the rich sculptural detail in the Town Hall in Amsterdam, built between 1648 and 1655. The fame of these decorations was spread by a magnificent book containing a long series of Quellin's etchings. These had considerable influence on Grinling Gibbons, who carried it a stage further by absorbing something of the character of Dutch flower painting, giving the wood, as Horace Walpole said, 'the loose and airy lightness of flowers . . .', chaining together 'the various productions of the elements with free disorder natural to each species.' Gibbons' first country house commission was for the staircase at Cassiobury, in Hertfordshire, the house altered for Lord Essex by Hugh May, between 1674 and 1680. In 1677, he made a brief appearance at Sudbury, carving the overmantel in the Drawing Room there (Fig. 278), and he then passed into Royal service at Windsor Castle.

Apart from some carving at Burghley, paid for in 1683, and at Badminton, paid for in 1684, and the Saloon overmantel at Ramsbury (Fig. 302), this is all that is known of his work in country houses before 1685. It was never as considerable as is generally supposed; and so Pierce, Selden, Samuel Watson, Thomas Young and Jonathan Maine, all men of great talent as carvers, will never receive their due.

PLASTERWORK

The great virtuosity of plasterwork after the Restoration was based on a revolution in technique. From Tudor times the elements of a ceiling or overmantel were cast from moulds transported by the journeyman from house to house. A section would be cast in a mixture of lime and plaster of Paris, and then applied in semi-plastic condition with the aid of nails. After the Restoration a harder, quick-drying plaster, called *stucco durro*, was introduced and used for the

37. *Astley Hall, Lancashire. The Drawing Room ceiling*, c. 1666.

elaborate naturalistic motifs, individually modelled fruit and flowers mounted on wire, wood or leather that then came into vogue. The ability to undercut created new possibilities of light and shade and new contrasts between plain and decorated areas.

Geometrical beamed and moulded ceilings had been introduced by Inigo Jones before the innovation of this new plaster. 'The most beautiful and commodious in my mind,' wrote Pratt, 'are those three which the Italians call *a la Cupola, a Padaglione* and *a Conca.* The two first are most proper for Chapels and Banqueting houses, but the latter is exceedingly graceful for rooms, especially if it be divided artificially into noble squares, ovals, or circles, and the like, and those either filled with painting, or absolutely without; but for the small divisions the plastering with Antikes, and other like devices, it is wholly ungraceful.'[1] For the Chapel at St James's Palace, Jones provided a coffered barrel-vault, and at Greenwich both the cove and the *conca.* Coved ceilings were not extensively used, however, being considered a waste of space. There is an early one in the chapel at Castle Ashby, erected in about 1624, and there was another of later date in the Saloon at Amesbury, which appears to have been a smaller version of the Double Cube Room at Wilton.

The development of plasterwork design may be studied

[1] Gunther, *op. cit.*, p. 67.

in the work of the Abbotts of Barnstaple, Devon, a dynasty of plasterers whose notebook designs survive. This was begun by John Abbott, the elder, about 1575, continued by his son, Richard, and by his grandson John, the younger. It was probably Richard who carried out the plasterwork at Forde Abbey, Dorset (p. 111), where the ceilings are a rich blend of the beam-pattern, of Jonesian origin, with lavish all-over ornament that harks back to the Jacobean tradition. The second John Abbott was born in 1639/40, and as a young man adopted the newly-introduced naturalistic manner. He executed a ceiling in the Exeter Custom House, in 1680/81, and may also have worked at Lindridge, Youlston and Dunsland, all in Devon (Fig. 318). The Abbotts came from a remote part of the west country and their work has not been identified outside this area.

Of the London plasterers perhaps the best known was Edward Goudge, a master craftsman much respected by William Winde, but there were others who enjoyed equal fame — John Grove, for instance, who did ceilings at the Queen's House after the Restoration, Henry Doogood, Halbert and Dunsterfield, who worked at Holyrood and possibly also at Holme Lacy and Eye Manor. Much of the plasterwork at Sudbury (p. 162) was executed by Bradbury and Pettifer; Edward Martin may have worked at Burghley and did the chapel ceiling at Arbury (Fig. 38) in 1678. Most of the well-known plasterers also worked on the City churches

38. *Arbury Hall, Warwickshire. The Chapel ceiling, by Edward Martin, 1678.*

and thus came within the orbit of Wren and the Office of Works.

Their exquisite work continued in vogue until the 1690s and later, in remote districts. Then wealthier patrons began to prefer the painted ceilings they had seen in Italy and France, or in the new State Apartments at Windsor. The change may be seen at Burghley where, on the ground floor, elaborate decorative plasterwork was employed, but for the State Rooms on the upper floor, begun in 1687, the celestial divinities of Verrio hold sway. Such Olympian scenes required no elaborate garlands or swags to set them off, and the plasterers eventually lost the battle to the painters. In 1702, Goudge lamented how 'the employment which has been my chiefest pretence has been always dwindling away, till now it's just come to nothing.'[1]

DECORATIVE PAINTING

The strength of Caroline interior decoration lay in its sumptous plasterwork and carved woodwork, and beside these crafts decorative painting played a subordinate role. This position was inevitable in view of the general pattern of country house building, for rich painting on walls and ceilings is essentially a courtly form of decoration, both in idea and cost, and the courtiers were generally timid patrons between 1615 and 1660. Not only were opportunities limited, but English painters were not of a calibre to surmount the difficulties.

As with plasterwork and woodwork, the most interesting commissions were those carried out in the last years of this period, and for the decades before 1660 the amount of surviving material is not considerable. In the catalogue of his

[1] Hist. MSS Comm. Earl Cowper, quoted by Miss Jourdain, and by Geoffrey Beard, *Country Life*, CXI, p. 1411.

first volume of *Decorative Painting in England*, Mr Edward Croft-Murray lists all the known work, but there are only three country houses where good quality painting survives. The earliest is Castle Ashby, where there is an attractive Painted Bower done after 1621 for the 2nd Earl of Northampton, perhaps by Matthew Gooderick. At Ham there is a ceiling painted in tempera by Clein in the former Miniature Room, some smaller inset panels by him in the North Drawing Room (Fig. 82) and another set after Polidoro da Caravaggio in the Marble Dining Room (Fig. 88).

Much more survives at Wilton, in the Hunting Room (Fig. 100), the Single Cube (Fig. 102) and Double Cube Rooms (Fig. 105), and this is sufficiently varied to show what was possible in England in the middle of the century. In the Double Cube Room, with its cove by the elder Pierce and three ceiling paintings by Emmanuel de Critz, the English admiration for Venetian art is displayed. The grotesque ceiling of the Single Cube Room, possibly by Gooderick, is very close to one in the Queen's Bedchamber at the Queen's House (Fig. 59) and inset in the panels of the dado are a series of small Schiavone-like panels by de Critz. The idea of the series of painted panels mounted in panelling in the Hunting Room is much simpler and there were other rather later houses that possessed rooms decorated in this way. Of these the best surviving one is at Old Wilsey, a house at Cranbrook in Kent, which is decorated with sporting and biblical scenes. The Wilton panels by the elder Pierce are more accomplished than the Old Wilsey scenes and in their derivation from Tempesta prints belong to a European current of ideas.

Wilton possessed more decorative painting than any other house until the rebuilding of Chatsworth and the redecoration of Burghley, both of which lie beyond the

39. *Powis Castle, Montgomeryshire. The Great Staircase, c. 1670. The ceiling possibly by Verrio after 1674, and the walls by Lanscroon, 1705.*

40. Charles II being presented by Mr Rose with the first pineapple grown in England, *by Danckerts. The house is thought to be Dorney Court, Weybridge.*

41. The Paston Treasure *The possessions and interests of Sir Robert Paston, painted c. 1665 by an unknown artist.*

terminal date of this study. There Verrio and Laguerre were the principal painters, but just as the south front of Chatsworth marks a breach in the Caroline tradition, the allegorical paintings on walls and ceilings within point to an English patron's strivings after the effects of contemporary French and Italian decoration. However, the way for this new style was prepared in Charles II's reign, mainly by Ralph Montagu, who brought over Verrio about 1672. The latter worked at Euston and Cassiobury before he began to decorate the new state rooms at Windsor Castle, but nothing now survives of these first two commissions. Laguerre did not arrive until about 1684 and so plays virtually no part in the history of decorative painting during Charles II's reign.

On a large scale one of the most important pieces of painted decoration is the ceiling of the staircase at Powis Castle (Fig. 39). This may be by Verrio and date from about 1675. Again, as with much of the Wilton decoration, the inspiration is Venetian, for the design is adapted from that of Veronese's *Apotheosis of Venice* in the Doge's Palace.

The part played by decorative painting in a country house of Charles II's reign was usually confined to the provision of overmantels and overdoors, for as Pratt said of the latter, 'if some little picture, but chiefly some pleasant landscape of ruins and trees be put, it will add much grace to the place where they are.'[1] Many examples of this fashion survive, notably at Ham, Thorpe, Denham Place and in more modest houses like the Parsonage at Stanton Harcourt, in Oxfordshire. However, they rarely possess the aesthetic quality of the Van de Veldes at Ham and often they look as if they have been copied from an engraving by the house painter, whose general line of work was what was then called 'vulgar painting', that is to say graining, marbling and other techniques that disguised the simple nature of the materials used.

This habit of imitating richer woods and coloured marbles was well established, and there are a number of references to such practices in the manuals like Smith's *Art of Painting in Oyle* (1676), but unfortunately little information on how they were done. Again Ham contains some of the best examples of graining, but there are well preserved grained rooms at Dunsland and examples of marbling at Belton, although these are not all of the 17th century.

[1] Gunther, *op. cit.*, p. 69.

IX. POLITER LIVING AND GRANDER MANNERS

As we have said, the Caroline house was evolved for the gentry rather than for the aristocracy. Domestic in character, it afforded limited scope for grandeur and display or for accommodating large households. Nevertheless, as wealth and security grew, 'the politer way of living' noted by Evelyn passed rapidly in many instances 'to luxury and intolerable expense'.

The taste for abundance, howbeit within a relatively simple setting, is no less obvious in the manners and dress than with decoration and sculpture of the age. It is evocatively illustrated in the large still life painting (Fig. 41) which Sir Robert Paston, later Earl of Yarmouth, of Oxhead Hall, Norfolk, in 1665 commissioned from an unknown artist, depicting some of his interests and possessions.

An essential part of the change in the way of life was the improvement in furniture design and the introduction of new pieces designed for special purposes. Before the Restoration, English furniture had been of simple construction, restricted in range to comparatively few types — tables, cupboards, chests, chairs and stools. A few Italian pieces had been introduced during the reign of Charles I, usually the gifts of ambassadors, but these found their way only into the royal palaces or the greater houses: native furniture was plain in the extreme. The Restoration had the same stimulating effect as in other spheres; more and finer examples were now demanded by the more elaborate social system, and by the more luxurious style of living. A considerable quantity, particularly of chairs, was imported from Holland. The typical Restoration chair with a tall back, the legs and arm-supports scrolled, and the stretchers broad and elaborately carved, is almost indistinguishable from Dutch examples; it was usually upholstered in gros-point or heavily fringed velvet, or had a seat and back of cane, a material introduced into chair-making about 1664. Cane chairs 'gave so much satisfaction to all the Nobility, Gentry and Common-alty of this Kingdom (for their Durableness, Lightness and Cleanness, from Dust, Worms and Moths, which insuperably attend Turkey-work, Serge and other stuff chairs and Couches, that they came to be much used and sent to all parts of the Europe'. The cresting of the high backs and deepened front stretcher rails were frequently carved with the device of *amorini* supporting the crown, a motif repeatedly mentioned in contemporary accounts as 'carved with Boyes and Crown'.

Of the new types, perhaps the most important were the chests of drawers, all but unknown before the Restoration, and pieces related to them, such as the cabinet, the cabinet-on-stand (Fig. 42), the bureau-table and the secretaire (Fig. 45). Most grand houses furnished during the latter half of the 17th century had such pieces, but few retain them today. Of those that do perhaps the most evocative is Boughton in Northamptonshire, remodelled by Ralph Montagu, the Ambassador to France. It has been said of this house that if a chronicler of England under the later Stuarts wished to environ himself with the true atmosphere of the age, nowhere could he do so better, for there the furniture largely retains its original upholstery and trimmings. Boughton has kept its contents and its atmosphere, because it remained virtually uninhabited from the mid-18th century until 1910. But to see the furniture of the period one must go to Ham House, where examples of the new types are to be seen, many of them employing materials and combinations of materials not used in England before; ebony tables with embossed and chased silver plaques and mounts (Fig. 46), walnut topped tables on gilt caryatid supports, taper stands and pier glasses decorated with floral marquetry. For the latter plate-glass was produced at the 2nd Duke of Buckingham's Glass House at Vauxhall, and at a considerably lower price than had hitherto prevailed. In 1664, Pepys noted that he had bought with satisfaction 'a very fair glasse for five guineas'.

These new combinations of material and techniques of decoration were part of the general adoption of walnut in place of oak for furniture; it was richer in both colour and texture, and lent itself to greater elegance of shaping and a higher polish. Among the woods used for marquetry, apart from walnut veneer laid in elaborate patterns, were laburnum and olive, box and holly; other colours were obtained by dyeing ivory or bone red, green or black.

The delicacy and richness of the new shapes and patterns was matched by the costly fabrics and trimmings used for the upholstery, Genoese velvet, or brocade, trimmed with galon and silk or silver-thread fringes. Time has mellowed the colour and texture of these materials so that they are now a pale reflection of their original state, but something of their original splendour may be seen in the state beds of the time, those towering structures of fantasy made gorgeous with hangings and upholstery. One of the finest is in the state bedroom at Drayton, Northamptonshire (Fig. 49), the hangings all worked in petit point and the interior lined with yellow watered silk. At the foot of the bed are placed two taper stands and an inlaid marquetry tablè, almost half a century later in date than John Webb's chimneypiece and overmantel, the design for which is shown in Fig. 48.

The tapestries that hang in the room are Mortlake, a product of the factory founded in 1619 under James I's patronage. Perhaps its most notable achievement was the weaving of tapestries from the Raphael cartoons (Fig. 181), bought for the purpose in 1623. The first director, Sir Francis Crane, collected a team of highly-qualified weavers, mainly from the Netherlands, although Philip Maeght, the chief weaver, was brought from Paris. Crane died in 1636 and for a time the factory was in the charge of Lady Harvey, acting on behalf of her brother, the Earl of Montagu, the Master of the Great Wardrobe, where weavers were engaged on the repair and maintenance of the tapestries in the Royal Collection. Weavers were occasionally transferred from Mortlake to the Wardrobe and others sometimes left and set up on their own account, as did William Benod at Lambeth; and since the factory's mark, a St George's cross on a shield, was often appropriated by these independent weavers, it is difficult to assign pieces with accuracy. Francis Poyntz, 'His Majesties' Chief Arras-Maker', signed some of the pieces at Hardwick and Houghton.

The extravagance of Restoration taste appears at its most obvious in its use of silver, not only for ornaments to be applied to furniture, but for encasing whole pieces. Apart from some at Knole, Burghley and in the Royal Collection, little of this has survived, for there was a strong temptation to melt it down. As early as 1696–97 Celia Fiennes records the Earl of Chesterfield turning it in, when William III offered 4s. 4d. an ounce. The tables at Windsor were presented to William III, but at Knole the pieces date from the 6th Earl of Dorset's time and look their richest against a tapestry background. As well as for sconces, silver was used for chimney furniture, where it would catch the play of flickering firelight. In the miniature closet at Ham the fender is of

42, 43. Inlaid walnut cabinet on stand, c. 1670, and opened to show needlework panels, including portraits of Charles II and Queen Catherine. At Groombridge Place, Kent (see page 123).

44, 45, 46. *Furniture at Ham House, Surrey. (Top left) A sleeping chair, with an adjustable back, c. 1670; (above) a scriptoire veneered with burr walnut and with silver mounts and handles, c. 1670; (left) a walnut table with an ebony top enriched with embossed and chased silver mounts and a central plaque bearing a countess's coronet, c. 1675.*

47. Mirror and table veneered with Chinese Lacquer, c. 1675, at Ham House.

and hinges became features of decorative importance. From about 1680 they were made in suites and cast in 'princes metal', a golden brass alloy invented by Prince Rupert, the plates being pierced, engraved and riveted to the lock face, with matching hinges, catchplates, escutcheons and keys provided *en suite*. Chandeliers of brass or latten, following familiar Flemish models, were made for wax candles, their socketed arms extending from baluster stems springing from large reflecting spheres.

The restricted vocabulary of ornament may account for the success of the imports of the East India Companies, which included porcelain, new fabrics and materials and a whole new vocabulary of ornament. As early as 1615, Lady Arundel had a 'bedde of Japan', but generally oriental goods in the first half of the century were called Indian. By mid-century, the porcelain trade was well under way and when John Evelyn was invited to a great supper by Lady Gerrard in 1652, he noted 'all the vessells, which were innumerable, were of porcelain, she having the most ample and richest collection of that curiosity in England'.

Apart from the leather hangings of oriental style at Honington, Warwickshire, and the lacquer panels in the Chinese closet at Drayton, Northamptonshire, no other Caroline room with oriental decoration has survived. The earliest example of an oriental wallpaper may be that at

48. Drayton House, Northamptonshire. Design for the chimney-piece in the State Bed Chamber by John Webb, 1653.

pierced and embossed silver, the tongs and shovel have silver mounts and the fire basket itself is all of silver (Fig. 93).

Towards the end of the century gesso was developed as a cheaper alternative for mirror frames and furniture, and particularly for the stands of cabinets. The composition, a mixture of calcium sulphate and parchment glue, was applied in successive thin coats to a previously roughly carved surface, and, when hardened, was recarved, sanded or, maybe, punched and then gilded.

An item of household equipment to which particular attention was devoted was door furniture; rim locks, bolts

49. *Drayton House. The State Bedroom, with the original Webb overmantel, a late 17th-century state-bed hung with embroidered hangings, and furniture in the style of Gereit Jensen.*

Longnor, Shropshire, which possibly dates from the 1690s (Fig. 267).

By then lacquer had become very fashionable and was being imitated in England, where it was claimed in 1683 that 'English varnished cabinets might vie with the oriental'. These cabinets are among the most representative pieces of the taste of Charles II's reign; they combine the aspiration of the day for exoticism and a liking for curiosities with brilliance of colour and elaboration of decoration. The strong contrasts of smooth surfaces with the rich carving and gilding of their stands had a particular appeal: in Stalker and Parker's *Treatise of Japanning and Varnishing* (1688) it was put forward that 'what can be more surprising than to have our chambers overlaid with varnish more glossy and reflecting than polisht marble? . . .'

New forms, materials and ornaments were a great feature of the country house of Evelyn's day, and contributed to the new elegance of life that the diarist noticed on his visit to Euston, Suffolk, in 1677. After describing the splendour of the apartments he mentions those 'for my Lord, Lady and Duchess with kitchens and other offices below, in a lesser form; lodgings for servants, all distinct, for them to retire to when they please, and would be in private . . . This seat is admirably placed for field-sports, hawking, hunting or racing. The mutton is small, but sweet. The stables hold thirty horses and four coaches. The out-offices make two large quadrangles, so as servants never lived with more ease and convenience; never master more civil. Strangers are attended and accommodated as at their home, in pretty apartments furnished with all manner of conveniences and privacy. There is a library full of excellent books; bathing rooms, elaboratory, dispensary, a decoy, and places to keep and fat fowl in. I believe he had now in his family one hundred domestic servants.'[1]

The Duke of Beaufort, who appears with his family in the

[1] *Diary*. September 10, 1677.

D

50. The 1st Duke and
Duchess of Beaufort
and their family, *by S.
Browne*, 1685.

portrait group by Browne (Fig. 50), kept even greater state at Badminton, Gloucestershire. He was visited there when 'in the midst of his building' by Sir Matthew Hale, who described the manner of life as being 'above any other except crowned heads, and in some respects greater than most of them, to whom he might have been an example. He had about 200 persons . . . all provided for.' In the servants' hall, according to Roger North, were 'the chief steward with the gentlemen and pages; the master of the horse with the coachmen and liveries; an under steward with the bailiffs and some husbandmen; the clerk of the kitchen with the bakers, brewers etc, altogether; and other more inferior people under these places apart' . . . 'soap and candles were made in the house; . . . and all the drink that came to the Duke's table was of malt, sundried upon the leads of his house.' At the Duke's table 'the meats were very neat, and not gross, no servants in livery attended, but those called gentlemen only; and in the several kinds, even down to the small beer, nothing could be more choice than the table was. It was an oblong, and not an oval; and the duchess with two daughters only, sat at the upper end. If the gentlemen chose a glass of wine, then civil offers were made to go down into

the vaults, which were very large and sumptuous, or servants at a given sign, attended with salvers, etc; and many a brisk round went about; but no sitting at table with tobacco and healths as the too common use is.' In a gallery where the ladies sat the Duchess had 'divers gentlewomen commonly at work upon embroidery and fringe-making, for all the beds of state were made and finished in the house.'[1]

After retiring from public affairs the Duke was said to have 'had always some new project of building, walling or planting' on hand, activities that extended beyond the gardens and over much of the countryside and which excited Celia Fiennes more than anything else. 'You may Stand on ye Leads', she noted, 'and look twelve ways down to Ye parishes and Grounds beyond all through Glides or visto of trees.'[2] The period described by John Evelyn was an age of pomp in which Englishmen delighted in a passion for display, and strove to enjoy life to the full.

The Ishams of Lamport, the Corbetts of Longnor and the Bickfords of Dunsland lived in a less spectacular manner, but their houses nevertheless express, though on more modest scale, the 'politer way of living'.

[1] Roger North, *Lives of the Norths*.   [2] *Diary* (ed. Morris), p. 236.

THE QUEEN'S HOUSE, GREENWICH

The Queen's House represents the nature of Inigo Jones's architectural revolution on a domestic scale. Begun in 1616 for Queen Anne, the consort of James I, building stopped in 1618 and was not resumed until 1629-35 when it was completed for Queen Henrietta Maria. (National Maritime Museum.)

During the Tudor and Stuart eras the Thames provided a ceremonial approach to London and on its banks were built several of the Royal Palaces, among them the old Tudor Palace at Greenwich. To this group of buildings by the waterside James I added the Queen's House, the first unit of a building complex that was to grow into England's grandest Classical architectual achievement. Initiated by Inigo Jones, it was continued by John Webb and brought to a splendid conclusion by Christopher Wren, with the assistance of Vanbrugh and Hawksmoor. Although the Queen's House is really too small to justify its position as the climax of the great vista from the river (Fig. 52), Wren's colonnades and twin domes appear to pay tribute to its peculiar position in the domain of English architecture.

Conceived partly as a Royal villa and partly as a conceit or fantasy, the Queen's House, although not a country house, opens our survey because it illustrates, as no other house, the quality of Jones's domestic work, and the nature of the revolution he brought about. His houses at Newmarket and Bagshot have disappeared and Stoke Park survives only in part, so that the Queen's House remains to demonstrate his European standing. In this building he succeeded in lifting English domestic architecture from a provincial, but none-the-less spectacular level, to one that stands proudly beside that of the 16th-century Italy.

Its building is a complicated story and the early stages are obscure, but from 1660 its history is well-documented and it is possible to trace successive alterations, modifications and spoliations that have continued until the present century.[1]

In 1616, the year after his appointment as Surveyor of

[1] *The Queen's House*, Survey of London, 1937.

51. *Inigo Jones. It is inscribed 'Vandyke's original drawing, from which the Print by Van Voert was taken, in the Book of Vandyke's Heads. Given me by the Duke of Devonshire. Burlington.'*

the Royal Works, Inigo Jones was called upon by Queen Anne to design a house for her on the site of an old gate-house at Greenwich that faced the Dover Road, which separated the gardens and park. In order that the Queen might step direct from the gardens on the river side to the

52. *The Royal Hospital, Greenwich, from the Thames, with the Queen's House in the centre.*

53. *The North Front facing the River.*

54. *The South Front. The projecting bay on the West Façade was added by Webb in 1660.*

55. *The Double Curved Stairway to the North Front.*

56. *The Loggia on the South Front.*

57. *The Entrance Hall. The floor design reflects that of the pattern of the ceiling.*

58. *The north west corner of the Hall.*

park on the other side without walking on the highway, Jones devised the idea of a house spanning the road.

None of the designs survive and the only dated Jones drawing of that year is that shown in Fig. 5. However, there is a sheet of sketch plans in the R.I.B.A. Library that may have been made with this house in mind; some of these recall Vignola's Villa Giulia, in Rome, a courtier's house not intended for permanent residence and one that could have given Jones inspiration for his unusual commission from the Queen.

Eighteen months later the Queen fell ill and further progress was halted; within twelve months she was dead, and work on the house was abandoned. The palace and the park were then granted to Charles, Prince of Wales, and, after his marriage to Henrietta Maria, were settled upon her. Stalbemts' picture, in the Royal Collection, shows Charles and his Queen in Greenwich park with the old Palace in the background, and the unfinished Queen's house appearing as a low, single-storey building.

In 1629 the new Queen decided to resume work, and Jones's original designs were then amended. It is likely that the upper part of the south, or park, front (Fig. 54) was revised, for it is doubtful whether he could have created so sophisticated a façade before he had tackled either Newmarket or Whitehall. Work continued for about six years,

59. *The Queen's Bedchamber. Detail of the painted cove, by John de Critz or Matthew Gooderick.*

but some decorations went on until as late as 1640, when the accounts record payments to carvers and statuaries, although the Queen was by that time in occupation.

In 1635 the house consisted of two rectangular blocks placed parallel to each other either side of the road and joined at first floor level by a central bridge. After the Restoration, the alterations made by Webb consisted of

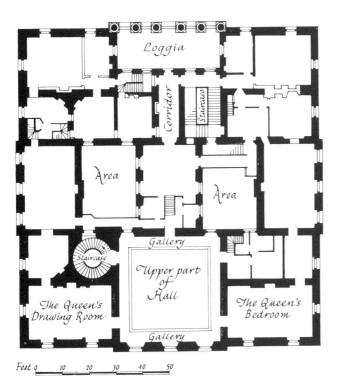

60. *Plan of the First Floor. (South to the top.)*

building two further bridges, so that it now appears from the outside as an unbroken rectangular block. The road has since been moved some distance south of the house and replaced by long doric colonnades connecting the Queen's House to later buildings on the east and west sides. Moreover, Webb's alterations have disguised the original character of the building and changed its internal arrangements. The house now consists of four ranges of rooms, instead of four separate suites linked by the loggia on the south front, the central bridge, and the galleried hall on the north front.

The riverside elevation (Fig. 53), built on a terrace and approached by curving stairways, has its two storeys clearly differentiated with rustication on the ground floor and rendering above. Originally, the first floor was of lime-washed brickwork, and when this was later stone-faced the architraves were partly obscured so that they now lack their former significance. The three central bays project forward and the windows here are slightly wider than the remainder. The balance of the design has also been slightly upset by the later lowering of the ground floor windows, and by the replacement of the original leaded casements with sash windows and thin glazing bars.

The façade (Fig. 54) facing the park is enlivened by the Ionic loggia placed in the slightly projecting centre bays of the upper floor. This creates movement in a sophisticated manner, through contrast of light and shade, and its design demonstrates Jones's study of Palladio's villas, revealing a knowledge and understanding that could only have been acquired from a study of them at first hand. It is one of the most convincing moments of the Classical phase in English domestic architecture, only equalled by the contemporary porches at Stoke Park (Fig. 75), and never recaptured, even by the Burlingtonians in the 18th century.

The entrance hall (Fig. 57) is a 40 foot cube two storeys high, with a gallery at first floor level connecting the rooms on

61. *Part of the Tulip Staircase.*

had seen at the Villa Capra, at Vicenza, for he noted against its description in his copy of Palladio: 'The Staires ar Parted with a raille of iorne so that you see through the parts underneath and so every waie.' The steps are of stone with moulded soffits, and the wrought-iron balustrade consists of alternating vertical bars and flat leaf scrolls with tulip heads, the tips being hammered to a tapering section. The effect achieved has a remarkable beauty, both of form and in the combination of material; there appears to be no other example of a stone staircase with wrought-iron balustrading until that made at Chatsworth towards the end of the century.

Great care and expenditure were lavished on the decoration of the principal rooms, but time, and the different uses to which the house has been put, have left only fragments. Some of the original ceilings survive and also a couple put up by John Grove, after the Restoration. The finest is in the Queen's Bedroom (Fig. 59) and probably dates from 1635–1637. Sir John Summerson[1] attributes its painting either to John de Critz[2] or Matthew Goodericke.[3] Its elaborate and colourful arabesques are clearly related to those decorating the cove of the Single Cube Room at Wilton (Fig. 103). The design includes a cartouche at each end, supported by *amorini* displaying the lilies of France, while at the sides the arms of England impale those of France. The large rectangular painting in the centre of the ceiling is later work, possibly from the studio of Sir James Thornhill. The original designs for some of the chimneypieces have survived; these and the ceilings give point to the remark of a contemporary observer who said the Queen 'hath so finished and furnished the house that it far surpasseth all other of that kind in England.' The rooms were at that time hung with fine pictures and contained a quantity of sculpture. It was intended to employ Jordaens to provide decorations for one of them to complement the Rubenses and Van Dycks in other palaces.

After the Restoration, Henrietta Maria returned to her 'House of Delight', as Queen Dowager, and came here periodically until her death in 1669. It was then granted successively to the consorts of Charles II and James II, but neither occupied the house.

In 1933 the Queen's House became incorporated with the National Maritime Museum, and its preservation is now happily ensured. Begun in the reign of the first Stuart king, whose son completed and transformed it into a treasure-house for his beloved consort, and whose grandson gave it the aspect it bears today, its destiny has been to become the casket for the safe custody of records of the men and ships of the Royal Navy, preserved from the days of the Tudors and Stuarts, the days of the *Golden Hind* and the *Sovereign of the Seas*.

either side. The balustrade retains its original painted and gilded decoration, uncovered in 1925 under no fewer than twenty-four coats of paint. We know that Jones employed ships' carvers on the house, and the detail of this balustrade is an indication of the shortage of skilled craftsmen. The panels of the ceiling were originally filled with decorative paintings by Gentileschi, who had been brought over from France by the Duke of Buckingham, but these were later removed to Marlborough House, where they are now.

The principal rooms occupy the first floor, those at ground level being given over to service. The main staircase (Fig. 61), which is of circular form, is placed at the south-east corner of the hall. Its design was probably derived from one Jones

---

[1] Edward Croft-Murray, *Decorative Painting in England*, p. 211.
[2] *op. cit.*, p. 198.   [3] *op. cit.*, p. 202.

62. *The East Front.*

RAYNHAM HALL, NORFOLK

The house was begun in 1622 by Sir Roger Townshend and completed some ten years later. In its combination of progressive and conservative features, this is one of the most remarkable of Caroline houses. (The Seat of the Marquess Townshend.)

Raynham is an exception to most of the theories concerning the Caroline country house put forward in the Introduction; and the history of its building is both complex and obscure. Roger Townshend had inherited an earlier house at East Raynham in 1603, when he was only about seven years old. Little is known of him except that he was created a baronet in 1617, presumably to mark his coming of age, and that later he served as Sheriff for the County and became a Member of Parliament. He held no other office and appears to have had no Court connections. According to Mr John Harris,[1] building was Townshend's hobby, which may be an explanation of the house's slow progress. Twenty-five years after his death, Pratt mentioned that Townshend possessed a number of fine volumes on architecture, which supports the view of his having been a knowledgeable amateur.

The first sign of his intention to build occurs in the accounts for August 30th, 1619, when it is noted that 'This weeke Beginne the Buildings.' Further references continue till April, 1620, and in the month following Townshend took his mason-draughtsman, William Edge, abroad, probably to the Low Countries. From March, 1621, there are records of payments to Edge for 'platts,' but early the following year the work was halted, and in April and May

the old foundations were discarded and new ones prepared. Townshend had used stone from Coxford Abbey, and, according to Sir Henry Spelman, a neighbour and the author of the *History and Fate of Sacrilege*, 1632, 'the wall reft from the corner stones — though it was clear above the ground.' This was taken as retribution for desecrating church property, and Townshend decided to start again.

On Lady Day, 1622, William Edge and Thomas Moore, a joiner, were paid for 'Clappboard deale & other necessaries for the modell of the building.' Further progress after the summer of that year cannot be followed, as no accounts have survived, but Spelman's account suggests that the house

63. *The South Facade.*

[1] *Archaeological Journal*, 1961, p. 180.

64. *The West, Entrance Front.*

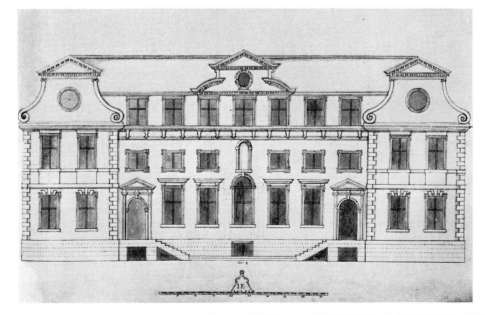

65. *Drawing showing the West Front in* 1671.

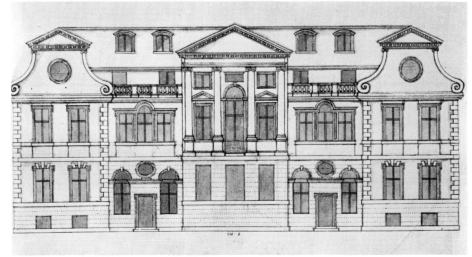

66. *Drawing showing the East Front in* 1671.

67. *The Doorway on the West Front.*

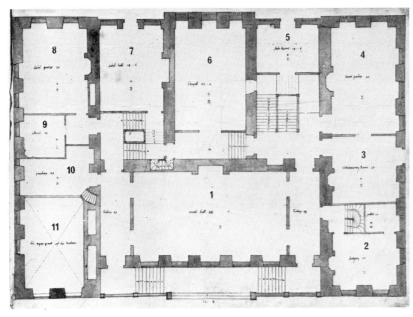

68. *Plan of the Ground Floor in* 1671.
1. *Great Hall.* 2. *Lodging.* 3. *Withdrawing Room.* 4. *Great Parlour.* 5. *Ante Room.* 6. *Chapel, with Belisarius Room over.* 7. *Little Hall.* 8. *Little Parlour.* 9. *Closet.* 10. *Pantry.* 11. *Kitchen.*

69. *The Belisarius Room. The ceiling* c. 1660.

was completed by 1632. During these years Townshend married a daughter of Lord Vere, but they never resided in the new house, and Pratt records, in a letter to Townshend's second son: 'Sir Roger left this house only decent and handsome as Augustus found Cleopatra after Mark Antoney's death in all her native beauty, which since your Lordship hath finished and furnished with all possible ornaments.'

Sir Roger Townshend died in 1636/37 and was succeeded by his eldest son, who died in 1648. Pratt's correspondent was Horace, Sir Roger's second son, who had been created a Baron in 1661 and was advanced to a Viscountcy in 1682.

A set of drawings made in 1671, in connection with Charles II's visit to the house, survives in the Library of the R.I.B.A. and there is also a drawing made by Edmund Prideaux[1] in 1716, which gives the appearance of the house before Kent's day. On the west, or entrance front (Fig. 64), the principal change has been the insertion of a central doorcase of late 17th-century type, replacing the original pair of doors that flanked the central bays. The windows and roundels, with their former Caroline mullions and transomes, have been replaced by Georgian sashes.

The façade must have appeared unusual and its various elements ill-disposed. The triple key-blocks in the lower tier of windows in the wings appear to have derived from one of Inigo Jones's designs at Newmarket. The pair of scrolled and pedimented gables, of 'Holborn' type, had their counterparts during the second decade of the century, possibly even in some of Inigo Jones's designs, but the central

[1] *Architectural History*, VII, 1964, pl. 88.

pediment was probably taken from an engraving. This feature is unrelated to any vertical support and merely rests on the architraves of the attic windows, above a poorly detailed entablature. The effect of the two ends of the façade being pulled apart sideways has been arrested and stabilised by the insertion of the central door, which also provides the needed focal point.

The evolution of the east front (Fig. 62) was even more complicated. Here the gabled wings are repeated, but the whole façade is dominated by a classic central feature entirely of stone and built in the form of a temple front. A comparison of the house today with the Prideaux drawing and the 1671 drawing (Fig. 66) shows an alteration in the form of a central doorway inserted by Kent in place of a window, and the remodelling of the bays that connect the central feature with the gabled ends, a change made between 1671 and 1716. The linking bays, shown in the 1671 set of drawings, have, as Mr Harris says, 'no stylistic relationship either to the centre or to the wings' and 'are consistent with a vernacular building style at the time of the Restoration.'[1] He suggests that 'Sir Roger may first have built the centre part of the present house of only two storeys and without the wings; then he may have added the wings and the second floor above the hall range; and as a final addition he may have built the chapel wing projecting from the centre of the east front. The temple feature in this position may not have been palatable to his successors for whom the most logical step would have been to fill in the spaces of the screen wall.' The source of design of the temple feature is the Prince's Lodging, at Newmarket, by Inigo Jones (Fig. 6), which Townshend must have seen on his journeys to London, and it is likely to have been the earliest example of Jones's influence on contemporary house building.

There is a plan (Fig. 68) among the 1671 drawings which follows the spirit of the elevations. The placing of the two entrances in the west front, leading into two screen passages, with the Great Hall between them, derives from traditional usage. The passages served the wings, the living rooms on the south side, and the staircases. Behind the Hall, and at right angles to its main axis, was the Chapel, and above it the Belisarius Room (Fig. 69), the largest apartment in the house. The plan thus assumed a T shape, for which there was Palladian precedent, but, by the addition of the linking bays, it became transformed to the double-pile type. The bays became lesser halls, unrelated either to the Chapel, Great Hall, the south range, or the offices, so that the house never achieved an arrangement that might have earned Pratt's approval. The plan, thus lacking unity and articulation, gives the impression of having been developed piecemeal.

Little decoration of the period has survived beyond a few chimneypieces and a carved doorcase. The most important survival is the ceiling in the Belisarius Room, a splendid affair that may be part of Sir Roger Townshend's work.

To the 2nd Viscount's generation the house was undoubtedly Jonesian, and so it was natural enough for him to turn to William Kent, the leading Palladian exponent of the day. His stately interiors, which are outside the scope of this book, are a robust compliment to Inigo Jones, whose work was so enthusiastically admired at the time.

[1] *Archaeological Journal*, 1961, p. 183.

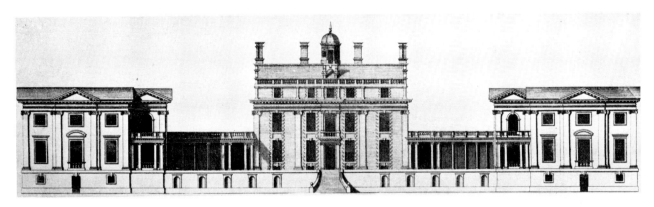

70. *The House and Pavilions, from* Vitruvius Britannicus.

STOKE PARK, NORTHAMPTONSHIRE

The pavilions, almost certainly by Inigo Jones, are all that remain of the house begun in 1629 for Sir Francis Crane, the manager of the Mortlake tapestry manufactory. It was the first appearance in England of the Palladian plan of a central block linked by curved colonnades to flanking wings. (The home of Mr R. D. Chancellor and Mr A. Revai.)

Northamptonshire was a favourite district among members of the Elizabethan and Jacobean Courts; a sporting county with great estates and large houses. Through it the monarch could proceed by easy stages from Castle Ashby to Holdenby or Althorp, and thence to Rushton, Kirby, Deene, or Apethorpe, and so to Burghley, by the Lincolnshire border. The preparations for suitable entertainment made by the Comptons, Spencers, Brudenells and Cecils were elaborate and costly, for the rewards of royal favour could be valuable and justify the expense entailed. By good fortune and careful husbandry, the descendants of many of the grandees of early Stuart times continue here, but their houses bear little sign of Inigo Jones influence. For the most part they had either been rebuilt before 1615, or the owners had remained loyal to the older manner until the Restoration. Only Kirby and Castle Ashby, where the date of the classical screen is uncertain, show signs of the new classicism.

Of the new men living in the county at the time, Sir Francis Crane was one of the most colourful. Rising from obscure beginnings, he became Secretary to Charles I when Prince of Wales, was made a baronet in 1617 and, a few

years later, first director of the Royal tapestry manufactory at Mortlake. For this he was well, but slowly rewarded both by James I and Charles I: at the time of the latter's accession he was owed some £6,000, and in consideration of this he was granted a pension. In 1629, in settlement of a debt, he was granted the 400 acre park at Stoke Bruerne, between Towcester and Northampton. A few years later Crane offered to forgo a further debt in exchange for land at Grafton, the adjoining property. Not much is known about Crane or the Mortlake manufactory. Its products were costly, and were apt to involve financial risk; for instance, in 1635–36 a warrant was issued to pay Crane £2,872 for

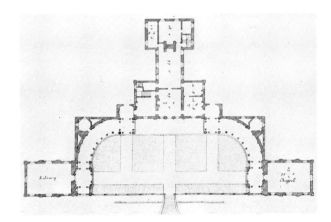

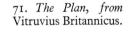

71. *The Plan, from* Vitruvius Britannicus.

72. *'Prospect of Mr Arundels house at Stoke Park taken in ye Garden'* c. 1725.

73. *The East Pavilion.*

74. *The Portico of the West Pavilion.*

75. *The West Pavilion from the east.*

three pieces of tapestry, one of which, woven from one of the Raphael cartoons, St Paul and Elymas the Sorcerer, cost £664.

Soon after 1629, Crane began the building of his house. Bridges, the 18th-century Northamptonshire historian, says that he 'brought the design from Italy, and in the execution of it received the assistance of Inigo Jones. . . .'[1] We have no proof that Crane ever went to Italy, but he went to France for his health in 1635. Bridges probably meant that the idea of the house was Italian, since it clearly stems from Palladio. The attribution to Inigo Jones, however, is convincing, and is borne out not only by Colin Campbell, but by the appearance of the colonnades and pavilions. Work continued until about 1635–36 and was thus contemporary with the second phase of the building at the Queen's House.

Conceived on an ambitious scale, the house consisted of a central block linked by Ionic colonnades to flanking pavilions (Fig. 70), a favourite Palladian motif, but revolutionary in

[1] *History of Northamptonshire*, Vol. I, p. 328.

England at that date; indeed it does not occur again until the erection of Hackwood, Hampshire, built by Talman for the 1st Duke of Bolton in 1683. It appears that the pavilions and colonnades were built first, for Campbell says: 'This building was begun by Inigo Jones: The Wings, and Colonnades, and all the Foundations, were made by him; but the Front of the House was designed by another Architect, the Civil Wars having also interrupted this work.'[1] Bridges notes that the house was finished before 1636, the year when Crane entertained the King and Queen. In this matter Campbell may well be trusted, but his engraving in *Vitruvius Britannicus* (Fig. 70) needs to be compared with a drawing in the British Museum[2] (Fig. 72), 19th-century and modern photographs. One of the British Museum drawings shows a three gabled building behind the east colonnade; possibly an older house on the site in which Crane lived while building the new one. The *Vitruvius Britannicus* plate shows the house as a five-bay block, with an unusual roof running

[1] *Vitruvius Britannicus*, III, p. 7.
[2] Add. MSS 32467, f. 237.

76. *In the East Portico, looking south.*

between what appear to be scrolled gables. This is not what one would expect from Jones in the 1630s, and was presumably the work of Campbell's unnamed architect. Moreover, the vertical linking of the windows by quoins is not characteristic of Jones. The drawing in Fig. 72 shows the central bay projected to form a porch with a window above, but the drawing is not of high quality, and the details of the main house are less carefully indicated than those of the pavilions.

The plan was unusual in consisting of a front range linked by a big room to a shorter cross range, a layout that survived till the house was destroyed by fire in 1886. There is a photograph in the Conway Library of the Courtauld Institute showing the back of the house with its original order of pilasters, and also the original roofing scheme. Campbell's engraving shows the colonnades with balustrades and no visible roofs; the drawing shows no balustrades, but is ambiguous as to the roofs. No balustrades appear in the 19th-century photograph, and the tiled roofs are set back from the entablature. This may have been the original arrangement, altered only at the junction of the colonnades and the house.

The west pavilion appears to have originally been a library and that on the east a chapel, as shown on Campbell's plan. The west pavilion still consists of one large room, but the east pavilion (Fig. 73) has recently been converted into a separate house, as part of the scheme of preservation and is the only one to have had its original fenestration restored. This has entailed replacing both the central windows, on the park front, so that it now appears as in Campbell's engraving, the only significant difference being the absence of pediments over the porches which were removed in an 18th-century re-roofing. The main parts of the pavilions now have hipped, instead of ridged roofs terminated by pediments on the west and east walls.

These modifications do not seriously detract from the extraordinarily accomplished design of the pavilions. They share with Whitehall and the Queen's House those qualities of excitement and flawless satisfaction that are the proof of genius in architecture. Their effectiveness is in part due to the selection of the materials used, whitish Weldon stone for the walls, capitals, consoles and frieze, and a brownish-purple ironstone for the pilasters, columns, architraves and cornice. Such use of colour reveals Inigo Jones's painterly approach to architecture and makes regrettable Soane's refacing of the Whitehall Banquet House in Portland stone, which has deprived that building of much of its former liveliness. At Stoke Park the colour of the stone has been used to complement the use of the orders. The combination of a giant and lesser order was derived from Michelangelo's Palazzo dei Conservatori in Rome.[1] A derivation of this kind, and the use, for instance, of solid over void in the vestibules, and the 'shadow' pilasters flanking the central pair on the park façades, show Jones's interest in mannerist architecture.

The basic scheme consists of a giant order, on the pavilions proper, with the central pair of pilasters slightly projected to emphasise the central pedimented bays facing the park. To these blocks are added single bay vestibules which face each other. It is in the conjunction of these two parts of the building, and in the colonnades, that Jones starts his play with the orders. The giant order is used on the west wall of the east pavilion and similarly, in reverse, on the west pavilion, while the corner of the building is marked not by a solid pillar, but by two pilasters, which reflect the shadow pilaster on the front when seen in perspective.

The piers of the lesser order of the porches repeat the use of pilasters. In the central bay the entablature is supported by a pair of pilasters and a pair of columns, but in the outer bays it is borne by half columns. The treatment of the central bay is repeated on the elevation facing the park, where the pair of columns is repeated again, three times, inside the porches, before continuing north into the colonnades.

The marshalling of columns, pier, impost and pilaster, with their responds, affords as many possibilities of variation as a Bach fugue. In these colonnades, with their play and interplay, Inigo Jones demonstrates his complete mastery of the language of classical architecture.

The loss of the house itself calls for no regret, since the two pavilions appear more effective as isolated survivors than as secondary incidents in a larger scheme. In a true sense they symbolise the unfulfilled promise of Inigo Jones's court architecture, and so are invested with an added romanticism. They are perhaps the most poetic instance of early Caroline buildings.

Restored, and linked by Victorian terraces and a fountain pool, their distinction is clear enough. But until recent years they lay derelict and in danger of destruction. Mr Marshall Sisson prepared a scheme for their reclamation that included the removal of the incongruous Victorian-Elizabethan house behind the east pavilion. The plan was published in *Country Life* in 1953; the present owners saw the article, acquired the pavilions and, with the aid of a grant from the Historic Buildings Council, have since carried out their restoration.

[1] Summerson, *op. cit.* (1963 edition), p. 80.

77. *The Entrance Front from the north.*

HAM HOUSE, SURREY

The Jacobean house was redecorated in the 1630s by William Murray and altered again in the 1670s by his daughter, the Duchess of Lauderdale. The decorations of both generations are of outstanding interest and well documented. The rooms contain a unique collection of furniture and fabrics that were acquired by the Lauderdales. (A Property of the National Trust.)

Ham lies in the meadows beside the Thames below Richmond Hill, a mile or so upstream from the Royal Palace of Rich-

mond. Its setting has remained unspoilt and, walking by the riverside, one can see why Sir Thomas Vavasour chose this site when he built his house in 1610. Behind the entrance front (Fig. 77) lie richly decorated rooms of both the 1630s and the 1670s, wherein we are able to observe the great changes that took place in both design and decoration of country houses of that time.

Vavasour's house was of the normal Jacobean type, a three storey house on the H plan, each floor containing a single range of rooms opening one into the other. The entrance

78. *The Garden Front. The seven central bays and the end bays were built about 1670; the bay windows are 18th century.*

79. *The West Façade, showing the junction of the 1670 addition and the Jacobean house.*

led to the Great Hall, then still the principal apartment, with the Great Chamber and Long Gallery both on the first floor, features that were out of fashion by 1670.

From Sir Thomas Vavasour, who was Knight Marshal to James I, the house passed to John Ramsay, Earl of Holdernesse, and some time after the latter's death in 1626, the lease, which was in the gift of the Crown, was granted to William Murray, later 1st Earl of Dysart. The son of the minister at Dysart, in Fife, he had been appointed whipping boy to the young Prince Charles, probably through the offices of his uncle, Thomas Murray, the prince's tutor. It was part of his duty to receive castigation on occasions when his princely companion's behaviour necessitated, the idea being that the real culprit would mend his ways when he saw another punished in his stead. According to Bishop

Burnet, Murray 'had great credit with [Charles] not only in procuring private favours, but in all his counsels. He was well tuned for a court, very insulting, but very false.'[1] He probably occupied the house for several years before the King granted him a lease, which accounts for his delay in redecorating until about 1637.

The work of his daughter, the Duchess of Lauderdale, was more extensive, but Murray's decorations are the more interesting, because so little of the decoration done for the court circle in the 1630s survives. Consequently Ham is placed early in sequence in this book and represents the 1630s rather than the 1670s. Murray was responsible for the great staircase, the North Drawing Room, the Green Closet and the repanelling of the Long Gallery.

The great staircase (Fig. 81), lies to the west of Vavasour's Great Hall and is linked to it by a wide arch, made to Murray's order. The stairs rise the full height of the house with a balustrade consisting of carved and pierced panels representing martial trophies, their design being presumably based on contemporary engravings; the panels were grained and partly gilded, but the gilding has since disappeared. Balustrade panels of this kind were a development from Jacobean strapwork, and are more usually composed of acanthus decoration, as at Thorpe and Sudbury. Unfortunately, the accounts do not reveal the name of the carver, although we know Thomas Carter, a joiner, charged £6 for making the 'great arch' between the Hall and staircase, carved with pendant trophies similar to the newel posts. He also charged £7 for 24 yards of wainscot on the stairs and £45 for five pairs of doors with their cases and 'frontispieces'. However, it is puzzling that the Duke of Lauderdale installed similar doors in the Ante-Room at Thirlestane Castle, Berwickshire, about 1671;[2] perhaps he and his wife enlarged the architraves at Ham, adding the broken pediments and busts. The original painting was carried out at a cost of £54

[1] *The History of the Reign of Charles II* (1823 edition), Vol. I, p. 423.
[2] Reproduced by John Fleming, *Scottish Country Houses Open to the Public*, p. 52.

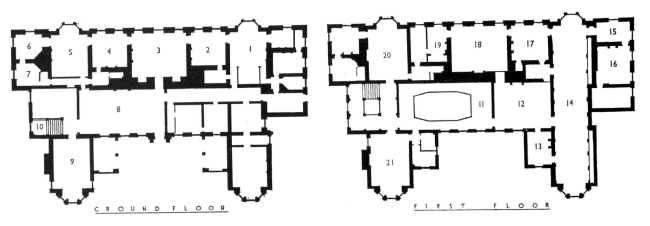

80. *Plan of the Ground and First Floor.* GROUND FLOOR. 1. *The Duchess's Bedchamber.* 2. *The Duke's Closet.* 3. *The Marble Dining Room.* 4. *Withdrawing Room.* 5. *The Volary.* 6. *The White Closet.* 7. *The Duchess's Private Closet.* 8. *The Great Hall.* 9. *The Chapel.* 10. *The Great Staircase.* FIRST FLOOR. 11. *The Round Gallery.* 12. *The North Drawing Room.* 13. *The Miniature Room.* 14. *The Long Gallery.* 15. *The Library Closet.* 16. *The Library.* 17. *The Blue Drawing Room.* 18. *The Queen's Bedchamber.* 19. *The Queen's Closet.* 20. *The Yellow Satin Room.* 21. *The Room over the Chapel.*

81. *The Great Stair-case*, c. 1637.

by Matthew Gooderick,[1] who worked at Court. The plaster-work was done by Joseph Kinsman in 1637–38, a craftsman working in the entourage of Inigo Jones.

Kinsman also executed the ceiling in the Vavasour's Great Chamber at the head of the staircase, which Murray seems to have used as a private Dining Room (the floor of this room was cut away only in the 18th century). Beyond lies the North Drawing Room, the most elaborate of Murray's rooms (Fig. 82). Here Kinsman charged £35 4s. for the

ceiling and frieze, and Carter £5 10s. for the wainscot and £12 for a pair of doorcases and doors. The room has been slightly altered — originally there were windows on both long walls — and now panelling of an elaborate kind remains only on the north wall, exhibiting contorted ornament of a kind associated with London artisan workmanship. It is possible that Francis Clein[1] influenced this part of the work; he painted the overdoors and may have suggested the twisted half columns flanking the fireplace, derived from the

[1] Croft-Murray, *op. cit.*, pp. 202–204.

[1] Croft-Murray, *op. cit.*, p. 196.

82. *The North Drawing Room, c. 1637. Decoration perhaps designed by Clein.*

Raphael cartoon, *The Healing of the Lame Man at the Temple Gate*. Prince Charles had acquired these cartoons in 1623, and Clein would have been acquainted with them through his work at the Mortlake tapestry factory.

Opening out of this room is the small Green Closet (Fig. 83), shown as it was when used as a Miniature Room. The ceiling and cove were painted by Clein *in tempera* on paper, based on engravings by Polidoro da Caravaggio (1490/1500–1543), an artist of considerable influence at the time. The woodwork is enriched with gilt carving, a fashion later followed at Wilton. The Lauderdales hung the room with 'Greene Damask with Green Silk Fringe', but the pair of ebony tables must have been made before their marriage for the embossed plaques on the tops bear Lady Dysart's cypher and a countess's coronet.

The Long Gallery (Fig. 84) itself is a survival from the Vavasour house, though the decoration is Murray's. Carter repanelled it in 1639, charging 4s. a yard for remaking the old work and 6s. for the new, and £10 10s. for the 20 Ionic 'palasters of my own stuff'. The furnishing of the gallery dates from the Duchess's time, as do the 'Two and Twenty Pictures with Carv'd and Guilt Frames', made between 1672 and 1675 at a cost of 70s. each.

Although Murray was created Earl of Dysart in 1643, he prudently suppressed his title during the Commonwealth, when he and his wife continued to be known at Ham as Mr and Mrs William Murray. He left no male heir, so that the

house passed to his daughter, Elizabeth, who had married Sir Lionel Tollemache of Helmingham, in Suffolk. It is not known whether she assumed the Dysart title before the Restoration, but after it she acquired it in her own right.

Bishop Burnet wrote of her as 'a woman of great beauty, but of far greater parts. She had a wonderful quickness of apprehension, and an amazing vivacity in conversation. She had studied not only divinity and history, but mathematics and philosophy. She was violent in everything she set about, a violent friend, but a much more violent enemy. She had a restless ambition, lived at a vast expense, and was ravenously covetous; and would have stuck at nothing by which she might compass her ends.'

After the Restoration the Tollemaches drifted apart, he preferring to live at Helmingham, leaving her at Ham. Sir Lionel died in 1669, but not before his wife was said to be aiming at enhanced power through one of Charles II's ministers, John Maitland, Earl of Lauderdale, a man whose ambition for power equalled her own. Lady Dysart was bent on getting the best of all worlds, and determined to use both husbands' fortunes for her own ends, a tendency that was as strong in Bess of Ham as it had been in Bess of Hardwick.

In 1650 Maitland had gone to join Charles II in Holland, and later accompanied him to Scotland. In the following year he was captured at the battle of Worcester and spent the next nine years in the Tower. The Restoration, however, brought him not only liberty, but office and, in 1661, he became

83. *The Green Closet or Miniature Room, c. 1637. (This shows the appearance of the room in about 1920.)*

84. *The Long Gallery. Wainscot of the 1630s and gilt-framed portraits hung in the 1670s.*

85. *(below) The Duke and Duchess of Lauderdale.*

Secretary of State for Scotland where 'he held the whole power and patronage for 18 years.' He seems to have been an enthusiastic builder judging by his correspondence[1] with Sir William Bruce about the work at Thirlestane, one of his Scottish houses.[2] This was in hand in 1671 and, in the same year, on June 27th, he wrote: 'I must entreat you to tell Sir Wm. Bruce from me that I much desire the hastening C. Dysart's gate at Ham. The King and Queen will be here this summer.' Perhaps this is the gate unopened since the flight of James II.

In February the following year, after the couple had been married in Petersham church, they proceeded to enlarge and to redecorate Ham. The building accounts show that work was begun in 1673 and completed in 1675, but the furnishing took a year or so longer.

[1] Burnet, *op. cit.*, p. 424.
[2] R. S. Mylne, *The King's Master Masons*.

86. *Overdoor panel by Francis Clein, c. 1637, in the Marble Dining Room.*

87. The Blue Drawing Room. Decoration, hangings and japanned chairs of the 1670s.

87. The Blue Drawing Room. Decoration, hangings and japanned chairs of the 1670s.

The builder in charge was Arthur Forbes (possibly a Scotsman), and under him were the bricklayers, Arthur Turner and Will Smith, and John Lampsine, the mason. From the accounts that survive it seems that Forbes was in charge of all the work as well as for keeping the records of the craftsmen's wages. In 1673, out of £1,618 5s. received he spent £1,281 19s. 6d. By 1675 Turner, the brickmaker, had supplied 400,000 bricks at 8s. 6d. per 1,000; Smith made a charge of £154 and Lampsine one of £413. Carpenter, plasterer, plumber and painter then needed about £500 to settle their accounts.

The Lauderdales made but few alterations to the north

front and did not change the original entrance door. They set the busts in the roundels above the windows, removed the cupolas above the loggias — which are shown in a miniature — and added hipped roofs and a modillioned cornice. (The bay windows on both the north and south façades are Georgian additions.) Their main undertaking was to fill the gap between the end bays on the south side with a new range of rooms (Fig. 78), thus doubling the depth of the house; they also made a small addition to the west end. They appear to have aimed at a rich effect, but with minimum expense.

It was on the interior, especially on the new apartments on

88. *The Marble Dining Room. The leather hangings date from the 1670s.*

89. *The Queen's Bedchamber. Decoration of the 1670s and 18th-century tapestries.*

the south side, that they lavished their care, and although the rooms are small the Duke and Duchess determined to make up for lack of space by distinction of style and a profusion of ornament. Here the effect of woodwork, ceilings, parquetry floors, rich furniture and marble chimneypieces, with their silver-mounted fireplace equipment, is sumptuous. Much of the furniture was made specially for the house and is without parallel elsewhere; its interest is enhanced by the fact that a considerable number of pieces can be recognised in the

inventories. The first of these was drawn up in 1679 and the second in 1683, a year after the Duke's death.

The walls of all the principal rooms, including the bed-chambers, were hung with tapestry, damask, velvet, mohair or sarsenet, suitably trimmed in matching or contrasting colours, which must have given them an effect of the greatest splendour. Much of all this has disappeared in the course of time but, notwithstanding, Ham in its hangings and uphol-stery is richer than any other contemporary house. The first

90. *Ceiling of the White Closet, by Verrio.* 91. *The Queen's Closet. Scagliola surround to the chimneypiece and marquetry floor.*

inventory gives the name and use of each of the rooms and also how they were decorated and furnished.

The principal rooms on the ground floor of the south front are contained in the Lauderdales' addition. The suite begins at the west end (within the original building) with their private apartments, the first of which is the Duchess's bedroom, partly hung with damask and partly lined with grained wood. To the left of the bed recess is one of a set of overdoors painted by the younger William Van de Velde, in 1673. A door beside the chimneypiece leads into a small closet with a painted ceiling by an unknown artist. The idea of ground-floor bedrooms was apparently less unusual then than now. East of the Duchess's bedroom is the Duke's closet and next, the Marble Dining Room (Fig. 88). This, the principal and central room of the suite, is on the axis of the entrance. It is an agreeable room, for the dark wood harmonises well with the faded gilt leather hangings, which were in place in 1679. Over the chimneypiece is an 18th-century copy of Danckert's picture of Rose, the royal gardener, presenting Charles II with the first pineapple grown in England at Dorney Court, near Weybridge, Surrey (Fig. 40). Above the doors are a series of paintings by Clein (Fig. 86), after originals by Polidoro da Caravaggio acquired by Charles I in 1637. Presumably the Duchess had inherited these from her father and had the positions prepared to receive them. The next room is a Drawing Room, beyond which is the Volary, so called from having been used by her as an aviary during her

widowhood. The suite ends with the White Closet (Fig. 92), where the ceiling (Fig. 90) was probably painted by Antonio Verrio, who at that time was working at Windsor. With the exception of this, and a few of the overdoors, the decorative painting at Ham is of rather indifferent quality. Behind the White Closet is the Duchess's Private Closet, an odd shaped room of small size, but interesting for its overmantel by William Ferguson, *A Sorceress among Classical Ruins*.

A small hidden door leads down a short corridor to the main staircase. The approaches to these rooms were contrived with some difficulty within the framework of the Vavasour and Lauderdale buildings, indicating the difficulty of adapting a Jacobean layout to the new standards of Restoration life.

The grander Lauderdale rooms fill the south range of the first floor. West of the Gallery is an ante-room leading to the Library and, to the east, the Blue Drawing Room (Fig. 87), overlooking the lawns. The grained wainscot of the latter is lavishly picked out in gold, while rather coarsely carved and gilt swags hang from ducal coronets. The damask hangings from which the room takes its name were originally blue with darker velvet borders and *appliqué* embroidery, but the colour has now faded to yellow. The chairs are an early example of the English taste for lacquer and chinoisserie.

Opening out of this room is the Queen's Bedchamber (Fig. 89), prepared, together with the Queen's Closet adjoining, for an expected visit of Queen Catherine. The walls are now hung with 18th-century Soho tapestries, after

92. *The White Closet and the enfilade through the south rooms.*

who are excellent joiners, and have made all my shapies and lyning of my rooms at Ham . . . and it may be they risk carrying with them a Dutch painter . . . with Paterns.' On April 15th he wrote: 'Germans have made the double chassee [sash] windows', and referred to their cabinet making. The reference to sash windows is the earliest so far known in England.

After her husband's death the Duchess continued to live at Ham and on her own death, in 1698, the house passed to her son by her first marriage, Lionel Tollemache, 3rd Earl of Dysart. He and his successors did little for the place (thereby ensuring its wonderful preservation) and when Horace Walpole visited his niece, the wife of the 4th Earl, he commented upon its unchanged and shabby state. The house continued with the Dysart Earldom until 1935, when Sir Lionel Tollemache and Mr Cecil Tollemache inherited it. In 1948 they presented the house to the National Trust, and the contents, which were acquired by the Government, were entrusted to the Victoria and Albert Museum, which is now responsible for their arrangement (very much sparser and less evocative than when a private residence). Some of the illustrations represent the interior in the time of the 9th Lord Dysart, while others show it in recent years.

Ham shows with particular clarity the manner in which country houses of the Charles II period were decorated, furnished and lived in. Even then visitors were struck by its sumptuousness, and John Evelyn was delighted with a visit he made there in the summer of 1678. 'After dinner I walked to Ham', he wrote in his diary, 'to see the house and garden of the Duke of Lauderdale, which is indeed inferior to few of the best Villas in Italy itself; the House furnish'd like a great Prince's; the Parterres, Flower Gardens, Orangeries, Groves, Avenues, Courts, Statues, Perspectives, Fountains, Avaries, and all this at the Banks of the sweetest River in the World.'[1]

[1] *Diary*. Vol. II, p. 126. August 27, 1678.

Watteau and Pater, but the ceiling, gilt carving and chimney-pieces date from the 1670s. The glory of the room was the marquetry floor, so prized that, from the time of its laying, it was protected by leather mats. Another marquetry floor, that in the Closet (Fig. 91), is in better condition and in its intricate inlay reflects the surrounds of the fireplace and the window sills, which are executed in scagliola, the earliest appearance of this type of work in England.[1] The Closet has a painted ceiling depicting Ganymede.

Unfortunately, we know less about the decorators employed at Ham than of the builders. Two of the joiners were Henry Haslow and Thomas Jelly; one of the painters was named Moor and there was a carver called Bullymore. Between 1673 and 1675 Haslow earned £890 and Jelly £572 12s., while Moor's account stood at nearly £500 and Bullymore's at £102. There were also two Dutch or German joiners — Lauderdale was not clear about their nationalities — employed about the house: perhaps they made the walnut caryatid tables in the Gallery. On April 3rd, 1673, he wrote to Sir William Bruce: 'I have agreed with two Dutchmen,

[1] *The History of Scagliola.* R. B. Wragg, *Country Life*, CXXII, p. 718.

93. *The fireplace in the Picture Closet. Silver fireplace furniture, c. 1670.*

94. *The South and East Fronts.*

WILTON HOUSE, WILTSHIRE

Wilton is the most important house of the Caroline period, and perhaps the most beautiful of all English country houses. The 4th Earl of Pembroke began to rebuild the Tudor house in 1636 to the design of Isaac de Caus, but with improvements apparently supervised by Inigo Jones. After a fire of 1647/48 the incomparable State Rooms were redecorated by Inigo Jones and John Webb. Some of their work was modified in the 18th century, and the north and west ranges replaced by James Wyatt. (The Seat of the Earl of Pembroke.)

'King Charles the first did love Wilton above all places and came thither every summer. It was he that did put Philip

first Earle of Pembroke upon making this magnificent garden and grotto, and to new build that side of the house that fronts the garden, with two stately pavilions at each end all *al Italiano*.'[1]

Philip, the 4th Earl, inherited Wilton on the death of his elder brother, William, in 1630. He was one of the great office holders of the time, being Lord Chamberlain, Lord Warden of the Stannaries, High Steward of the Duchy of Cornwall, Vice Admiral of South Wales and Lord Lieutenant of Kent,

[1] Aubrey's notes for *The Natural History of Wiltshire*, edited and elucidated by John Britton, 1847, p. 83.

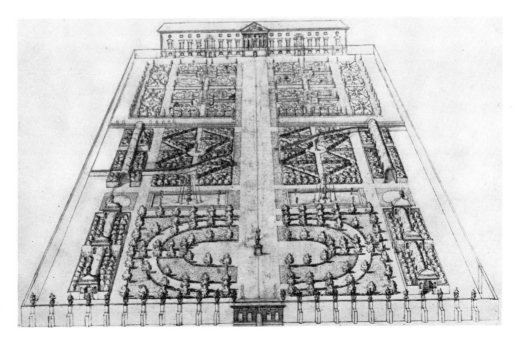

95. *The Grand Design. de Caus's Garden layout and design for the South Front*, c. 1635.

96. *Proposal for the reduced South Front, attributed to de Caus,* c. 1638–40.

Wiltshire, Somerset and Cornwall. The profits of these offices almost doubled his income, for Aubrey says he had about £16,000 from his estates, but £30,000 'with his offices and all. . . . And, as the revenue was great, so the greatnesse of his retinue and hospitality was answerable. One hundred and twenty family uprising and down lyeing, whereof you may take out six or seven, and all the rest servants and retayners.'[1]

He 'did not delight in books or poetry; but exceedingly loved painting and building, in which he had singular judgment.'[2] And so, within a year or so of coming into Wilton, he began to consider the alteration of the courtyard house, created over the previous ninety years by his forbears. The ancient Nunnery of Wilton Abbey had been granted to Sir William Herbert by Henry VIII in 1544, and some of its buildings were probably incorporated in the new Tudor house. Aubrey continues: 'His Majesty intended to have it

[1] Aubrey, *op. cit.*, p. 88.   [2] Aubrey, *op. cit.*, p. 91.

all designed by his own architect, Mr Inigo Jones, who being at that time, about 1633, engaged in his Majesties buildings at Greenwich, could not attend to it; but he recommended it to an ingeniuse architect, Monsieur Solomon de Caus, a Gascoigne.'[1] Solomon had left England in 1613 and Aubrey obviously meant Isaac, his son or nephew.

Isaac de Caus had already worked at Court, and also on the scheme for Covent Garden, but his speciality was garden design. He published engravings of his scheme for the great formal garden at Wilton about 1640 (which was swept away by the 9th Earl), but these do not show the house. Mr Howard Colvin, however, has discovered a drawing[2] (Fig. 95) showing a façade of considerable length with the garden, as engraved, depicted in front of it. The front, of 21 bays, is

[1] Aubrey, *op. cit.*, p. 83.
[2] In a volume of *Vitruvius Britannicus* in Worcester College Library that had belonged to Dr Clarke, the former owner of the Jones and Webb drawings.

97. *The South Front. Similar to the design above except for the corner towers presumably suggested by Inigo Jones.*

*98. The central window
on the South Front.*

shown centred on a hexastyle portico, with breaks at the fifth and seventeenth bays in the form of Venetian windows.

This would have provided a stately foil to the elaborate parterre, a contrast that was doubtlessly intended. There was no English precedent for such a design and, had it been executed, the range of State Rooms would have been comparable to those projected by Inigo Jones for the Palace of Whitehall. This drawing presumably passed to Webb, for he quoted from it in the designs he made for Belvoir Castle in 1654 (Fig. 18). We shall refer to it here as the Grand Design.

There was no documentary record for de Caus's building of the garden front, till recently Mr A. A. Tait[1] found confirmation that work began in 1636. In the Earl of Pembroke's

[1] *Burlington Magazine*, February, 1964, p. 74.

Warrant Book he had discovered an instruction to 'Mr Isaak De Caux to take downe (with the advice of Mr Boules) that side of Wilton house which is towards the garden & such other parts as shall bee necessary & rebuild it anew with additions according to ye Plott which is agreed.' This is dated March 14th, 1635 (old style), and evidently refers to the existing façade, which corresponds to the eight right hand bays of the Grand Design. The garden had been begun some four or five years previously, no doubt with this background in mind.

About 1638/39 Lord Pembroke had second thoughts about the Grand Design; he may have sensed danger ahead, or possibly he expected the breach with the King which culminated in his dismissal, in 1640, from the office of Lord

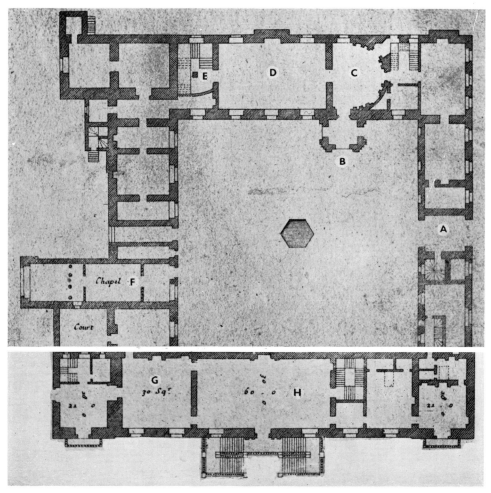

99. *An 18th-century ground plan showing the north (top) and west ranges demolished by Wyatt, combined with the plan of the first floor of the south front.*
A. *East Entrance Front.*
B. *Holbein Porch.*
C. *Vestibule.*
D. *Great Hall.*
E. *Great Stairs.*
F. *Chapel.*
G. *Single Cube Room.*
H. *Double Cube Room.*

Chamberlain. Alternatively, he may have considered it undiplomatic to build on so magnificent a scale when the King himself was plunging into bankruptcy. Whatever the cause, his change of heart came at a time when de Caus was preparing his engravings of the garden, which is probably the reason why the Grand Design was not engraved and included in the set.

There is a drawing attributed to de Caus in the Library of the R.I.B.A., showing his suggestion of how the Grand Design might be curtailed, and the eight uncompleted bays terminated (Fig. 96). One of the problems was how to emphasise the central feature: the drawing shows the suggestion of a dormer breaking the balustrade above the Venetian window. Another problem was the design of a feature to balance the end bay on the right, and to provide a stairway from the *piano-nobile* to the garden. His solution was a bay, repeating that on the right, in front of which he proposed a double flight of steps to the garden, which, however, would not have corresponded with the garden's axis. That he could not achieve the symmetry such a project demanded points to one feature having already been in existence, or at least decided upon, as early as 1640. This must have been the large room called by Evelyn, in 1654, the Dining Room, and known to us as the Double Cube Room. The steps shown in the design suggest an ante-room, corresponding to the

present Hunting Room, in place of the central apartment of the Grand Design.

Aubrey further records, after mentioning the fact that de Caus was a Gascon, that he performed his work at Wilton 'very well; but not without the advice and approbation of Mr Jones.' It may very well be that the R.I.B.A. drawing was de Caus's solution, and that he submitted it to Jones, on whose advice the dormer, with its hipped roof and cornice, was omitted, and the end bays altered. These comprise pavilions 'all *al Italiano*' and were almost certainly Jones's idea, demonstrating his knowledge of Scamozzi (Part I, Book III, page 284) and possibly his reaction to the Elizabethan east façade, then the entrance front.

This combination of Italian fashion and English tradition, together with Inigo Jones's refining influence, has resulted in the superb façade we see today. Its classical balance and harmony has no need for the support of the orders and, apart from the mouldings, its only embellishments are the figures carved in relief above the central feature.

Both the Grand Design and the south façade, as it exists, became a source of inspiration to 18th-century architects, but, through Campbell's attribution exclusively to Jones in *Vitruvius Britannicus*, de Caus's part was forgotten. The façade inspired those of Houghton, Hagley and Croome, to name only three great Georgian houses.

100. *The East (original Entrance) Front.*

101. *The Hunting Room. Painted panels by Edward Pierce the elder, c. 1640, with painted trophies added by Clermont, c. 1730.*

102. Partridge Netting *by Edward Pierce. One of the panels in the Hunting Room, c. 1640.*

The south range, contrived by de Caus and Inigo Jones, did not last long, for Aubrey records that it 'was burnt ann. 1647 or 1648, by airing of the rooms. In anno 1648 Philip re-edifyed it, by the advice of Inigo Jones; but he, being then very old, could not be there in person, but left it to Mr. Webb, who married his niece.'[1] It is uncertain how much was des-

[1] Aubrey, *op. cit.*, p. 84.

troyed by the fire, and it is probable that the range was not completely gutted. A comparison of the R.I.B.A. drawing and the existing façade shows them basically the same, and no drawings for the exterior appear to survive. The existence of a number of designs for elaborate ceilings dated 1649 suggests that the reconstruction was by then well advanced.

Much of this decoration in other parts of the house was swept away during the 18th and 19th centuries, but the original arrangement of the rooms can be followed from the 18th-century plans (Fig. 99), one of which is given in *Vitruvius Britannicus*. The approach to the house, which can be seen in both Kip's engraving and also in the painting by Knyff, was by way of a forecourt leading to the east front (Fig. 100). Having passed through the east gate-tower, the house was entered on the north side of the court by way of the Holbein porch, which Jones persuaded Lord Pembroke to retain. This gave into a vestibule with a semicircular east wall, presumably of the 4th Earl's time. To the west of it lay the Great Hall, which had a gallery at first floor level, probably similar to that in the Whitehall Banqueting Hall and that in the Queen's House at Greenwich; it may have occupied the site of the Tudor Great Hall. In its west wall a doorway led to a staircase that rose by three flights to the level of the State Rooms on the *piano-nobile*. A small gallery comprised the prelude to a suite, filling the west side of the courtyard.

In this approach to the south rooms, it may be seen from the plan that the Hunting Room lay to the west of the axis of these western rooms, partly occupying the position of the centre room of the Grand Design. This suggests that it was formed when the Grand Design was curtailed, but it is also related axially to the Cube rooms, which open from it one

103. *The Single Cube Room. Part of the painted cove, late 1630s (?).*

104. *The Single Cube Room. The chimneypiece and wainscot,
c. 1650.*

105. *The Single Cube Room. Detail of the decoration on the
west wall, showing part of a series of painted panels inset in the
dado illustrating Sidney's* Arcadia.

into the other. East of the Double Cube some of the apartments have been altered. As originally planned, the imposing
doorcase in the centre of the east wall of the Double Cube led
to a staircase, and a door to the right, since removed, into a
passage room. These were replaced in the 18th century when
the Great Ante-Room was formed. At the same time, the
Colonnade Room was contrived from the former King's
Bedroom and its two closets. The frieze and chimney (Fig.
113) here date from about 1650, but the columns were
inserted at the time of the alterations. The suite terminates
with the Corner Room, where the direction changes north to
the little Ante-Room, which looked onto the original east
forecourt.

For all its grandeur, there are several confusing aspects of
the plan, especially the relation between the Grand Design
and the old quadrangular house. It would appear that the
original approach to the Cube Room was via the west range
(since rebuilt by Wyatt) ending in the Single Cube, which
would thus then have formed an ante-room between the
central room of the Grand Design, and the Double Cube.

106. *The Double Cube Room, looking west.* The Family of the 4th Earl of Pembroke *by Van Dyck on the end wall.*
The painted cove by Edward Pierce and two of the three central panels by Emmanuel de Critz, c. 1650.

107. *The Double Cube Room, looking east, showing part of the series of Van Dyck portraits.*

One of the results of the curtailment of the Grand Design is the lack of a staircase comparable in scale and magnificence to the Cube Rooms. Another is that the house is over-weighted with ante-rooms and deficient in big rooms. This no doubt accounted for the need of Wyatt's alterations.

Our description of the State Rooms begins with the Hunting Room (Fig. 101), which Mr Christopher Hussey has suggested may have survived the fire of 1647–48.[1] It is panelled in pine, designed as two orders in almost mannerist fashion, but originally had no fireplace. The oak leaf entablature is decorated with shields supported by the out-stretched wings of the Herbert wyvern, which take the place of the capitals to implied pilasters in the decorative scheme. The series of painted panels depicting hunting scenes was painted by Edward Pierce, senior, after engravings by Antonio Tempesta, but with figures dressed in the fashion of Caroline England. In the *Partridge Netting* panel (Fig. 102) the mounted figure of Lord Pembroke appears in the middle distance. There is no precedent for such a decorative scheme in England, but there is a hunting room at Villa Lante at Bagnaia decorated with hunting scenes by Tempesta. As Mr Hussey has written, 'the costumes, indeed the whole conception and the idyllic rural scenery of these panels, pertain much more closely to 1640 than to the last grim year of Lord Pembroke's life (1649). Also I find it hard to believe that such

pictures, which must have taken several years to execute, and showing the Earl hunting and hawking, would have been undertaken in the year of the King's beheading, or if they were, would have been continued with after the Earl's own death.'[1] The panels between the hunting scenes representing sporting trophies were painted by Clermont in the 1730s.

Panelled double doors, similar to those in one of Jones's drawings (Fig. 117), open into the Single Cube Room (Fig. 104). This has a painted ceiling with a cove of arabesques, similar to that in the Queen's Bedchamber at Greenwich (Fig. 59), which is presumed to have been painted by Matthew Gooderick in about 1635; the close resemblance of the two seems to point again to an early date for this one, rather than one about 1650, which is the presumed date of the panelling and frieze. The chimneypiece and overmantel are certainly part of the post-fire decorations, the overmantel being derived from Jean Barbet's *Livre d'Architecture, d'Autels et de Cheminées* (Paris, 1633), a source frequently drawn upon by Jones. The dado panels contain a series of paintings illustrating Philip Sidney's *Arcadia*, which he wrote at Wilton, for his sister was Mary, third wife of the 2nd Earl and step-mother of Philip, the 4th Earl. Their painter was Emmanuel de Critz, and their inspiration 16th-century Venetian painting, then in fashion at the English court.

East of the Single Cube is the Double Cube Room (Figs.

[1] *Country Life*, Vol. CXXXIII, p. 1112.

[1] *Country Life, loc. cit.*

108. (*above, left*) *The Double Cube Room chimneypiece and overmantel.*

109. (*above*) *Detail of the decoration at the north-east corner of the Double Cube Room.*

110. (*left*) *The east wall of the Double Cube Room.*

111. *Detail of the carved entablature to the east door in the Double Cube Room.*

112, 113. *The chimney-pieces and overmantels in the Corner Room and Colonnade Room, c. 1650.*

114. *The ceiling of the Little Ante-Room*, c. 1650. *The* Birth of Venus, *by Sabbatini.*

106 and 7). It is without question the noblest room of the period and perhaps the most distinguished in any English country house. The decoration dates from about 1650, when the room was restored after the fire, and was designed to display Lord Pembroke's incomparable series of Van Dyck family portraits, brought here from Durham House, the Pembroke town house. (The date of their arrival is uncertain, and Evelyn does not mention them in 1654.) They could not be more splendidly housed, and their character must undoubtedly have influenced the designers of the room, inspiring them to create a setting in harmony with their Flemish, Genoese and Venetian qualities. With the added support of the Kentian gilt furniture, introduced in the following century, also in an Anglo-Venetian manner, this aim had been triumphantly achieved.

The design of the central doorway in the east wall (Fig. 110) can be traced back to earlier drawings for Whitehall, but nowhere was this type more splendidly carried out than here, where it is partly of stone and partly of wood. Designs for its capitals are in Webb's *Book of Capitals* at Chatsworth. Again the chimneypiece (Fig. 108) derives from one of Barbet's designs, but unfortunately the name of the craftsman responsible for the high quality of the marble carving is unknown. Nicholas Stone or his son might be hazarded, for they were the usual suppliers of chimneypieces to Jones and Webb.

Sir William Chambers likened the great carved clusters of fruit hanging from French-inspired masks to 'bunches of turnips'. Although they are not to be compared to the later trophies of Grinling Gibbons, they are boldly conceived and vigorously carved. They, like the rest of the carving in these rooms, seem to have something of the same character as that lavished on Stuart galleons: the figures atop the doorcases and chimneypieces and the cartouches tilted forward between them recall the decoration of the stern galleries of those vessels. In spite of the handicap imposed by the lack of more skilled carvers, these drops are astonishingly effective, for the painting and gilding is carefully articulated so that the light illuminates and plays on the gilding, breaking on the rougher surfaces and reflecting from the smooth. Particularly is this so in the gilding of the carved drapery on the overmantel and the figures of Plenty and Bacchus guarding it, which is carried out in two shades of gold leaf. This contributes a subtle liveliness to the whole suite of white and gold rooms, which achieve a marvellous combination of splendour and spontaneous gaiety that is most rare in palace rooms and surely stems from Jones's and Webb's close ties with the theatre.

There is a curious discrepancy in the plan of the Double Cube Room, for the chimney is not on the axis of the Venetian window opposite. This may have arisen because Isaac de Caus had to incorporate some older walls in his 1630 fabric, to which the decorators had to conform as best they

115, 116. *Designs, possibly for one of the Cube Rooms, by John Webb. (Victoria and Albert Museum.)*

could. As we have seen, Aubrey recorded that: 'In anno 1648, Philip re-edifyed it, by the advice of Inigo Jones; but he, being then very old, could not be there in person but left it to Mr Webb . . .' Webb certainly consulted his master, and Jones wrote comments on the drawings, but the latter was not likely to have been too anxious at the time to work for a former client whom he must have regarded as a traitor to his royal master. Judging by Pembroke's reference to 'Iniquity Jones', they were no longer on friendly terms.

Although the Van Dycks have dictated the character of the decoration, their courtly and royalist significance might have been embarrassing in the 1650s; indeed the overmantel did not always contain the portrait group of Charles I's children. Their parents hang rather insignificantly above the two door-cases at the west end of the room, where they are eclipsed by the parade of Pembrokes below. Perhaps this was intentional, for Earl Philip had broken with the King.

The superb family group at the west end, designed and hung to create the illusion of the sitters being present in the room, is of the 4th Earl's family. Lord Pembroke and his wife, Lady Anne Clifford, are seated to the right of the centre; beyond them, on the right, stand his daughter Sophia and her husband, Lord Caernarvon; in the foreground is the young Mary Villiers, the wife of Charles, Lord Herbert; he appears with his younger brother, later the 5th Earl, to the left of the centre, and there are several other young sons on the extreme left. On the north wall to the left of the fire-place are hung full-lengths of Isabella, Lady Rich, and the 3rd Earl and, to the right, portraits of the 4th Earl and his first wife, Penelope Naunton. On the east wall, either side of the large doorcase, are portraits of Mary Villiers as Duchess of Richmond (she married the Duke after the death of Lord Herbert) and of the Duke himself.

The three central panels of the ceiling, by de Critz, depict the story of Perseus, which may in some obscure way refer to the Herberts below. They surmount the deep cove

117. *Design for a doorcase for one of the State Rooms by Inigo Jones.*

decorated with *putti*, vases, swags of fruit and foliage, and shields bearing the monogram P M H for Pembroke, Mont-

118, 119. *Designs by Inigo Jones for the ceilings in the Passage Room and the Countess of Pembroke's Bedchamber.*

120, 121. Designs by Inigo Jones for the ceilings of the Countess of Carnarvon's Bedchamber and the Cabinet Room, 1649.

gomery and Herbert, all painted to an unusually large scale by the elder Pierce. Although the quality of this ceiling is not particularly distinguished, its effect is impressive and there is no other example of the kind from this period in England.

The last rooms in the series are the Corner Room and small Ante-Room, both of which retain their 1650 decoration. They are hung with some of the finest pictures in the collection formed after the dispersal of the great earlier collection by the 6th or 7th Earls. The Corner Room (Fig. 112) contains another chimneypiece based on Barbet, and the Ante-Room an elaborate ceiling with the *Birth of Venus* by Sabbatini, surrounded by exceptionally free decorative plasterwork of about 1650 (Fig. 114). The only other rooms of this period are two on the ground floor in the east front, to the north of

the gate. They both retain their original friezes and chimney-pieces.

Visitors nowadays approach the State Rooms by the stair-case in the east front, passing through from east to west, which is the reverse of de Caus's and Webb's intention.

The 4th Earl died before the refitting of the house was finished and was succeeded by his son, another Philip, who completed the work in about 1652–53.

The Herberts have always lived up to their tradition of being assiduous builders, and with the exception of the 6th and 7th Earls, who neglected and largely despoiled the great house, rarely has a generation left it or the gardens untouched. The enthusiasm of the 4th and 5th Earls was inherited by the 8th and his three immediate successors, who, between 1700

122. The Stables. Designed by de Caus, c. 1635–40.

123. *The façade of the Garden House, formerly that of de Caus's Grotto.*

and 1850, created the present setting of Wilton. The 9th 'Architect' Earl altered the house in the 1730s and, with the help of Roger Morris, built the Palladian bridge; the 11th Earl was the patron of Wyatt. His widow, and her son, Sydney Herbert, gave the gardens their final form. In the present century, the 15th Earl remodelled Wyatt's north front and de-gothicised some of his interiors, while the present Lord Pembroke has modified more of Wyatt's work.

Unfortunately, there is no record of the Jones-Webb work swept away and all we have are a number of isolated drawings. There is a design in the Worcester College Library for what could well be the Chapel at Wilton which projected from the west front. Judging by its elevation it was an ambitious concept, comparable with Inigo Jones's Queen's Chapel, built in 1623. In the Victoria and Albert Museum there are two designs (Figs. 115 and 116) formerly attributed to Brettingham, but now convincingly to Webb, which bear similarities to the Double Cube Room as executed, but it is not certain that they refer to Wilton: the division into two storeys suggests a hall like that at Lamport (Fig. 144), but the grandeur of the decoration indicated is comparable with Wilton. There are other drawings at Worcester College for ceilings, one of them inscribed 'Ceiling of the Great Staire, Wilton'. The most elaborate of them is entitled a 'Ceiling of ye passage room into ye Garden' (Fig. 118); it bears the monograms of the 4th or 5th Earl on its border, and might conceivably be a design for the ceiling of the Hunting Room (of which the existing ceiling is by Clermont); this shows a knowledge of 16th-century *quadrature* paintings and anticipates the Ashburnham House staircase. There are designs for the ceiling of the Cabinet Room, including one dated 1649

(Fig. 121), and two for ceilings in the suite of the Countess of Caernarvon, the daughter of the 4th Earl, one being for her Bedchamber (Fig. 120), and the other for her Drawing Room, and one for the ceiling of the Countess of Pembroke's Bedchamber (Fig. 119).

Of the Caroline garden layout, nothing remains beyond a few incidental buildings and features such as the fantastically carved façade of de Caus's grotto (Fig. 123), now in the Rose Garden. To the south-west of the house lie the attractive brick and stone stables 'of Roman architecture' which Aubrey says were designed by de Caus, presumably in the 1630s (Fig. 122): behind the pair of balustraded pavilions linked by an arcade is an enchanting courtyard, which, according to Aubrey, was decorated with 'pictures of the best horses as big as the life, painted in several postures, by a Frenchman,'[1] an idea presumably taken over from Guilio Romano's decorations at the Palazzo del Te at Mantua. The other survivors include the column of Venus Genetrix, formerly in the east forecourt, a number of statues now in the north forecourt, and a pair of rusticated columns, once fountains, in the south garden and now set up near the Orangery. Although all have been moved to new positions, they enable the visitor to visualise something of the 17th-century setting of Wilton.

Today, the mellowed garden front of Wilton, so admirably set off by the green velvet of the lawn, broken only by sombre-toned cedars, the limpid river and its phantom bridge leading nowhere but to the water meadows beyond, so casually disposed that they emphasise to perfection the symmetry of the house, compose a scene that must surely be the most poetic of any among English houses.

[1] Aubrey, *op. cit.*, p. 87.

124. *The Entrance Front from the east.*

COLESHILL HOUSE, BERKSHIRE

The masterpiece of Sir Roger Pratt, begun in 1649 and completed in 1662, was destroyed by fire in 1953.

The building of Coleshill was contemporary with the decoration of the State Rooms at Wilton. The correspondence is significant historically, for the two houses were the supreme expression of the taste of the two most important classes of English society of that day, the aristocracy and the gentry. Wilton was decorated by Jones and Webb for one of the most informed connoisseurs at the court of Charles I, while Coleshill was the first architectural enterprise of Roger Pratt, an educated man with first-hand knowledge of European architecture, and cousin to its owner, Sir George Pratt. The taste displayed in each was advanced for the period: both

125. *Design for a house from Serlio's* Architettura (*Book VII, page* 33).

Wilton and Coleshill are untypical of their generation, brilliant exceptions to the general level.

We know little about Sir George Pratt. Late in life he married a daughter of Sir Humphrey Forster of Aldermaston, who had built a house in the 1630s of advanced type. Sir George's grandfather had been a Cirencester clothier and his father, Henry, a City merchant. The latter must have been successful, for he rose to be Alderman and was made a baronet on relinquishing this appointment in 1641. He had bought Coleshill, then an old house, in 1626, and it was the destruction of this house by fire, in about 1647, that led Sir George to build a new one.

He had already made a start on this before seeking the advice of his cousin, Roger, who in 1649 had recently returned to England after six years abroad, where he had studied Italian Classical and Renaissance architecture at first hand. Invited to come and give advice on the new house, he found it so far removed from his ideal that he induced Inigo Jones, then an aged man, to visit Coleshill with him. He considered Inigo Jones to be the one and only English architect; and the only remarkable buildings in England those for which Jones had been directly responsible: the Banqueting House, the portico of old St Paul's and the Queen's House at Greenwich.

It was decided to discard the partly built new house and start afresh. Jones himself may have given assistance with the plans and also such details as the ceilings and chimney-pieces, for there is a design by John Webb in the R.I.B.A. for the dining room chimneypiece, but the latter cannot have been carried out during Jones's lifetime. The plan thus produced was an unbroken parallelogram of four storeys; the

126. *The Entrance Doorway and Steps.*

127. *(left) The Central Bays of the Entrance Front.*

128. *(below) The cupola on the roof.*

129. *The Garden Front.*

130. *The Saloon, originally the Great Dining Room.*

131. *The Great Staircase.*

lowest partly below ground level and the third contained in the hipped roof, which rose to a balustraded lead-flat surmounted by a cupola. The silhouette was probably inspired by one of Serlio's plates, but its horizontal emphasis complied with the English preference for length. The hipped roof, balustrade and cupola were derived from foreign examples. They could have been copied from Serlio (Fig. 125), or maybe had been seen in France. Such features occur at Balleroy, basically an oblong house, but divided into three sections in the French fashion, built in about 1626 by Francois Mansart.

The idea of the cupola providing access to a flat roof,

however, was not a new one in England, for at both Longleat and Burghley there were cupolas and roof-top promenades. The eight massive chimney stacks were an important feature of Coleshill, defining and emphasising the form of the cube, and although they appear large in the illustration they were not unduly so, for the house was 124 feet long and 62 feet deep (Thorpe Hall, see p. 102, is 88 feet by 74 feet). Pratt doubtless benefited by his knowledge of continental building when designing them, but adapted his experience in the light of the English tradition, for both Tudor and Jacobean designers had made great play with the composition and decoration of their chimneys.

The striking quality of Coleshill, which was evidence of Pratt's talent, was that although it appeared to be completely English, it was, in fact, a full-blown classical house in a land without a building tradition in that manner. Moreover, being the first essay of a man steeped in the classical style, a rash of columns, pillars and pilasters might have been expected, but there were none. The house was classical in the harmony of its proportions, and so strongly had the discipline of the orders been ingrained that there was no need of their appearance.

The long front of nine bays (Fig. 124) was saved from monotony by the rhythm of the fenestration, in sets of three, the three centre windows being spaced slightly wider apart than those at the ends. The central pedimented door (Fig. 126), the string courses, the rusticated plinth and the quoins, were all sensitively detailed, and great care bestowed

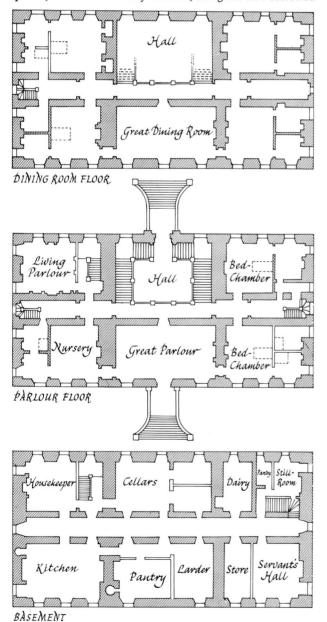

132. *Plan of the house. (North to the left.)*

on the panelled chimneys with their carved egg and dart moulding.

The plan was what Pratt called a double-pile — i.e. a block with two ranges of rooms separated by a corridor, an uncommon arrangement in England at the time. The offices were contrived in the basement together with the kitchen, while the Great Dining Room was on the upper floor, the living parlour (presumably the normal dining room) being on the principal floor. The Italian custom favouring this arrangement allowed for a flight of steps leading up to the entrance. The setting of the Great Dining Room above the parlour was not unusual in England, where State Rooms were occasionally placed on the upper floor.

At Coleshill the hall (Fig. 131) contained both entrance and staircase, an unusual arrangement in the 1650s. At Thorpe, for instance, the hall was a survival of the old Great Hall, and lay to one side of a cross-passage. The axial relationship of hall to parlour was of importance to future development, for it is the key of the typical Restoration plan of the Ramsbury-Belton type (see pp. 180 and 198); it was an ideal arrangement, though rather restricting in grander houses.

The idea of paired flights either side of the hall was recommended by Palladio,[1] 'so that people may go up and come down both ways, which makes them very handsome and commodious.' A more recent source of inspiration could have been Longhena's staircase of S. Giorgio Maggiore, in Venice, built in 1643–45; if this is so, it shows Pratt's interest in contemporary architecture, as well as in monuments of the past. The stairs started on either side of the entrance door, the wide and easy treads being bounded by great newels and a broad rail supported on enriched balusters. The newels had sunken panels carved with lions' masks and fruit drops, while the string was embellished with a series of ribboned swags springing from the side of a central cartouche, and extending to draped female heads at the corners. The work is referred to in a bill, dated May, 1662, from Richard Cleave or Cleeve, who worked later for Wren on the City churches, especially at St Olave's Old Jewry. Cleave charged £1 a yard for the festoons, of which there were 20½ yards; they were sent down from London in large baskets in the charge of a man who was paid 26s. 'ffor his goeing down to set up the festoons on the stayres.'

The boldly designed doorcases formed a feature of the decoration, as did the laurel-wreathed roundels in the walls, containing busts of the Roman Emperors, a gesture to Italianate taste. The ceiling (Fig. 133), with heavy beam-like ribs, had enriched soffiting characteristic of Inigo Jones's work: we are told he 'was also consulted abt ye Ceilings.' They took the form of two pairs of cross beams running from end to end and side to side, forming nine panels; the large oval in the centre overlaid the rectangle, an arrangement that had been similarly used by Jones at Whitehall. The oval was left plain, but perhaps intended for a decorative painting; the side panels were enriched with wreaths of oak or bay leaves.

In the ceiling of the Library the beams were shallower and their soffits embellished with scrolled floral enrichment; the segmental panels were ornamented with linked dragons, while the side panels had cornucopiae. Far richer treatment was

[1] Book II, chapter 13.

133. *The Hall ceiling.*

134. *Detail of the Saloon ceiling and frieze.*

135. *Design for the chimneypiece in the Great Chamber by John Webb.*

136, 137. *Gate-piers guarding the approaches. One of a pair at the entrance to the park and one of a pair on the drive.*

bestowed on the ceiling of the Great Dining Room (Fig. 130), latterly the Saloon. Here the ribs were of similar depth to the cornice; the soffit of the oval was enriched by a fruit and flower garland, while the beams had acanthus foliage in which amorini disported themselves between whorled rosettes at the intersections (Fig. 132). The frieze, festooned with ribboned swags of fruit and flowers in full relief, had forward-tilting cartouches accenting the centres.

Sir George Pratt lived another eleven years after paying Cleave's bill in 1662, and thus had time to enjoy the 'green walke with all sorts of dwarfe trees', on which Celia Fiennes commented.[1] He would also have seen his four sets of imposing gate-piers set up; the noblest being those alongside the road (Fig. 136), through the gates of which a glimpse of the house could be seen. Here the panels are formed with nail-head rustication and enriched with the same egg and dart as was carved on the chimneys of the house. On the park side the panels have recessed roundels containing classical busts,

while shell-headed niches are arranged as seats; the same shell-head, with variations, appears on the other sets of piers.

Sir George's son died six months after his father, without an heir, so that the house passed to the son of his sister, who had married Thomas Pleydell. In 1728 Mark Pleydell inherited, and from him the house came by descent to the Earls of Radnor. These photographs were taken in about 1919, when the house was the home of the widow of the Hon. Duncombe Pleydell-Bouverie. In 1945 Mr Ernest Cook acquired it with the idea of bequeathing it to the National Trust, but while some repairs were being executed in 1953 a fire gutted the interior, and it was decided to demolish the shell, an irreparable loss, for besides being one of the most beautiful and architecturally the most accomplished of country houses, Coleshill was the most important of Pratt's works. As Sir John Summerson has said:[1] 'Massive, serene, thoughtful, absolutely without affectation, Coleshill was a statement of the utmost value to British architecture.'

[1] *The Journeys of Celia Fiennes.* (C. Morris edition), p. 24.

[1] Summerson, *op. cit.*, 1963, p. 87.

138. *The West Front. John Webb's building, flanked by Francis Smith's additions of 1732 and 1741.*

LAMPORT HALL, NORTHAMPTONSHIRE

In 1654 John Webb added a new wing to the Tudor manor house for Sir Justinian Isham. A unique collection of letters and drawings relating to the work have survived. (The Seat of Sir Gyles Isham, Bt.)

The Ishams have lived at Lamport since 1560 and during the succeeding centuries have taken unusual care of their family papers. These give a particularly complete picture of an old county family in the third quarter of the 17th century when the first Sir Justinian was squire, revealing the sense of uncertainty hanging over the gentry during the Commonwealth, and details of their financial difficulties and arrangements. There are also full details of Sir Justinian's additions to his house.

Sir Justinian, who inherited in 1651, was the 2nd baronet and head of the fourth generation of Ishams to live in the house that had been built in 1568 by John Isham, a successful member of the Mercers Company and younger son of one of the oldest families in the county. The house had been altered in 1610/11, but by 1650 was considered so out-of-date that Dorothy Osborne, whom Justinian wished to marry, called it 'a vile house'. After he inherited he married, as his second wife, Vere Leigh, a daughter of Lord Leigh of Stoneleigh, in Warwickshire. Then he restored the chancel of Lamport church 'that it may be both made and kept a house of praier, and the common tomb of our family'; and after this turned his attentions to the house.

For a design he first approached a neighbour, David Papillon, an amateur architect and engineer who lived nearby at Lubbenham in Leicestershire. This gentleman produced two schemes for a new house in the form of a cube, with cross corridors similar to Thorpe. Although they indicated a handling of space exceptional at the time, Sir Justinian decided, possibly for reasons of economy, to adapt the old house. The Lamport estate was then probably worth about £1,000 a year, and Shangton, a second estate which had been acquired in 1637, brought in a further £645. In addition to

these, the mortgages purchased by his father yielded another £360 a year, so that he was well able to contemplate building. (These figures compare with the Pembrokes' £30,000 a year, or the Spencers' £6,000 to £8,000.)

On 28th February, 1654, Justinian wrote to Bishop Duppa of Winchester: 'My cheifest imployment at present seems to me as naturall as to ye very birds and crowes about mee, to be busy in building my nest against my Wife lies downe, nor with much greater designe than they, raising no proud structure to sett my heart upon it, but such as if these stormy dayes chance to blow away yet my rest remains on a City not built with hands.' Despite the constant threat of the 'stormy dayes' he went to John Webb for a design. The present owner, Sir Gyles Isham, suggests that he may have known

139. *Webb's design for the West Wing.*

140. (*above left*) *The façade of the Webb building.*

141. (*above*) *Detail of the masonry at the south-east corner of the Webb building.*

142. (*left*) *Lamport in 1761. A drawing by James Blackemore showing the stables, the old manor house and the north end of the West Front.*

143. (*below*) *Plan of the Ground Floor. Webb's work is hatched.*

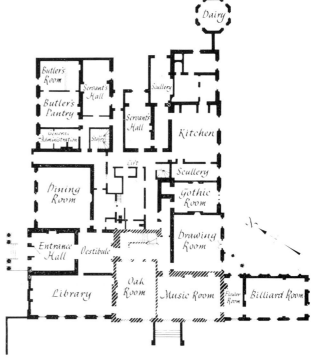

Webb through Henry Cogan, who was one of the two over-seers of Inigo Jones's will. If this is so, he would have approached Webb privately and not through any official connection, which had been the usual way of obtaining a design from either Jones or Webb. It is an indication of the times that Webb was free to carry through such a comparatively small undertaking and to devote all the attention that his letters and the 33 drawings testify.

Work was begun on the new range in 1654 (Fig. 138), in strong contrast of style to the older house, to which it stood at right angles (Fig. 142). It included a great room of three bays rising two storeys high, a new staircase, and a parlour with a bedroom above. Webb's elevation (Fig. 139) was faithfully carried out, but this pediment was replaced in 1828–30 by Henry Hakewill, who added the inscription (this superseded an earlier pediment by Smith of Warwick, which in turn replaced that designed by Webb). These minor alterations, together with the reglazing of the windows, are the only departures from the original conception, which may be seen in Fig. 139.

The foreman, Sargenson, and the masons, John Greene and Robert Grumball (or Grumbold), all local men, were directed by Sir Justinian himself. Judging by his books, still

144. *The Music Hall, showing Webb's chimneypiece and doors, wainscot of 1685, and plasterwork of 1738.*

in the Library, he had a good knowledge of architecture, for among them are *Le Muet's* volume, together with Rubens's *Palazzi di Genova* and du Cerceau (acquired in 1660). Seven of Webb's letters date from the period 19th June, 1654, to 31st May, 1655. Then Sir Justinian was imprisoned in St James's Palace for the summer, but the building continued, its progress being reported from time to time by Sargenson. Later in the same year Sir Justinian wrote to Sir Ralph Verney, who had been a fellow prisoner, signing his letter 'Architrave, Freeze and Cornice.' On November 2nd, he wrote again, this time from Lamport, 'where you may see what the want of my prescence hath now necessitated me to in very ill season, my house not yet all covered.' During that year Pierre Bennier (or Besnier)[1] carved the cartouche bearing the Isham arms over the central doorway, and Sargenson visited Thorpe to inspect its lead roof and to see how the rainwater was carried away without the use of external down pipes.

The fitting of the interior had come under discussion before Sir Justinian had been arrested, and in February, 1655, Webb wrote that he wished the chimneypiece in the High Room

'were wrought here in Towne by Mr Marshall.' Isham would have preferred it 'after ye fflemish manner carryed on Cartooses', a notion disapproved of by Webb, who replied: 'My design is after ye Italian manner.' The lower half of this chimney (Fig. 146) is of stone, carved by C. G. Cibber, while the upper part is of wood incorporating the Isham arms and a swan; the inset picture is a copy of a Titian. Apart from the doors and their cases, that is all that remains of Webb's decoration, but his design can be followed in the four drawings of the walls and the separate details of the chimneypiece and ceiling (Figs. 145, 147–9). The walls would have been divided into two sections by a bold cornice supporting busts, while classical figures and reliefs were to be set in recesses in the lower part. One of the drawings shows a pendant drop sketched in faintly, similar to those in the Wilton Double Cube Room.

The statuary was in all probability executed, for there are records of Bennier having been employed. Webb had objected to a foreigner, but agreed it might be better to employ one rather than entail the expense of obtaining one from London 'especially if you intend statues in the neeches as I designed, but then also lett him cast them for you out of Antique moulds for ffrench fashions are you know fantasti-

[1] Appointed Sculptor in Ordinary to Charles I, 1643. See Rupert Gunnis, *Dictionary of British Sculptors*, p. 50.

145, 146. *Webb's design for the Music Hall chimneypiece and overmantel and (right), as executed by Cibber. The copy of the Titian double portrait of George d'Armagnac, Bishop of Rodez and his secretary Guillaume Philandrier was bought for this position.*

call.' Vertue refers to a sculptor of the name of Andrew Keane, who 'carved many statues for Sir Justinian Isam.'

The present decoration of the room is of two periods; the panelling was installed by Henry Jones, a local joiner, in 1685, and the ceiling by John Woolston, of Northampton, in 1738. The two portraits of Charles I have been in the house since Sir Justinian's time. The equestrian portrait of the King, with Monsieur de St Antoine, is a copy acquired in 1655 for £250 from the dealer Maurice Wase, who was recommended by Webb; he also supplied a number of works, including the Van Dyck of *Christ and John the Baptist*. The position of the portrait of Charles I was probably specially prepared for it, and being hung close to the floor, follows Van Dyck's baroque intention when he painted the original for the gallery at St James's. Maurice Wase's letter relating to this picture is dated 24th May, 1655, and it was on 9th June that Isham was arrested. Opposite hangs a copy of the portrait of Charles as a country squire, the original of which is in the Louvre. This may have come from Holdenby House, also in Northamptonshire, together with one of Anne of Denmark, whose house it had been.

All that remains of Webb's staircase are some of the balustrade panels; neither the parlour nor the bedrooms retain any trace of his work. His last letters, dated 1657, are concerned with a family depository or mausoleum which Sir Justinian was anxious to provide, but the idea was not proceeded with. In 1672–73 the present chapel was built, on the north side of the church.

Sir Justinian and his wife both lived to enjoy the new wing and to bring up a large family in the house. He became a member of the Royal Society, lived to see his old friend Elizabeth Murray become Duchess of Lauderdale, and Althorp remodelled by the Earl of Sunderland, the son of another friend, Dorothy Sidney. He died in 1675, at the age of sixty-four, leaving the estate to his son Thomas, then a minor still at Oxford.

In October, 1676, however, Thomas abandoned his studies and set off for Italy where he spent seventeen months, returning with twenty pictures, of which eighteen are still in the house; nine are originals, and the others copies after Raphael, Domenichino, Guercino, Lanfranco, da Cortona, Poussin and Maratta. The originals are by Lauri, Salvator

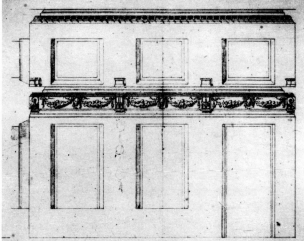

147–149. *Webb's designs for the Music Hall. The inner and outer walls, and the two end elevations.*

150. *One of a pair of Neapolitan cabinets decorated with painted glass pictures, acquired in Italy by Sir Thomas Isham.*

Rosa and others, and there is a splendid portrait of himself, by Maratta. These pictures complement the Italianate building put up by his father. The European character of the Isham taste is further exemplified by a marble urn, an inlaid marble-topped table that possibly belonged to Sir Thomas, and the two elaborate Neopolitan cabinets (Fig. 150), which he had brought back.

When Sir Thomas died, on the eve of his wedding, in 1681, Lamport was architecturally unique among the houses of local squires, and only surpassed in grandeur by Althorp. In the 18th century the Smiths of Warwick extended the Webb front, retaining its scale and sympathetically allowing its richly worked masonry to project slightly beyond their own additions. In 1842 further additions were made behind the eastern half of the long front by Henry Goddard, replacing work by Hakewill, who had been employed in 1821. The original manor house was largely rebuilt by Burn in the 1860s, when it assumed its present form. While these alterations have inevitably changed the outward aspect of the house it still largely reflects the tastes and interests of Justinian and Thomas Isham.

151. *Thorpe in 1721. A drawing by Tillemans showing the house with the cupola that originally crowned the roof.*

THORPE HALL, NORTHAMPTONSHIRE

Designed about 1653 by Peter Mills for Oliver St John, Thorpe Hall is the outstanding country house of the Commonwealth. Apart from a mid-19th-century restoration and the removal of a room in about 1920, the house has been little altered. (Occupied by the Peterborough and Stamford Hospital Board.)

The four lofty chimney-stacks of Thorpe are a landmark in the flat country to the west of Peterborough. Built of Weldon stone now weathered to a creamy-white, they rise above the trees and catch the sunlight. Even today the tall pile of the house seems alien to its setting and must have been even more surprising when John Evelyn passed it in 1654. 'Got this evening to Peterborow,' he wrote, 'passing by a stately palace of St John's (one deepe in ye blood of our good King) built out of the ruins of the Bishop's palace and cloister.'[1]

Oliver St John, who was related to the builder of Cold Overton, in Leicestershire, was a great-grandson of the 1st Lord St John. He was among those who turned against the Stuarts in the 1620s, going to the Tower for a short time in 1629. A successful lawyer, acting as such to the 4th Earl of Bedford, and defending Hampden in the Ship Money case, he was thus well placed when Parliament seized control in the 1640s. Perhaps he was helped by his two wives' connection with Cromwell, the second being a cousin of the Protector. In 1648 St John became Lord Chief Justice of Common Pleas, but, contrary to Evelyn's remark, he played no part in the execution of the King. In the 1640s he was very close to Cromwell, but became less and less in sympathy with his regime in the 1650s and claimed that he never made a penny out of it.

He obtained a lease for the land at Thorpe from the Dean and Chapter of Peterborough, and in 1653 the freehold of the manor. He may have obtained the idea for his house from a trip to Holland, in March, 1650, where he went on an embassy with John Thurloe, who later built a smaller, but similar type of house at Wisbech (Fig. 16).

The design for Thorpe must have been prepared in 1653,

[1] *Diary*. Vol. I, p. 305. August 30, 1654.

for a contract dated 8th February, 1653/54, refers to 'a draught or map of the said intended House' and 'the Place in Hill Close aforesaid where the said House is to be built'. Work proceeded rapidly as Sargenson, the foreman at Lamport, visited Thorpe in the summer of 1655 to see the way rainwater was carried off the roof. There are more rainwater heads, on the low wing, dated 1656. The 'draught' was for a house of a type rare in England, a tall block-like shape of four storeys in strong contrast to the longer front of Wilton or Coleshill. Its origin may be traced to the plates in Rubens's *Palazzi di Genova* and to St John's recent acquaintance with Dutch architecture.

Like many other important houses of the 1650s, Thorpe was once attributed to Webb, but Mr Colvin's discovery of the 1653/54 contract in the British Museum (Add. MSS No. 25302, f. 153) shows the designer to have been Peter Mills.

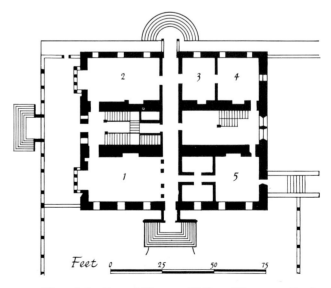

152. *Plan of the Ground Floor. 1. Hall. 2. Library. 3. Study. 4. Dining Room. 5. Kitchen. (North to the bottom.)*

153. *The West and South Elevations.*
154. *(below) A drawing for Rubens's* Palazzi di Genova: *Nicolo Spinola's palazzo.*

The London surveyor thus emerges as an architect of un-expected power. The other parties to the contract are the masons, John Ashby and Sampson Frisby, both local men.

The house lies at the centre of an elaborate layout of some five or six acres enclosed by a high wall. Gardens lie to the east and south of the house, an office court to the west, and a forecourt on the north. A raised walk along the western section of the layout enables one to look down on a parterre and across the wall to the surrounding countryside. Considerable play is made with gate piers and arches in the enclosing wall and within the garden itself. The most ornate of the piers are those flanking the entrance to the forecourt (Fig. 157). Their niches are filled with a stunted version of the Raphaelesque twisted column, and they are crested, like their responds on the south side, with the handsome coroneted falcon of the St Johns. A rusticated archway terminates the western axis, and there is another, more mannerist in character, between stable-yard and garden. Running west from the house is the long office and stable wing, which has a version of the Holborn gable with a clock cupola above. Beyond this was another range running north and south, but all that remained in 1920 was the façade of a garden pavilion.

155. *The Porch and the central window on the South Front.*

156. *(below left) The South and East Elevations. The fenestration on the East Front was altered in* 1854.

157. *(below right) The gate piers at the entrance to the North Forecourt from without.*

158. *The Dining Room. A detail of the east wall.*

159. (*below*) *The Drawing Room door.*

160. (*below right*) *Detail of the Main Staircase at the Drawing Room landing.*

Such a layout is a unique survival. It shows an attitude to architecture and landscape contrary to that of the 18th century, set on foot by Kent when he leapt the wall and saw all nature was a garden. At Thorpe the feeling is almost medieval, with the house rising like a castle-keep from its system of ramparts. There is no attempt to link it to the landscape; indeed, it is impossible to obtain satisfactory photographs of the house in its setting, a difficulty that is illustrated by a drawing in the British Museum attributed to Tillemans, showing the house rising above the garden walls (Fig. 151).

This drawing also shows the cupola and balustrade that once crowned the roof, similar to that at Coleshill and other houses. Its presence explains the scale of the chimney-stacks, which now appear awkwardly dominant. Apart from this, the south, north and west fronts have not been altered except in the matter of the glazing of the windows. The south front consists of seven bays and twenty windows, one more than the number specified in the contract, a departure possibly explained by the existence of a separate contract, now lost, for the more elaborate central window linked to the doorway beneath (Fig. 155). This gives onto the roof of the porch, itself a rare feature. Unfortunately, the iron balustrade shown here is no longer in position; it was probably inspired by the 'pergolas' at Arundel House, London, erected thirty years previously by Inigo Jones. The north front is identical to the south, except that the porch carries a stone balustrade. The west façade (Fig. 153), facing the office court, is of simpler design and less dependent on foreign inspiration: the strange double window here might be expected to light the main staircase, but this is not so.

161. *The Library Door and the foot of the Staircase.*

162. *The Main Staircase at the Second Floor.*

163. *The upper stair leading to the roof cupola.*

The east front (Fig. 156), facing the garden and containing the principal rooms, is of unusual design; it is dominated by the pair of two-storey bay windows, which have no counterparts in other houses of the period. In the past doubts about the authenticity of this façade were raised, and recently Sir Gyles Isham has shown that certain alterations were made when Hakewill restored the house for the Strongs between 1851 and 1854. A note dated 14th April, 1851, records 'the sill of the window in the Drawing Room (East) [the upper room in the right hand bay in 1920 and probably in 1850] was also partly fixed; commencing the restoration and alteration of the stone frame-work.'[1] Unfortunately, there is no record of how extensive these works were, but in all over £4,000 was spent.

The formality of the garden layout is continued within the house, where the basic elements are a corridor running north and south on the axis of the entrance and garden doors, staircases lying at either end of the east–west axis, and the principal rooms filling the corners of the cruciform plan. In some ways this was an old-fashioned arrangement, for the north–south corridor assumed the nature of a screens passage, dividing the living and serving rooms. This would have been more apparent before 1850, when the four columns were introduced half-way down the corridor and the ways to the staircases opened up. On the 1850 plan the room to the left of the front door is marked Hall, but it was probably never open to the corridor and was used as the Dining Room; it is opposite the Serving Room, which connects with the Kitchen range.

The Hall, which is panelled for two-thirds of its height, contains a large chimneypiece surmounted by the arms of the Strongs carved on a Cromwellian cartouche. A door at the south-east corner leads to the main staircase hall and beyond it lies the Parlour, which, in 1920, was known as the Library;

[1] Sir Gyles Isham. Northants. Antiquarian Soc., Vol. LXII, 1958–59, p. 37.

167. *The Library.*

168. *The Billiard Room door.*

the photographs (Figs. 164–7) show it as it was at that time. Avray Tipping said of it that: 'Next to the bigger and more sumptuous Cube Rooms at Wilton it is the most remarkable room of its age to come down to us.'[1] After the Strongs sold the house, this panelling was unfortunately removed, and it is now installed at Leeds Castle in Kent. The scheme is based on vertical panels surmounted by palm sprays set beneath independent cornices; their complex rhythm is best seen on the end wall (Fig. 167), where the central doorcase is flanked by pilasters supporting an entablature that breaks forward from the main cornice. The scrolls either side of the key-block in the doorcase are an unusual detail, which is echoed in the inverted scrolled-ends of the architraves surrounding the panels. These are turned outwards and rest on the dado capping. The dado mouldings, both capping and skirting, are also terminated by scrolls, as may be seen in the chimneypiece illustration. The chimney-piece (Fig. 165), which is placed off centre, is of marble with a wooden overmantel. In places the design of the woodwork does not exactly fit the walls, as in the north-east corner, but strange things also happen in the corners of the Double Cube at Wilton. In this room it is possible that Mills had some French or Dutch prints to draw upon and used them elsewhere in the house, particularly in the design of the

[1] Avray Tipping, *English Homes*, Period IV, Vol. I, p. 42.

doorcases with their long runs of guilloche carving and the use of painted panels or niches in the overdoors.

The Library is balanced on the south front by two smaller rooms, which in 1920 were called the Study and Dining Room respectively. The Study is lined with the characteristic bolection panelling of the Restoration period, and the ceiling has an enriched cove of moulded plasterwork. In contrast to such advanced decoration, the chimneypiece here is rather crude in design. The Dining Room (Fig. 158) is wainscoted in a manner similar to the Library, but rather simpler.

The main stairs have a splendid balustrade (Fig. 160) of carved, pierced and scrolled foliage, with newels surmounted by miniature baskets of fruit standing on inverted brackets. They terminate at first floor level and, before the 1850 restoration, led only to two rooms, of which one was the Drawing Room. During the restoration the first floor arcading was inserted and a way made through to the other staircase serving the upper floors.

The balustrading of the first flight of the western stair is less imposing, but becomes more elaborate at first floor level. The balusters are turned and carved, while the newels with their low relief carving are surmounted by ball finials (Fig. 162). From the first floor to the attic in the roof the stair rises in a series of straight flights, but continues, into what was the cupola, in a spiral (Fig. 163) that gyrates around a central post, a spectacular *tour de force* in carpentry. From the cupola one could step out onto the roof to survey the countryside.

The most important room on the first floor is the Drawing Room. This retains traces of its original decoration and appears to have been hung with tapestry. It is wainscoted only between the windows on the north wall; pier glasses are inset in the wainscot, apparently one of the earliest instances of mirror decoration. The carved enrichment above is of the 1650s, which appears to confirm that these mirrors formed part of the original work. The doorcases are surmounted by niches for busts. The ceiling is an 1851 copy of a Webb design in the Library at Worcester College, Oxford. (One of the arguments for attributing the house to Webb was this ceiling.)

Despite his unpopularity with the restored monarchy, and Clarendon's covetous eye, Oliver St John managed to retain possession of Thorpe, but in 1664 he deemed it wise to go abroad. He died in voluntary exile nine years later. His descendants retained the house until 1793, when the last of them, Mary, wife of Sir John Bernard, died. From then until 1850 the house belonged to the Fitzwilliams of Milton, who sold it to the Rev. William Strong, who carried out the 1850 restoration.

The illustrations show the house as it appeared during the occupation of his grandson, Brigadier-General Strong. He sold it after the 1914–18 war. After the Strongs left, the Library panelling was removed and then the late Mr Meaker bought the house. For some years it has been used by the Peterborough and Stamford Hospital Board, who have taken care to protect its unique decoration.

169. *The South Front. A remodelling of medieval and early 16th-century monastic buildings in the 1650s.*

FORDE ABBEY, DORSET

The monastic buildings were acquired by Edmund Prideaux in 1649 and in the following years were transformed into one of the most impressive houses of the Commonwealth. It contains interesting decoration of the period. (The home of Mr and Mrs Geoffrey Roper.)

The houses described in this book illustrate the reactions of patrons and architects to the classical style. But Forde is unique among them in showing Edmund Prideaux's reaction not only to the classical, but also to the gothic. Like many great houses its origins were monastic and to this day there remain the 12th-century chapter-house, the early 13th-century dorter range, and the splendid early 16th-century buildings of Thomas Chard, the last Abbot.

When the abbey was dissolved, in 1539, the buildings were leased and later granted to Richard Pollard, who sold them to Sir Amias Paulet. They then passed to William Rosewell, Solicitor-General to Queen Elizabeth, whose son Henry sold them in 1649 to Edmund Prideaux. The latter came of an old West Country family and, like his father, Sir Edmund Prideaux of Netherton in Devon, was a lawyer. He was more interested in politics and sat as a member for Lyme Regis in the Long Parliament. A loyal supporter of Parliament against the King, he subscribed £100 in 1641 for its defence. Office followed, and for a few months in 1648 he was Solicitor-General. He resigned when the King's trial became imminent, but was made Attorney-General in April, 1649. Besides holding these appointments, he organised a weekly postal service in England, no mean achievement at the time, and perhaps he deserved the fortune he is reputed to have made from its profits. In all probability it was from them, as well as from the law, that Prideaux was enabled to acquire Forde and transform it on so elaborate a scale.

By careful adjustments he managed to pull the disparate monastic buildings into a balanced and ordered façade (Fig. 169). Perhaps he had no desire for a true classical front, but he seems to have followed a favourite theme of Palladio, an elevation consisting of five elements, a central block and terminal pavilions linked by lower ranges. To emphasise its centre, he built the three-bay section containing the Saloon, which projects in front of Chard's gate-tower and is set just to the right of it. In order not to compete with this splendid feature, he kept his centrepiece a little lower in height. Above the old chapter-house at the east end of the façade he built another storey with three windows on the upper floor, the central one having an arched head. To balance this on the west, Prideaux refaced Chard's building, and placed a matching round-headed window in the centre of the upper tier. He also altered the westernmost bay of Chard's great hall, dividing it into three bays and two storeys, and to give unity to the hall range he placed a pedimented sundial above the west window. This lower section balances the cloister range, east of the Saloon, which he heightened by building bedrooms above. The manner in which this long façade is ordered shows considerable skill, besides being one of the most interesting examples of mid-17th century building.

We do not know in what state Prideaux found the house, or how much of the monastic buildings he destroyed. The date when the church which lay to the south of the main range disappeared is also unknown. It is regrettable that parts of Chard's exceptional carving above the hall windows were taken down in the 1650s, when several of its stones were reset in the west wall. Despite this, Prideaux undoubtedly had a sympathy for late gothic building, for, apart from placing a large cartouche bearing his arms above the porch and removing some of the mullions from the double-tiered oriel above,

170. *The west part of the South Front. Mid-17th-century re-facing of earlier fabric.*

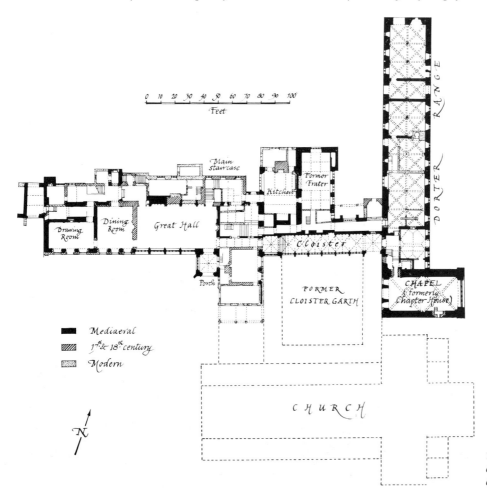

171. *Plan showing the 17th-century work in relation to earlier building.*

172. (*above*) *Detail of the woodwork on the east wall of the Great Hall. Compare the treatment of the niche with the centre of the engraving in Fig.* 173.

173. (*above right*) *Plate* 157 *from Dietterlin's* Architectura.

174. *The Chapel Screen, looking west.*

175. *The Dining Room.*

176. *The Drawing Room.*

177, 178. *Chimneypieces in the Dining Room and Drawing Room.*

he preserved Chard's tower. He also retained the beautiful cloister, adding a plaster vault in an unusual gothick manner. A gothic vault might be expected in the conservative west, where the style was retained as the vernacular until the mid-17th century. Probably Chard had not completed the cloister when he surrendered the abbey, and perhaps Prideaux's vault replaced its temporary roof.

Since the south front of the house displays such architectural sense it is odd that no such discipline was applied to the north. Prideaux did not attempt to bring unity to the varied parts and his main addition was built to contain his grand staircase. Since then several further additions have been made at different times.

Like other 17th-century houses, Forde has sometimes been connected with the name of Inigo Jones, but there appears, however, to be no clue to the identity of its designer. There are no links with Captain Ryder's wing at Cranborne Manor, of 1647, nor with Anthony Ashley-Cooper's St Giles's House, of about 1650. Forde's connections seem to lie rather with Thorpe, Wisbech and Tyttenhanger. The name of Peter Mills has been suggested in connection with Forde, a not unlikely attribution on political as well as visual grounds. A number of features may be compared with Thorpe, such as the simplicity of the window frames with their slightly projecting bases. The arrangement of the

Saloon frontispiece with its *œil-de-bœuf* windows, the round-headed central one between a plain pair, bears a striking resemblance to the front of the now ruined garden house at Thorpe. If Mills worked on Forde one would have expected bold chimney-stacks, but these are insignificant and play no part in the general scheme, which is unusual in a house of this date.

The interior shows abundant artisan detail, particularly in the woodwork. The centrepiece in the east wall of the Great Hall (Fig. 172) is Prideaux's work, and its elongated form, broken pediment and complicated patterning are typical of artisan-mannerism. The other woodwork in the room is advanced in character for its date, the panels being of an unusually large size. This apartment is still a Great Hall, despite its truncation to provide a dining room beyond.

Prideaux must have intended this room, the Drawing Room at the west end of the house and the bedrooms above as the private rooms of the house, as they are to this day. They are served by a secondary, but still spacious, staircase rising from the corridor on the north side of the range. This is separated from the Great Hall not only by a door, but by a pair of dog-gates as well.

The Dining Room (Fig. 175) is impressive, with a definite attempt at a classical scheme, the pilasters of the panelling being aligned with the ceiling beams. Even so, it lacks the

179. (*left*) *The Great Staircase.*

180. (*right*) *Detail of the Great Staircase, showing* trompe l'œil *painting repeating the design of the carved balustrade.*

integrated quality of the best of the Thorpe rooms, and the detailing suggests that the West Country craftsmen were less skilled than those of Northamptonshire. There is a distinct provincial feeling about the figure of eight motifs in the centre of the long panels and in the enrichment of the overmantel. The marbled wooden chimneypiece (Fig. 177) is more disciplined in design and is somewhat reminiscent of that formerly in the library at Thorpe.

The plasterwork of the ceiling, like that in many of the other rooms, is vigorous, if rather coarse, and was certainly executed by West Country craftsmen. Richard Abbott of Barnstaple, the second of three generations of plasterers, may conceivably have been employed, for some of the ceilings bear a close relationship to the drawings in his family notebook. Their layout is of more advanced character than some others that have been attributed to Abbott, but, if he was employed, he was probably working under a London designer. The detail is typical work in the 'Jacobethan' manner.

The Drawing Room (Fig. 176) beyond is a room of comparable size, but the original panelling scheme is now mostly hidden by the tapestries. Their soft colours, the old gilding

181. *The Saloon. The Mortlake tapestries woven after Raphael's cartoons.*

182. *Detail of the Saloon ceiling.* The Sacrifice of Isaac; *the figures wear contemporary costume.*

of the overmantel and the brown paint of the woodwork give this room what one imagines to be an authentic Commonwealth atmosphere and, if more austere furniture was introduced, the room would appear much as it must have done in Prideaux's day.

There is a nice sense of separation between these rooms at the west end of the house and the Saloon on the first floor in the centre. The latter lies at the head of the three flights of the Grand Staircase (Fig. 179), which is built out on the north side of the house, opposite the main entrance. Double doors face the arch of Chard's porch across the Great Hall and immediately behind them the first flight starts to rise. The balustrade consists of a series of pierced panels carved with acanthus foliage set between newels topped with baskets of fruit. Originally it must have created a rich effect, for the carving was picked out in gold. This is now hidden beneath layers of brown paint and varnish and to judge its original appearance one must look at the *trompe l'œil* painting on the dado (Fig. 180). The quality of the carving is good and is of considerably higher standard than work carried out in the first years of the Restoration, such as the staircase at Eltham. This stair was probably completed in 1658, for that year is inscribed on the ceiling.

Double doors at the head of the stairs lead to the Saloon (Fig. 181), the grandest of the Prideaux rooms, and hung with five Mortlake tapestries after the Raphael cartoons. These were presented by Queen Anne to Francis Gwyn, a later owner of Forde, but being so characteristic of the mid-17th-century taste of both courtiers and parliamentarians alike, they are in complete harmony with their setting. *The Healing of the Lame Man* has been slightly cut down to enable three of the tapestries to fit the west wall, thus giving the impression that the room was built to receive them. Dating products of the Mortlake factory is no easy matter, but the borders of this set are not unlike those on a set at Boughton, which Marillier[1] attributed to the period of 1640–50. The *putti* climbing the pilasters and also the top border are consistent with Francis Clein's work.

[1] MSS notes in the Victoria and Albert Museum.

The panelling has been removed from the west wall, but survives on the others. The ceiling beams here correspond with the pilasters and frame Abbott's delightfully naïve roundels depicting subjects such as *The Sacrifice of Isaac* — in Commonwealth dress (Fig. 182). The large central relief (Fig. 183) bears the Prideaux arms, combined with those of his son and his wife, who were married in 1658. Although heraldically incorrect, they provide a clue for dating the work.

Edmund Prideaux died in 1658. It was perhaps fortunate, because the Restoration government might well have enquired into his affairs. His son lived till 1702, when the estate went to a daughter, Margaret, and her husband, Francis Gwyn, a lawyer and politician. The house remained with their descendants, not all direct, until 1846, when John Francis Gwyn died. At the sale of the contents the new owner, Mr Miles of Bristol, bought a few items, including, fortunately, the Raphael tapestries. In 1864 he sold the house to Mrs Bertram Evans, from whom it passed by descent to the present owner, Mr Geoffrey Roper. Little has been done to alter Prideaux's work and Forde remains today the most interesting of the Commonwealth houses still lived in.

183. *The centre of the Saloon ceiling. The painted armorials are those of Prideaux quartering Ivory and Fraunceis.*

184. *The South Front, originally the entrance.*

TYTTENHANGER, HERTFORDSHIRE

This impressive brick house was built by Sir Henry Blount, probably in about 1655-60. (A Seat of the Earl of Caledon.)

There was considerable building activity during the 1630s in the counties around London, and although interrupted in the 1640s, it revived during the next decade. Tyttenhanger, probably begun in the mid-1650s, belongs to this group, and is linked both by scale and detail to those erected by leaders of the Commonwealth — such as Thorpe, Forde and Wisbech Castle. Wisbech has long been demolished, and Tyttenhanger takes its place as third of the triumvirate, although Sir Henry Blount, its builder, did not share the same background as the other proprietors.

Brought up as a well-endowed younger son, Sir Henry inherited the property in 1654 on the death of his elder brother, a bachelor, who had succeeded his father in 1639. He had already made some mark in the world, having travelled in France and Italy and in the lands east and south of the Mediterranean during the 1630s, and had published his experiences in *A Voyage to the Levant*, seven editions of which appeared during his lifetime. His fame as traveller and writer led to his knighthood in 1640. Seven years later he married Hester, Lady Mainwaring, a widow and heiress.

His inheritance of Tyttenhanger had been unexpected, but it provided him with the means to build a new house on the estate, which the Blounts had inherited in 1591 on the death of Lady Pope. Born a Blount, she married Sir Thomas Pope, who had been in the service of Henry VIII and thereby acquired Tyttenhanger at the Dissolution.

The exact date of erection is unknown and no details survive of its building. The appearance of the house, however, suggests that it was built in the years 1655–60, and this is supported by a certificate, dated 1684, recording the Chapel as having been dedicated by Ralph, Bishop of Exeter, 'in the time of the late rebellion.' The house conforms to the H-plan, the south wings projecting one bay forward, but those on the north only a few feet. The principal entrance has since been moved from the south to the north side of the house, entailing certain changes within. The centre range was always a double pile, however, with the principal rooms on the west and the offices on the east side.

The house was evidently intended to be seen from the south (Fig. 184), where the impression of mass is emphasised by the large hipped roof, the chimney-stacks and central

185. Part of the South Front.

186. The West Front.

187. Doorcases on the first floor landing.

188. *The Principal Staircase.*

189. *Plate 25 from Dietterlin's* Architectura. *Compare the centre of the engraving with the design of the right hand doorcase in Plate* 187.

to be expected in so important a house. The name of Mills has been suggested as a possible designer; a London man, he was used to working in brick, but his Hitcham building, at Pembroke College, Cambridge, bears no visible relation to Tyttenhanger.

The interior of the house was redecorated in the mid-18th century and again later and, except for the main staircase, the Caroline survivals are fragmentary. The entrance led to a large Hall; the main stairs (Fig. 188), reached by a door at the north-west corner, rise the full height of the house. The balustrade is of the familiar acanthus type, with pierced carving, which is vigorous rather than distinguished. The panels are set between stout newels supporting baskets of fruit. The joiner appears to have abandoned all restraint at first floor level, where he provided doorcases of varying design (Fig. 187), which display little taste beyond an unfortunate study of Dietterlin's engravings.

The Chapel and Long Gallery are on the second floor, the latter being considerably narrower than its Jacobean predecessors; in fact it is surprising that one should have been provided in a house of so late a date. Its walls are lined with wainscot, presumably salvaged from the older house.

Sir Henry made Tyttenhanger over to his wife in 1678 and, at her death, it passed to their son Thomas, the first baronet. The house remained with his descendants until the third baronet's death, when his niece, who married Charles Yorke, inherited it. Their son was created Earl of Hardwicke and, after his death, the house was settled on his daughter Caroline, who married the first Earl of Caledon.

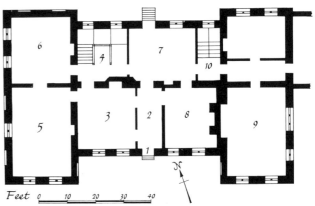

190. *Plan showing the original layout of the ground floor.*

1. *Front Entrance, now garden door.* 2. *Passage behind screen.*
3. *Hall.* 4. *Principal staircase.* 5 *and* 6. *Drawing Rooms.*
7. *Hall.* 8. *Library.* 9. *Kitchen.* 10. *Stairs.*

cupola. The virtual absence of a visible basement storey also contributes to the effect of mass, for the central doorway is almost at ground level. Consequently, there is nothing of the strong vertical thrust so characteristic of many Commonwealth houses, and the pediments above the first floor windows accentuate the horizontal emphasis. The other façades are simpler. The windows on the first floor of the west side (Fig. 186) are pedimented, but oddly arranged with segmental pediments of different sizes, suggesting a division of the house into a front range three bays deep and a back range of only two.

It is not possible to achieve the same precision of moulding in brickwork as in stone. This is apparent in the window architraves, which appear to lack something of the confidence

191. *The house reflected in its moat, seen from the north-west.*

GROOMBRIDGE PLACE, KENT

The house was built soon after the Restoration by Philip Packer. Nothing is known of the designer or the craftsmen employed. (The home of Mr S. W. Mountain.)

Groombridge is as perfect an example of a house of the early Restoration period as can be found, having remained unaltered since its building. Age has added a softening patina to the brickwork and mellowed the tones and outlines of the roof, and generations of gardeners have bestowed their care on the yew-planted parterres of the terraced garden. The house sleeps on drowsily in its lovely valley, mirrored in the still waters of a moat, disturbed only by its sentinel swan. It looks very much as it must have looked in the second King Charles's days, and certainly no other house so conspicuously evokes the spirit of that age.

The peculiar charm of Groombridge lies in the quiet

192. *The Entrance Front from the bridge across the moat.*

194. (*above*) *The porch projecting from the loggia.*

193. (*above*) *One of the gate piers at the entrance to the forecourt.*

195. *The porch and loggia.*

196. *Within the loggia, looking north.*

dignity of its composition. It is built on an H-plan with the end bays of the entrance front treated as projecting wings, leaving a recessed centre of four bays (Fig. 192). From the point of view of symmetry, problems are inherent in this even number, but they are overcome with delightful ingenuity. The stone porch (Fig. 194), which projects from the centre of the colonnaded and balustraded loggia suggests a central doorway, and yet there is none: instead, there are two of equal importance, in the first and fourth bays. The design of this colonnade is unique, exemplifying the English genius for adaptation and improvisation. The whole façade is triumphantly successful.

The glazing of the windows contributes much to its quality. When built, these had the usual leaded lights set within iron casements fitted in wooden transomes and mullions, in the early Stuart manner; some of them remain on the north side. The sash windows were probably inserted early in the 18th century, when someone scratched initials, with the date 'Sept. 1713', on one of the panes. The way the old glass catches the light adds liveliness to the soft texture of the brickwork, while the broad and flat white-painted glazing bars effectively echo the scale of the quoins.

The house was built about 1660, on the site of an earlier one. The moat, which sets it off so admirably, originally surrounded the medieval house of the Wallers, who lived here until 1607. They were succeeded by the Sackvilles of Knole, who in 1618 sold it to John Packer, a man who had enjoyed both their and Buckingham's patronage. A Clerk to the Privy

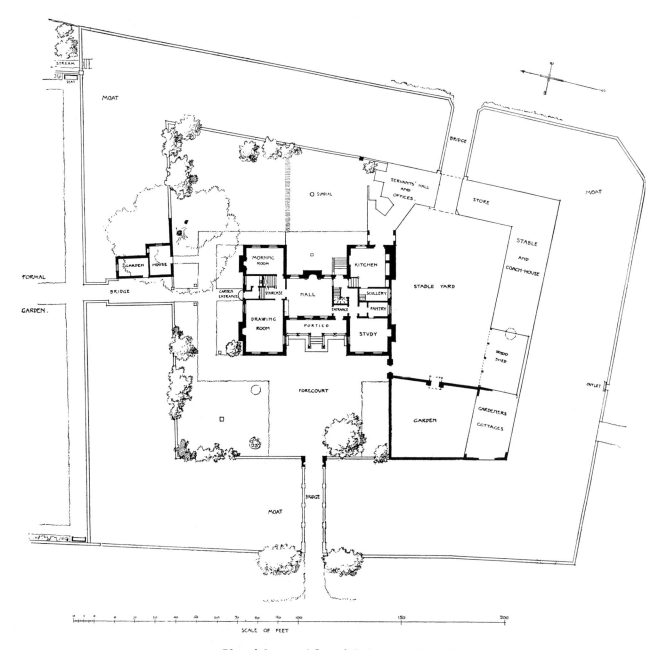

197. Plan of the ground floor of the house, and its setting.

198. *The Drawing Room chimneypiece. (The cabinet on the right is shown in Figs. 42 and 43.)*

199. *Packer portraits in the Drawing Room.*

Council, he sided with Parliament in the Civil War and died in 1649, leaving Groombridge to his third son, Philip, the builder of the present house.

Little is known of Philip Packer, and nothing of the team who built his house, except that he was a friend of John Evelyn, his fellow student at the Middle Temple. Evelyn records two visits to Groombridge; the first on a Sunday in July, 1652, when 'I heard a sermon at Mr Packer's Chapell at Groomsbridge, a pretty melancholy seate, well wooded and water'd . . .' By the time he went again, on 6th August, 1674, the house had been rebuilt and he records it as 'built within a moate in a woody valley . . . The old house now demolish'd, and a new one built in its place, tho' a far better situation had ben on the South of the wood, on a graceful ascent.'

The house is approached across the moat by a bridge flanked by gate-piers (Fig. 193), surmounted by stone pine-apples, and through wooden gates with a wrought iron cresting

200. *The Drawing Room.*

201. *The Hall Chamber, 16th-century panelling reused.*

202. *The House from the north.*

203. *The Kitchen.*

204. *A painted glass sundial in a bedroom window.*

on the swept top-rail. At either side are niches with carved stone shell-heads accommodating seats. Immediately opposite is the colonnaded loggia (Fig. 195). The detailing of this feature is delicately conceived and not the least interesting point is that the front pair of columns, which are set forward on the lower part of the balustrade, are consequently a couple of feet taller than the others (Fig. 194), of identical girth, yet they do not appear incorrectly proportioned. Mr Arthur Oswald,[1] in describing this loggia as 'a little piece of Italy in Kent', considered it likely to have been suggested by Evelyn.

The house is entered through the right-hand doorway in the loggia, by way of a lobby, a relic of the screens passage. The Parlour occupies the right-hand projection, with the Kitchen quarters behind, opening onto the stable court. The Hall is in the central section of the house, in the traditional position of a great hall, with the main staircase and a small Library beyond it. The entrance to the garden is beneath the

[1] *Country Life*, CXVIII, p. 1525.

stairs and the Drawing Room is in the left-hand projecting bay, balancing the Parlour. The principal room on the first floor is the Hall Chamber, a late descendant of the Tudor Great Chamber; both Hall and Hall Chamber fill the whole centre of the house, with windows on both sides. The conservative planning suggests that the house was built by a Kentish team rather than by a London master-builder.

Both the Parlour and the Hall Chamber are lined with woodwork salvaged from the earlier house. The panelling in the Hall is mostly plain, but some of the panels are inlaid; the fireplace is Tudor and the overmantel Jacobean. The Parlour panelling is earlier and resembles that in the Old Parsonage at Brenchley, where one of the panels, dated 1573, bears the initials EF carved above the quartered shield of Hendley. Elizabeth Hendley was first married to William Waller, whose son bought Brenchley as a dower house for his mother. Her second husband, George Fane, died in 1571. This family connection explains the resemblance of the two sets of panelling. That at Groombridge has been reset, signs of which are particularly visible around the chimneypiece. The woodwork in the Hall Chamber (Fig. 201), dating from the end of the 16th century, constitutes a remarkable example of panelling painted in black and gold to imitate inlay. This use of old materials may suggest a certain lack of means.

The Drawing Room (Fig. 200), is a magnificent apartment with oak wainscot, a bolection-moulded fireplace of black and white marble and an enriched plasterwork ceiling. The walls are hung with family portraits which have remained here since the Packer's time, among them one of Philip, the builder. From the ceiling hangs a fine glass chandelier and around the room are notable pieces of late 17th-century furniture. To the right of the fireplace is an exceptionally fine inlaid walnut cabinet on a stand (Fig. 42), *circa* 1670, veneered with oyster pieces and with marquetry doors of sycamore and ebony. The interior is lined with superb stumpwork, including portraits of Charles II and Catherine of Braganza, while Herod and Salome, with the head of John the Baptist, and other allegorical subjects, cover the drawer fronts (Fig. 43). When opened, the central recess reveals a miniature temple-like compartment with gold columns and a chequered ebony and ivory floor delightfully reflected by a cunning arrangement of mirror walls.

Incorporated in the glazing of one of the windows of the bedroom above the Library are a pair of beautifully painted glass sundials (Fig. 204), no doubt inserted by Philip Packer. One bears the inscription *Lumen Umbra Dei*, with a fly painted for deception, a familiar 17th-century conceit in window dials.

Philip Packer lived to enjoy his inheritance until 1686, but his son John, and grandson Philip, for only eleven and twelve years respectively. The house then passed to the sisters of the latter, and in 1754 the Packer connection ended. The rooms contain many fine pieces of contemporary furniture, mostly collected by the present owner's father, Mr H. S. Mountain, who acquired the house in 1919. Groombridge owes much to the care bestowed upon it by Mr Mountain and his son, who have restored the old garden and adorned the interior with objects of rare loveliness and of a quality comparable to their setting.

205. *The South Front. Nicholas Stone's block (1632–33) between the Tudor wing and the end of May's range of 1666.*

CORNBURY PARK, OXFORDSHIRE

In 1633 the Earl of Danby added a wing designed by Nicholas Stone to the old house and after the Restoration Hugh May designed additions for the Earl of Clarendon. These include the stables built in 1663, a new entrance front begun in 1666 and the Chapel begun in 1677. Much of the interior has been re-modelled. (The home of Mr and Mrs Oliver Watney.)

From the time of Henry I until the 17th century Cornbury was a royal hunting lodge in the forest of Wychwood, and visited by almost every king. It was frequently granted to prominent ministers and favourites, together with the Rangership of the Forest, and consequently has been associated with many famous names — Nevilles, de la Poles, Tudors and Dudleys. In the 17th century it was granted to Henry Danvers, Earl of Danby, and later to Edward Hyde, Earl of

Clarendon, both of whom made significant alterations and additions to the Tudor house, which had probably been built by John Dudley, Duke of Northumberland, in the mid-16th century.

Danvers was the second son of a Wiltshire knight and began his soldiering career as Sir Philip Sidney's page, being probably present at Zutphen in 1586. During his life he held many commands, was advanced to a barony by James I and to an earldom by Charles I. Cornbury was granted to him after the death of Charles's elder son, Prince Henry, and he seems to have occupied it from about 1617; he made no alterations until 1632, when he was almost sixty. That he should have decided to start building at that age is rather surprising, since he was a bachelor; possibly he was encouraged to do so by his inheritance of property from his mother.

206. *The South and East Fronts.*

207. *The central bays of the East Front.*

208. *The 1st Earl of Clarendon, from a portrait after Gerard Soest.*

In 1631 Nicholas Stone 'agreed with the Right Honbl. Lord Earell of Danby for to mak 3 ston gattes in to the phiseck garden Oxford and to desine a new hous for him at Corenbury in Oxfordsheer and to dereckt the workmen and mak all ther moldes'.[1] Stone had worked under Inigo Jones at Whitehall and on several subsequent occasions. From Jones he had learned what he could of classical architecture, and early in life had spent some years in de Keyser's workshop at Antwerp. His work at Cornbury is such as one would expect from a master-mason — careful and accurate, but lacking particular distinction.

His work here consists of the seven-bay south front (Fig. 205), set between the 16th-century Leicester wing and the Restoration addition of Hugh May. Stone's design has been altered, according to Mr John Belcher, who restored the house for Mr Vernon Watney after 1901: May altered its roof-line and redesigned the first floor windows, to conform to his own on the east front. It is possible that Stone's fenestration was similar to that surviving at the west end of the range, a row of *oeil-de-boeuf* windows with small rectangular ones above, following the spacing of those on the ground floor. The porch, however, remains as Stone designed it.

The wing took two years and Stone was paid £1,000. He visited the site no fewer than thirty-three times, though he

[1] Walpole Society, Vol. VII, p. 70.

209. *The East Front from the north-east.*

210. *May's stable building, 1663.*

employed his cousin, Gabriel Stacey, to superintend the work. This is the earliest record of Stacey, whose name re-occurs in the accounts for the Queen's House and Somerset House. The contractor was Timothy Strong, of Barrington, Gloucestershire, the founder of a dynasty of quarry owners and mason-contractors who worked in Oxford, the City of London and at Blenheim. Timothy's son, Thomas, carried out May's designs at Cornbury in the 1660s.

Little of the original interior remains; it was remodelled by May and has since been altered. Before May's time the left half of the range comprised a dining room with bedrooms over it, and the right half a Great Hall rising through both storeys. Although Stone's building is only a fragment, it is a document of considerable interest as being the earliest surviving classical façade of a country house. (The Stoke Park pavilions were begun earlier, about 1629, but of the house they flanked we know little.)

Lord Danby died in 1644, two years after Charles I had granted him the estate 'for ever', but instead of descending to his heirs, Cornbury reverted to the Commonwealth government and, at the Restoration, to the Crown. The claims of Danby's heirs were not accepted, and in 1661 the house, together with the Rangership of the Forest, was granted to Edward Hyde, soon to be created Earl of Clarendon.

Apart from building the stables in 1663, Lord Clarendon did not begin work on the house until 1666, when his Clarendon House, in London, was almost completed. The latter was considered at the time one of the marvels of England and was widely copied, but it was short-lived, being demolished in 1683. Soon after its completion Lord Clarendon fell from power and went into exile in 1667, dying abroad in 1674.

The Cornbury stables (Fig. 210) appear to be May's earliest surviving building, and, as far as we know, his first commission. Their front is surprisingly sophisticated, relying on the balance of the five parts: far more advanced than the Wilton stables designed by de Caux in the 1630s, they constitute the first classical stable block attached to a country house.

Evelyn visited Cornbury with May in 1664 to advise about some planting in the park. 'The house', he notes, 'is of excellent freestone abounding in that part; 'tis of ample dimensions, has goodly cellars, the paving of the hall admirable for its close laying. We design'd an handsom chapell that was yet wanting; as Mr May had the stables, which

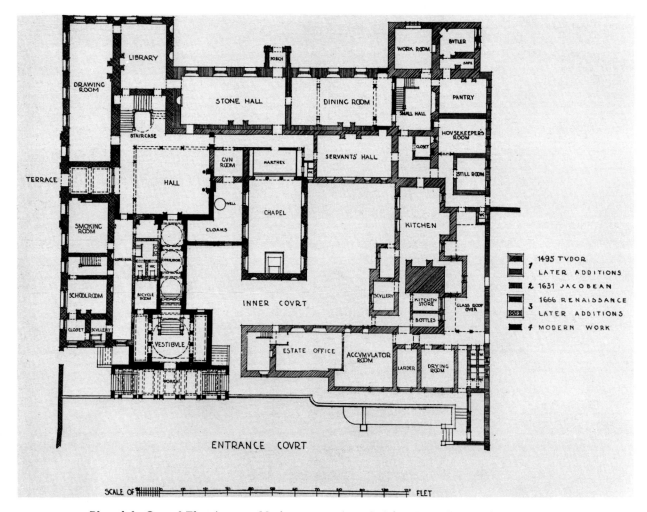

211. *Plan of the Ground Floor in 1910. May's east range is on the left and Stone's south-facing block at the top.*

212. *The Chapel, seen through the Ante-Chapel gates. Designed by May and Evelyn 1664; built 1677.*

213. *The Chapel.*

indeed are very faire . . .' The chapel was not erected for another thirteen years.

The next addition to the house was the building of the east front (Fig. 206), begun in 1666. In January of that year Lord Clarendon wrote to Evelyn: 'Mr May (who you know governs at Cornbury) hath made a design for a very convenient house there, and splendid enough, which will be begun this spring.' The long façade of eleven bays stands at right angles to the Danby building and projects beyond it to form a narrow flanking wing. Its design is an expansion of the Eltham façade (Fig. 247), of two years earlier, and, like that, centres on a pedimented feature inspired by the buildings of Van Campen (Fig. 26), which May had seen in Holland during the Court's exile. But here he has omitted the basement that is normal in his Palladian models and the main rooms are at ground floor level. Consequently the façade appears over-long for its height, but nevertheless achieves an elegance and dignity rare for its time. It was a design that obviously appealed to May, for he repeated it in the next decade at Cassiobury, Hertfordshire.

The building was unfinished at the time of Clarendon's fall, and was completed only in 1677 by the 2nd Earl, who then turned his attention to building the chapel that May had designed thirteen years earlier. This is attached to the Tudor south range and fills much of the original court. Externally it is a plain, well-mannered, but unremarkable building; the interior, however, is a complete example of May's manner (Fig. 212). As Mr Christopher Hussey[1] has said, 'the interior, which has much of the character of a small college chapel or the hall of a city company, reminds us how little Wren originated of the decorative style associated with his name'. The building achieves a harmony and dignity characteristic of the best Restoration architecture and decoration, a style singularly well suited to the demands of a country house.

In 1694 the 2nd Earl sold Cornbury to his brother, the Earl of Rochester, whose descendants retained it until 1751. It was then purchased by the Trustees of the 3rd Duke of Marlborough and remained Spencer-Churchill property till 1896, being acquired by the present owner's father, Mr Vernon Watney, in 1901. He employed Belcher and Macartney to restore the house, and to remove the incongruous Victorian tower and a portico that masked May's front.

[1] *Country Life*, CVIII, p. 926.

214. *Ashdown House and its pavilions from the east.*

THE COUNTRY HOUSES OF LORD CRAVEN

Ashdown House and Hamstead Marshall, Berkshire, and Combe Abbey, Warwickshire.

What survives of these buildings, and of the documentary material concerning them, forms one of the most illuminating chapters in the history of Caroline country house building. Ashdown alone has remained intact and is now a property of the National Trust; Hamstead Marshall was burnt in 1718 and only its gate-piers survive; while Combe Abbey is now but a fragment, stripped of its former splendour.

The first Earl of Craven's service to Queen Elizabeth of Bohemia, the sister of Charles I, is among the most touching stories of the Stuarts, and it provides a thread of continuity through sixty years of his life. Craven first met her in about 1632, when she and her husband were in exile in Holland after they had lost the Bohemian throne and the Palatinate. But he must have known of her years before, for she had been brought up at Combe, the Warwickshire house acquired by his mother in 1610 from the Countess of Bedford, daughter of the Earl and Countess of Harington, who were the Princess's guardians. From their first meeting until her death in 1662, he supported her as occasion arose, providing her with money during the years of the Interregnum, even when his own estates had been sequestered, and, at the Restoration, placing his houses at her disposal. An attractive legend records that Hamstead Marshall was built, as a compliment, to resemble her castle at Heidelberg, but it was not completed till long after her death. Neither was Combe, where work only finally ceased during the last decade of the century. Her spirit seems still to linger by the famous gate-piers of Hamstead Marshall, as it surely used to wander from room to room at Combe, where the walls were hung with portraits of her children and of her brother's family.

Craven did not belong to the circle of the old court families. His Yorkshire father had amassed a fortune in London and

risen to be Lord Mayor. Only after his death did his widow invest this in land, buying Combe in 1610 for £36,000 and Hamstead Marshall eight years later. During his youth Craven showed no particular interest in building, but spent most of the years before the Civil War serving on military expeditions in Europe. After the Restoration, however, he turned to the repair of his numerous houses and estates. Besides the three places already mentioned, he owned Caversham Park, Reading, and a large house in Drury Lane.

The building of Ashdown may have been his first venture, but there is no evidence either of its date or of the architect or craftsmen employed. The elderly Gerbier or the young Winde might conceivably have been responsible, but not

215. *Ashdown in its setting on the Downs.*

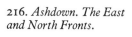

217. *Ashdown. The West Front.*

218. (above) Ashdown. The cupola.

219. (above right) Ashdown. Inside the cupola.

220. (right) Ashdown. Plan of the Ground Floor.

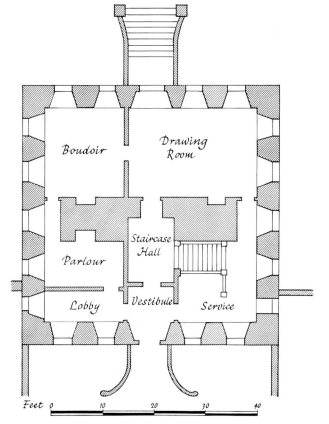

enough is known of either of them to justify an attribution.

The house is remotely situated (Fig. 215) high on the Berkshire downs near the White Horse Hill, three miles north of Lambourn and seventeen from Hamstead Marshall. The upper part of the tall white block may be seen above the trees in a dip in the rolling landscape, formerly heavily wooded, where four rides converge, so making a suitable site for a hunting box. Its appearance comes as a shock of surprise, on closer approach, however (Fig. 214), the two lower blocks on the entrance side anchor it to the site, their long, low proportions constituting an admirable foil to the tall Dutch nucleus. The main building (Fig. 216) rises four-and-a-half storeys to the balustraded roof-platform and the gilded ball on the cupola, its striking silhouette emphasised by the strong contrast of the chalk of its ashlar walls and the white painted woodwork with the contrasting blackness of the glass in the casements. The chalk has retained its luminosity and the house appears almost as new as the day it was built.

In spite of its Dutch look, the detailing is unsophisticated. The string courses are simple, and the central doorcases, on both façades, lack boldness of scale and moulding, but the joinery has a robust and pleasing simplicity. The cupola, with its slight batter (Fig. 218), and the staircase leading to it of loneliness. Hamstead Marshall makes a different appeal, springing from a sense of vanished magnificence expressed in the richly decorated, but isolated gate-piers, which now rise from a pastoral landscape setting. Surmounted by splendid vases, they indicate the pattern and extent of the former layout, as recorded in Kip's bird's eye engraving of 1707 (Fig. 223). This shows the house as it appeared before it was burnt, and helps to piece together the jig-saw of the stranded piers.

The vanished house consisted of a range of eleven bays, three storeys high, with projecting wings of the same length and height, and a hipped roof surmounted by three cupolas. Although both roof and cupolas would have appeared appropriate at the time, the bays and the mullioned and transomed windows of the lower storeys look earlier in date than the Restoration period, and indeed hark back to Jacobean fashion.

The Kip view is supplemented with a series of about forty drawings in the Bodleian Library, some by Gerbier, who was in charge from 1662 until his death in 1665, or 1667,

221. Ashdown. The Staircase from the Hall.

222. Ashdown. The Drawing Room door in the Hall.

(Fig. 219), have the air of having been made by a shipwright. One senses that Caroline joiners might have felt equally at home working in the dockyard or at a country house.

The simplicity of the exterior is maintained within the house, which forms a forty-foot cube. The entrance door leads to a passage-way little wider than the Drawing Room doorcase (Fig. 222), which is enriched by a boldly scrolled and broken pediment. To the left a small Parlour, with a similar sized room beyond, communicates with the Drawing Room; to the right, the staircase occupies a quarter of the plan. The stair is bordered by a particularly wide moulded handrail with turned balusters between massive newels (Fig. 221). Originally carved drops were applied to their recessed panels, similar to those used not many miles away at Coleshill.

The house remained a seat of the Earls of Craven until 1956, when it was given by Cornelia, Countess of Craven, to the National Trust. It has since been restored, and the later additions enclosing the forecourt removed.

The magic of Ashdown comes in part from its atmosphere

223. *Hamstead Marshall. Kip's view of the house and garden layout* c. 1707. *The letters marking the gates indicate those illustrated here. A, Fig. 237; B, Fig. 235; D, Fig. 240; E, Fig. 239; F, Fig. 238.*

and others by Winde, or by the craftsmen concerned. Among the plans is one (Fig. 227) for a quadrangular house with longer wings than that shown in Kip's view, and another for three ranges with shorter wings. The plan for the quadrangular house is unusually interesting because the uses of the rooms are inscribed. They thus indicate the scale of living

Gerbier had in mind, recalling that of great noblemen's houses in the first years of the century rather than the more straitened circumstances of the 1660s. A large central Hall was placed in the front range, with 'the Little Parlour or Ordinary Roome to eat in' on the left, and beyond a 'Withdrawing Roome or Roome for the Lord to eat in'. To the

224, 225. *The 1st Earl of Craven, and Queen Elizabeth of Bohemia.*

226. *'Designe for the Front Portall att Hamsted'*.

yard (Fig. 235), and also with a second pair between the former garden and orchard (Fig. 238), to the west of the house. The vases above them are not shown; they would appear to have been added by Edward Pierce in the 1670s, for there is a drawing of the 'Peers at Hamstead Marshall neare the Church Yard' (Fig. 234), which shows them in outline with fully delineated urns atop.

Another drawing (Fig. 236) of a similar type, dated 1673, presumably by Pierce, but not inscribed with his name, shows one of the piers before the portico, which can also be compared with surviving work. The same richness of carving is found on another pair of piers where shields and coronets spill from upturned cornucopiae (Fig. 240), and also in a single pier now built into a wall (Fig. 239), where acanthus leaves swirl up the central panel towards the crowning pine-apple.

One of the best drawings of the interior is for the Dining

right of the hall, as if to suggest life below the salt, were 'Roome for the Gentlemen to eat in' and 'Roome for the servants to eat in'. Such generous provision and careful segregation was matched by the elaborate kitchen offices in the right-hand wing, including 'a Great Kitchen, a Privy Kitchen or Pastry, a Roome for the Confectioner, a Spicery, and the Apothecary Office or Distill House.' Elsewhere there were a 'Roome to Bathe' and 'Roome for to Repose after Bathing'.

This elaborate scheme must have been modified quite early, for the first floor was begun on 27th July, 1664. The revised plan survives, as do a number of others of the same set, including those for the roof and the platform. None is signed by Gerbier, or appear to be by his hand; his style of draughtsmanship, although coarse, was vigorous and colourful, as in his designs for the Great Piers, for the front portal (Fig. 226) and for the ornament between the windows (Fig. 229), which is influenced by Rubens's plates in *Palazzi di Genova*. Among the more interesting of the drawings, and apparently from his hand, is a design for the west portico (Fig. 228), which would have linked the two projecting wings. This is hidden by the main part of the house in Kip's view, but it must have been built in that, or a similar form, for the design of its ceiling was approved by Winde in 1686.

The garden was being laid out simultaneously with the building of the house; a design for the base court was made in 1665, but a start must have been made before then since the design of the north gate-piers is dated 1663 (Fig. 233). Apart from slight differences in the execution of the mouldings, these piers are identical with those next to the church-

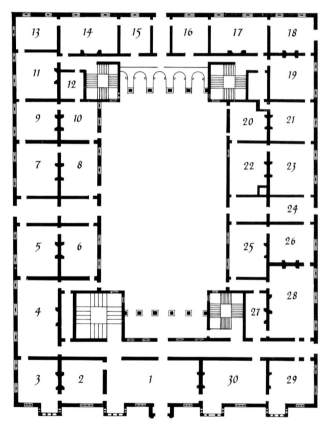

227. *Hamstead Marshall. Plan of the intended house:* 1. *Hall.* 2. *Little Parlor or Ordinary Roome to Eat in.* 3. *Withdrawing Roome or Roome for the Lord to Eat in.* 4. *Great Parlor.* 5. *Withdrawing Roome.* 6. *Lodgings below stairs for the Steward.* 7. *Withdrawing Roome to repair the records.* 8. *Lodging roome for the Butler.* 9. *The Lords Records.* 10. *Secretary.* 11. *the Gentleman of the Horse.* 12. *Boxes.* 13. *Furniture for the Gentleman of the Horse.* 14. *Footmen.* 15. *Pages.* 16. *Gentleman Usher.* 17. *Roome for to Repose after Bathing.* 18. *Roome to Bathe.* 19. *Distiller.* 20. *Spicery.* 21. *Apothecary's office or distill house.* 22. *Clark of the Kitching.* 23. *Confectioner.* 24. *Lardery.* 25. *Scullery.* 26. *Pastry.* 27. *Pantry.* 28. *Great Kitching.* 29. *Roome for the Servants to eat in.* 30. *Roome for the Gentlemen to eat in.*

228. *Design for 'the West Portico at Hampsted Marshall' possibly by Gerbier.*

229. *'The Ornament of the windows att Hampsted Marshall' possibly by Gerbier.*

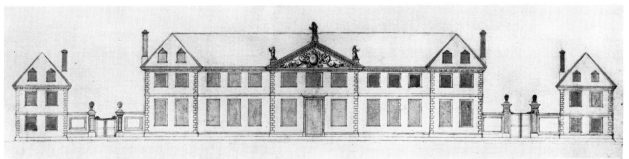

230. *Design for the stables at Hamstead Marshall.*

231. (above) Hamstead Marshall. Design for the Dining Room ceiling by Goudge, and 'allowed' by Winde, 1686.

232. (left) 'The Garden Gate at Hamstead Marshall', 1677.

233. (below) 'The North peers at Hamsted Marshall 1663'. Compare with Fig. 235 (B in Fig. 223).

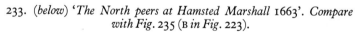

234. (*right*) *'The peeres at Hamstead Marshall neare the churchyard' signed by Pierce, who designed the vases. Compare with Figs. 233 and 235* (B *in Fig. 223*).

235. (*far right*) *Hamstead Marshall. One of the gate piers by the church. Compare Figs. 233 and 234.*

Room ceiling (Fig. 231), a design almost certainly by Goudge. This was accepted by Winde on 22nd June, 1686, and gives proof of Goudge's accomplishment not only as a craftsman executant, but as draughtsman-designer as well, and justifies Winde's estimation of his skill. The plastering was spread over many years, some of the designs are dated 1678 and 1683, and that for the Withdrawing Room ceiling 22nd June, 1686.

Since there are no papers to supplement or explain these drawings, it is particularly fortunate that those for Combe Abbey can be related to a volume of letters, also in the Bodleian, from Sir William Craven and others concerned in its building; these give a rare insight into the way in which country houses were built in Charles II's reign.

During the 1660s and 70s Combe Abbey had been let to Sir Isaac Gibson, who, in 1667, built the three-bay gabled block at the south end of the west front (Fig. 241). According to a plan of 1678, this balanced a block at the north end of the façade, which backed on to the old cloisters. About that year the house reverted to the Craven family and appears to have been occupied by the Earl's nephew, heir and namesake,

236. *'The peers before the portico at Hamsted Marshall, 1673', possibly by Pierce.* (A *in Fig. 223*) 237. *The Piers as they are now.*

238–240. Examples of other piers at Hamstead Marshall (F, E and D in Fig. 223).

Sir William Craven. Some work must have been done that year, for there is a drawing by Goudge, dated and signed by Winde, who was the architect, for the ceiling of the great staircase, and there is another of the same year for the Hall ceiling. These first steps appear to have been rather half-hearted attempts to repair the old house, which was apparently in a poor state. Among letters from Winde is a report of March, 1680, on the west front, which is described as an 'old decayed building, supported with ten buttresses to prevent the old wall from falling; which wall in some places hangeth over at least a foot and in other places leaneth inward as much . . .'

Early the following year Sir William wrote to Winde about a design for a new west wing. Complete rebuilding does not seem to have been envisaged and apparently Sir William wanted a new range of rooms backing on to those on the old west and north sides of the cloister court. There is no mention of adding a further range to the outer side of the east wing or remodelling the inner face of the open cloister court, which was, and still is, the entrance front of the house.

Sir William was anxious to get started: it would take all the

spring, he said, to pull down the old building, clear the site, and sort out the material, and he hoped that the foundations would be laid in May. Then 'there will be 5 or 6 months time after to raise the intended building, which if it can be brought up to ye first storie, will I imagine, be as much as can be expected in the Summer, and then the Worke will have ye more time to settle against another season . . .' By 15th March, Winde had sent down two designs for Craven's approval; the work of demolition was begun in May, and on the 9th of the month Craven wrote he hoped the foundations would be laid by June 12th. He also wanted Winde to send Cooles, the mason, with his design for the elevation.

All did not go well with Winde's plans, largely perhaps because he had not visited the site, and everything had to be done by correspondence, a slow and inefficient method. Towards the end of June James Morris, the carpenter, was sent to London with a drawing connected with the proposal to lengthen the house by seven feet. Another of Winde's suggestions was to send down 'a window for first and second storie, a door case, one lutheran window, and a yeard of Cornish'. The problems encountered in June proved difficult,

241. *Combe Abbey. A 17th-century drawing of the West Front showing the Winde building (1681-2) and the Isaac Gibson building (1667).*

241. *Combe Abbey. A 17th-century drawing of the West Front showing the Winde building (1681-2) and the Isaac Gibson building (1667).*

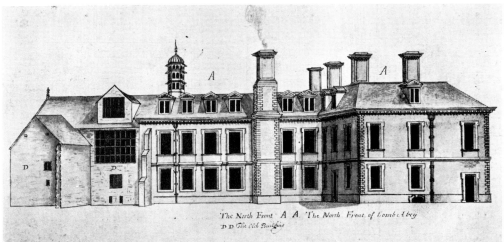

242. *Combe. A 17th-century drawing showing the north side of the house, with the Winde building.*

and in July Cooles went to see Winde, who sent him back without corrected drawings or directions. Having already made the major alteration of adding the seven feet to the elevation, Winde now proposed a frontispiece, a feature rejected by Craven many months before. Despite delays and changes of mind, the building was up to the level of the first floor window sills by 21st October and 'as much as had been intended had been accomplished.' Work was brought to a halt towards the end of the month, the walls being thatched for the winter, the workmen disbanded and Cooles sent back to Berkshire.

By February, 1682, Craven was thinking of the new season and what he hoped to see done; he wanted Cooles to come again and begin on the Great Hall in the north range. Decoration, too, was on his mind, for he mentioned a plasterer recommended by Pierce and the architect, but did not give his name. Later in the month he wrote to Winde again to say that he hoped that Wilcox would come down, and also Currie, the plumber; also he wanted to know how much lead would be needed for the roof and gutters. In the spring and early summer Craven's letters refer to Winde's desire to heighten the main storeys, which seems to have been done. On 7th July, he wrote that the kitchen was 'high as the topp of ye windows of ye 2nd storie' and his thoughts were turning

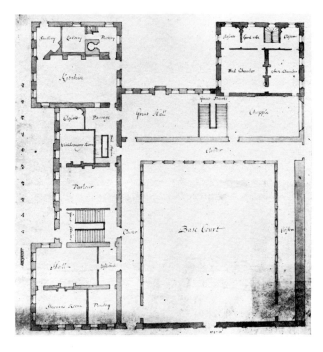

243. *Plan of Combe (north at the top).*

ye withdrawing room' and Craven wanted Winde to buy more wood, pile it up for the winter and then send it by boat to Gainsborough, whence it could be brought down the Trent to a spot only twenty-five miles from Combe. A fortnight later, on 24th November, he wrote about chimney-pieces, wainscot and sash windows, 'which according to Wilcox you intended should be made in Towne by Mr Simms and Mr Pearce'. They were to be sent down the same way, by sea and river. When the roof was completed work on the interior continued, and in early December Craven wrote that the rooms were being prepared for the plasterers' arrival in the spring.

The letters break off at this point, but there are two drawings dated 1686 — one for a door for the Great Hall and another for a door in the cloisters — and also an undated design for a carved overmantel by Pierce.

Something of the splendour of the rooms can be gathered from photographs of the house taken in about 1920 (Fig. 246), when the rooms were still lined with portraits of the Stuarts and Cravens, and when the ceilings, the wainscoting and the overmantels were still *in situ*. There was a fine balustraded staircase similar to that at Powis, the border castle of one of the Earl's kinsmen.

244. *Combe. The carved Overmantel in the Gilt Parlor (no longer in situ).*

to the proposed frontispiece, a feature mentioned in several letters that summer. Pierce was consulted by Winde about this, as it was intended he should carve it. Work may have been held up by the plumber's failure to appear, but Craven wrote in September, with considerable satisfaction, that Wilcox 'saies wee have exactly and substantiellie pursued ye directions in everie particular thing . . .' and a week later that Wilcox and Currie 'both bid me tell you that the more they looke upon ye new building, the better they lik it, and declares hee did never see more performed better both by carpenters and masons.'

When the west wing was begun there had been no suggestion of demolishing Gibson's block, and as late as October, 1682, Sir William wrote to Winde, 'if he [Lord Craven] will please have the other wing made answerable to this new building I shall be glad to receive yr directions in it.' Goudge is mentioned at this time and also a painter named Holmes. Pierce was expected to come down to carve the frontispiece, the stones of the pediment being in position and the cornice almost finished by 24th October.

Meanwhile, material was being acquired for completion of the interior. Craven and Wilcox had bought 'walnutt planks . . . which we conclude will be sufficient to waynescot

245. *Combe. Design for a doorcase in the Great Hall, 1686.*

246. *Combe. The Brown Parlour in* 1920 (*no longer* in situ).

These rooms largely survived alteration in the 18th century, when new chimneypieces were installed. When Eden Nesfield was called in towards the end of the last century, he made towering additions to the east range and also laid out extensive gardens, but left the Caroline rooms intact.

On the death of the 4th Earl, in 1923, the estate and the house were sold. The sale catalogue makes sad reading, describing, in auctioneers' jargon, rooms with such evocative names as the Van Dyck Room, Brocadilla Room, Gilt Parlour, Bohemian Room, Cornelian Room, Parrot Room, Paradise Room, Griffin Bedroom and Palatine Room, wistfully recalling the days of the 1st Earl.

The new owner removed the Nesfield range and modernised the remainder, unfortunately destroying the proportions of the Winde front by removing the high roof and chimneys. He also demolished the kitchen block. Before carrying out these changes he sold the panelling and ceilings of the main rooms, so that virtually nothing of decorative interest remains. The house is now in use as a hostel of the General Electric Company.

247. *The North Front.*

ELTHAM LODGE, KENT

The house, designed by Hugh May, was built in 1663-65 for Sir John Shaw. (The Property of the Crown and occupied by the Royal Blackheath Golf Club.)

The unpretentious, but carefully detailed façades of Eltham have a confidence and authority that puts the house among the outstanding buildings of the decade. Apart from Coleshill, the only earlier works of similar size that can compare with it are the Jones-Webb drawings given in Fig. 9. There is no evidence to suggest that Hugh May had any connection with Jones or with Webb before the Restoration; and it is more likely that he learnt his architecture in Holland, where he is known to have been in the 1650s in the service of the 2nd Duke of Buckingham. This would account for the marked Dutch appearance of Eltham, which is strongly influenced by the Mauritshuis at The Hague (Fig. 26).

May's patron, Sir John Shaw, had given financial assistance to the exiled King and, in return, benefited after the Restoration. In 1661 he was knighted; he became a Member of Parliament for Lyme Regis and, in the following year, was appointed one of the farmers of the customs. The State Papers record that payments were made to the farmers in compensation for advances to the King, and Shaw received more than one warrant for repayment of monies expended on secret service work. For these services he was granted the lease of the Royal Manor of Eltham. He needed a country house within easy reach of the City, and one suitable for his second wife, the former Dowager Viscountess Kilmorey, whom he had recently married.

The house was begun in 1664, and in July of that year Evelyn visited Eltham 'to see Sr. John Shaw's new house now building; the place is pleasant if not too wet, but the house is not well contriv'd, especially the roofe and rooms

too low pitch'd and the Kitchen where the cellars should be' — an unjustified criticism.

The entrance front is a particularly happy composition. Attention is concentrated in the centrepiece, comprising an order of Ionic pilasters with cartouche and swags in the

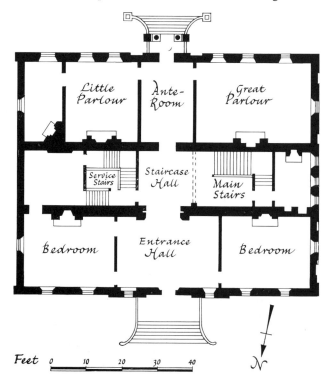

Feet

248. *Plan of the Ground Floor.*

249. *The North and*
West Façades.

250. *The South Front.*
The porch is a 19th-
century addition.

251. *The Main Staircase,*
looking west.

tympanum of the pediment (Fig. 247). A modillioned cornice
continues round the house, and the hipped roof has been
given an attractive bell-cast enhancing its silhouette. Whether
the house was originally capped by a balustraded roof-
platform is not known. The other elevations are simpler,
only relieved by the shallow-arched recesses in the brickwork;
others are more effective since there are neither quoins nor
moulded architraves: they create a pleasant rhythm on the
west façade where the ends project slightly, in the nature of
pilasters.

The plan is a variant of the double-pile, which became
standardised after the Restoration. The Hall leads to the
Staircase Hall, and through it to a garden hall in the centre
of the south front. To the right and left lie other rooms, that
in the south-west corner being the larger: the principal room
is on the upper floor, as was the State Dining Room at
Coleshill.

Since Sir John Shaw's time a number of rooms have been
redecorated, including the Hall, which is now linked to the
staircase by a screen of columns. The Parlour, on the left of
the Hall, was redecorated about 1750. Until recently, both the
Staircase and Garden Hall were hung with late 18th-century
wallpaper painted with landscapes and mythological figures
framed in an architectural setting, but this has since been
removed.

There is sufficient of the original decoration, however, to
show the appearance of the house in Shaw's time. The
Staircase (Fig. 251), the most significant feature, is contrived
in an unusual manner to embrace a subsidiary flight, serving
the south-east and north-west rooms, leading off the second
landing. It is an early example of the newly-introduced type
comprising balustrades composed of pierced and carved
panels, capped by the usual wide moulded handrail, flanked
by sturdy newels surmounted by floral urns. The panels
(Fig. 252), which are carved from four inch slabs of pine,
reveal a high accomplishment of craftsmanship; little boys
play amid the convolutions of the acanthus foliage, while

252. *Detail of the carved*
balustrade.

253. *The Main Staircase, looking east.*

254. (*left*) *Part of a secondary staircase.*

255. (*above*) *Detail of the Great Parlour ceiling.*

256. *The Great Parlour overmantel. The carved cypher inside the laurel wreath is that of the builder, Sir John Shaw.*

the surrounding margins and mouldings are articulated with competent and convincing authority.

The stairs ceiling comprises a central ellipse framed by a bold wreath, and set within a rectangle above a plain cove; the end sections are filled with acanthus enrichment with mermaid figures. The ceilings in some of the rooms, inventive in design, but coarsely executed, constitute a transitional phase between the stiffness of the first half of the century and the marvellous freedom achieved in Goudge's generation.

The Parlour on the first floor is a splendid room. The walls are panelled and subdivided horizontally into three sections, and surmounted by a carved acanthus cornice, while enriched architraves surround the door and window openings. The chimney-breast is given dignity by a splendid black and white marble bolection moulding surmounted by an inset architectural landscape, above which is Sir John's cypher flanked by carved festoons, and some delightful ribbon decoration (Fig. 256). The carved drops that must have formerly hung either side of the picture have unfortunately disappeared. The carving reveals the characteristic rigidity of contemporary work before it had become unloosened by the magic of Grinling Gibbons' influence.

Eltham was completed in 1665, the year Sir John was created a baronet. He died in 1680 and was followed by three successive Sir Johns, the last of whom died in 1779. He was succeeded by Sir John Gregory Shaw, the fifth baronet, who let the house until 1839, when it reverted to the Crown. The house is now the clubhouse of the Royal Blackheath Golf Club and, after considerable damage suffered in the Second World War, has been restored by the Ministry of Works.

257. *The North Front. The roof altered and the dormers added c.* 1840.

LONGNOR HALL, SHROPSHIRE

Begun before 1670 by Sir Richard Corbett and completed by his son, Sir Uvedale, in the 1690s. (Formerly the home of Colonel and Mrs Evelyn Arthur.)

At the time of the Restoration Shropshire was still a remote district and, like other distant counties, did not enjoy the same benefits as those nearer the metropolis. When writing about the glazing of windows in a house, Aubrey recorded that: 'Even in my remembrance, before the Civil Warres, copy-holders, and ordinary people had none. Now, the poorest people that are upon almes, have it. In Hereford-shire, Monmouth, Salops, it is so still.'[1] Although glass came to the windows, vernacular architecture remained conservative and Longnor was a house of advanced character for the district.

Sir Richard Corbett was the type Pratt had in mind when compiling his notes. His ancestors had held half the manor since 1454, but it was not until 1610 that his great-great-grandfather, Thomas Corbett, had been able to obtain possession of the whole. Edward Corbett, Sir Richard's grandfather, had married Margaret Waties, an heiress, and had been given a baronetcy. He died in 1653, a few months after his son, another Edward, and Longnor passed to Richard, his grandson, then a boy of thirteen or so, who came of age soon after the Restoration.

He must have been fairly wealthy, because the Corbett property had been joined by that of the Waties family. In about 1663, he married Victoria Uvedale, the daughter and co-heiress of Sir William Uvedale, of Wickham in Hampshire, Treasurer of the Chamber to Charles I. Presumably they lived in the old moated manor beside the church, now marked merely by a hump in the ground, but by 1667 they seem to

[1] Aubrey, *Brief Lives* (ed. Powell, 1949), p. 7.

have moved away to Frodesley Lodge, in the next village, where they remained while the new house was building.

This was probably begun in 1668 or 69, for the date 1670 is carved on the soffit above the entrance. A manuscript

258. *The Doorway on the North Front.*

259. *The South Front.*
The dormers added
c. 1840.

260. *The doorway on*
the South Front.

poem dated 1692[1] records 'This wondrous pile shall be begun, soon as this Knight shall seen the sun', the future tense being used to disguise the riddle of the family history as a prophecy, a strange conceit of the time. The Knight referred to is Sir Richard's son, Uvedale, who was born in 1668 or 69.

The 'wondrous pile' lies away from the church and the village across the Cound brook, on what had been common land, a site probably chosen for the view it afforded over the fields, now deer park, to Caradoc, the lofty ridge dominating the country to the south of Shrewsbury. At first sight the house conforms, both in outline and material, to conventional contemporary houses, a cube of red brick with stone dressings and a hipped roof, but no London designer would be likely to have proposed the central gable with its three windows (Fig. 257): a pediment in the Eltham manner was the accepted treatment, and the Longnor gable is evidence of the survival of 'Jacobethan' detail. The original silhouette, shown in a water-colour of 1792,[2] was altered in 1840 by Edward Haycock, who was also responsible for the lamentable dormers that disfigure the roof. The latter, presumably reconstructed at the same time, no longer oversails the walls.

Whoever the designer, he appears to have been unacquainted with classical practice, for he not only distributed pediments above windows in unorthodox manner, but ran into difficulty with the mouldings and the pilasters of the doorway on the south front (Fig. 260). The entrance door (Fig. 258) on the north side is bolder, but there again difficulty arose in placing it between its flanking windows. However, in spite of these shortcomings and Haycock's insensitive treatment, the house has considerable charm and character.

The south front (Fig. 259) has been slightly altered by a

[1] National Library of Wales, MSS 15548, poem 1692.
[2] Belonging to Mrs Arthur.

subsequent lowering of the ground floor windows, and the insertion of too slender glazing-bars. The five-bay side elevations are very simply treated and are without ornamental features.

A combination of London and provincial practice is evident in the plan, where the basic arrangement conforms to the double-pile. The relative proportions of the Hall and

261. *The Great Hall, looking west.*

Drawing Room are unusual, however: the Hall (Fig. 261) occupies five of the seven bays of the façade, instead of the usual three, and its unusual size, only equalled by that at Court of Hill, another Shropshire house of the period built a few years later, suggests a late survival of the Great Hall tradition. The two ranges of rooms are separated by an unusually thick spine-wall containing the staircases and chimney-stacks. Access from Hall to Drawing Room is by way of a small vestibule, contrived in the thickness of the spine, and aligned on the two entrance doorways. The

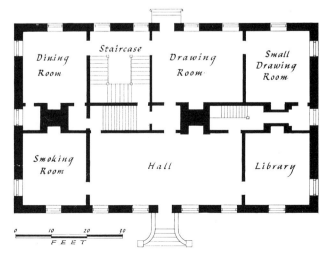

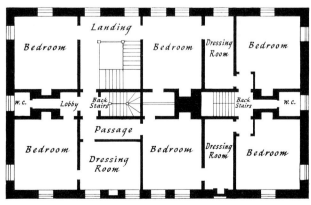

262. *Plans of the Ground and First Floors.*
(*North to the bottom*)

263. *The Staircase, looking north-west, showing the inlaid treads and risers.*

264, 265. Doorcases at the head and foot of the Stairs.

Drawing Room, which is considerably smaller, has its fire-place off-centre. The main staircase lies to the east of the Drawing Room, but is so oddly related to the Hall that it appears to represent a change of intention at some time.

Had the building of the house proceeded to plan, it is likely that it would have been completed, at the most, within four or five years, say in 1672–74. But it appears that Sir Richard had not moved in by 1675, for in October of that year he went to another house in Shrewsbury. A comparison of the accounts for the years 1666–68 and 1668–70 shows an increase in overspending from £79 to £656; the reason could well have been the costs of building. There are no figures for the next few years and perhaps the work was then halted. Lady Corbett died in 1679 and Sir Richard four years later; their finances at the time cannot have been in good shape because the servants were owed more than a year's wages. Sir Richard had been considered, however, to be of sufficient standing to be elected a Member of Parliament for Shrewsbury.

His heir, Sir Uvedale, was still a minor in 1683; three

years later he went abroad to complete his education, not returning till 1689 or 90. The verse quoted below giving an account of his adventures states that he returned home with William and Mary, but makes no mention of his marriage in 1693 to Lady Mildred Cecil, the youngest daughter of the 3rd Earl of Salisbury, who brought him a dowry of £10,000. Sir Uvedale seems to have resumed the work at Longnor before his marriage:

> *A people too he shall command*
> *Of stature small number'd as sand*
> *who daily labour on his land*
> *and architecture understand*
> *Their discipline shall outdo art*
> *which they to none shall e'er impart . . .*

The team employed on the house appears to have been supervised by a man named Young, described in the poem as 'one man whom old and young . . .' He is identified in notes attached to the poem as Thomas Young, who appears in an account compiled by Lady Mildred after her husband's

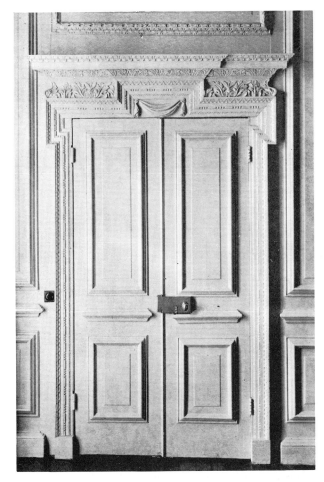

266. *A Doorway in the Drawing Room.*

death, in 1701, showing that she had paid all but £5 of the £248 16s. 8d. due to him. The dates are puzzling, because Waties Corbett says the house took twenty-four years to build, which would mean it was completed about 1693, yet Lady Mildred seems to have paid accounts incurred before her marriage. There are other craftsmen listed in the account, but their names are unfamiliar and the arrears owing them are smaller than those of Young. When Avray Tipping wrote of the house, he wondered whether it had been finished before 1683, when Sir Richard died, but he had not seen either the accounts or the poem. The new evidence mystifies rather than clarifies the position, because it is impossible to assess how much was completed before 1683 and how much after.

Bolection-moulded panelling occurs throughout, and more than one carver appears to have been employed on its ornamentation. The carving in the pediments of the Hall doorcases is of the scroll type, distinct from that in the Drawing Room and Dining Room overmantels, which conforms more closely with that on the main stairs. The only decorative plasterwork in the house is on the Drawing Room ceiling, where the four-times repeated cypher is presumably Sir Richard's.

The main staircase (Fig. 263) has been dated about 1670, but several factors suggest it to be a later one, more probably in the 1690s. Prolifically carved and also elaborately inlaid, it would appear unlikely to have been ordered by Sir Richard if he were short of money. Its old-fashioned character can be explained by Young's age; it is likely that an old man would have worked to a pattern several decades behind the current London fashion. The scrolls on the doorcases look old

267. *The Dining Room. Panels of Chinese wallpaper, supposedly late 17th century.*

268. *The Dining Room.*

fashioned for 1690. They are more akin to carved woodwork of the 1650s as, for instance, in the Thorpe Library, or in the Gallery at Chirk Castle, just across the Denbighshire border, which was panelled in 1678. Despite the care lavished on these stairs, they show little sense of scale, this being particularly noticeable in the truncation of the pediment of one of the doorcases on the upper floor. The inlay on the treads and landings, which is hardly apparent in the illustration, was a rare extravagance, but one occasionally found in the decade 1690–1700. The cypher on the second landing is presumably Sir Uvedale's.

In each corner of the ground floor are small rooms; that lying towards the south-west is a Drawing Room partly panelled and hung with damask. Behind lies the Library, re-decorated during the 18th century in the Adam style, balanced by a room lined with wainscoting presumably removed from the older house. The most interesting is that at the south-east, the Dining Room (Fig. 268), on the walls of which three panels of Chinese wallpaper (Fig. 267) of an early type were discovered in 1952. They seem to have been altered or rearranged by an English hand, and it is likely that they were installed by Sir Uvedale in the 1690s, for the Corbetts then had a bed with 'chiney hangings' and also, in one of the

closets, some Indian pictures. This paper is not mentioned in the 1701 inventory, when the room was possibly used as a parlour or, since it had a closet adjoining, as a bedroom when required, a usual practice at the time. The first floor retains its original lay-out. The main stairs lead to the principal bedrooms at the south-east end of the house and communicate with the other bedrooms by a passage-way. These rooms are partly panelled, and one contains an inner porch enabling the adjoining bedroom to be reached.

Longnor is a remarkably complete example of its type and date and has survived breaks in the Corbett inheritance. Sir Uvedale's son, Sir Richard, remained a bachelor till his death in 1774, when the estate, but not the baronetcy, passed to his kinsman, Robert Flint, who adopted the surname of Corbett, as did the latter's nephew, Archdeacon Plymley, who inherited in 1804. It was the Archdeacon's son Panton who called in Haycock. The house thence continued by direct descent until the death, in 1948, of Major Corbett, whose son sold the property. Colonel and Mrs Arthur, who acquired it in 1952, laid out a considerable garden to replace the original one, swept away in the 18th or 19th centuries. Mrs Arthur sold the house in 1964, after the death of her husband the previous year.

269. *The Entrance Front.*

SUDBURY HALL, DERBYSHIRE

One of the most individual of Charles II houses. Begun by George Vernon *c.* 1665, but not completed until the early 1690s. The rich decoration includes work by Grinling Gibbons and Edward Pierce. (A Property of the National Trust.)

Sudbury is full of paradoxes: in idea it is a courtier's house, yet built by an obscure country squire combining in a unique way both Jacobean and Restoration motifs. For its decoration many of the best-known craftsmen of the day were employed, but no architect seems to have been consulted, and the fully documented building accounts make no mention of either foundations or the start of the work. Lying at the west end of its village, the Hall stands proudly, even ostentatiously, facing the road for all to see, its massive scale emphasised by the crowning cupola and bold chimney-stacks. A short drive, aligned on the front door, originally led to the forecourt, between parterres laid out in the form of a heraldic fret, one of the Vernon armorials.

Sir John Vernon inherited the manor in 1513, from his father-in-law, the last of the Montgomerys, its medieval owners. Sir John's grandson, another John, married late in life Mary Vernon, widow of his kinsman Walter Vernon of Houndshill, and died without issue in 1600. The masterful Dame Mary had induced him to leave Sudbury to his step-son, Edward, her son by her first husband. Only sixteen at the time, he did not marry until 1613, nine years before his mother's death. His grandson George, who inherited in 1658, held the estate for forty-four years and was responsible for the house we see today.

Edward's inheritance in 1600 had not been accepted without a struggle, and a long and costly lawsuit ensued. A

270. *The Frontispiece, carved by William Wilson,* 1670.

271. *The West Front and garden lay-out in 1700, from a painting by John Griffen.*

solution was found in 1613 by his marriage to Margaret Vernon, the daughter of his step-father's younger brother. These quarrels and arrangements are recorded in a poem (not entirely trustworthy) written by John Harestaffe, a man who acted as steward and man of affairs to successive generations of the Vernons in the 18th century. It records that Mary Vernon built a manor house at Sudbury, which is confirmed by her son on her monument in the village church, where in the porch there is another tablet, dated 1646, referring to Sudbury Hall. A manor house close to, or on the site of, the present house is shown on an estate survey of

1659. These references suggest that Dame Mary not only built, but completed her house, but nothing definite is known of its appearance. It is uncertain whether the present house was built anew by George Vernon, but according to one theory he completed the house begun by Dame Mary, which had been left unfinished for forty years.

We incline to the view that the present house is exclusively George Vernon's work, but perhaps incorporates the foundations of Dame Mary's house. He began building on the estate soon after 1660 and was probably at work on the house itself by about 1665. It does not appear that he travelled

272. *The Cupola.*

273. *The West Front.*

274. Inside the Cupola.   275. The Great Hall, looking South. Plasterwork by Samuel Mansfield, 1675.

abroad, and the most advanced local buildings with which he could have been familiar were the Elizabethan and Jacobean Hardwick and Bolsover. With the exception of the roof and chimney-stacks, the scale of Sudbury, the use of diapered brickwork, and the detailing of the lower cornice with its brackets and strapwork, are consistent with late Jacobean work in the Derbyshire tradition. These trappings of the day-before-yesterday apparently satisfied Vernon, for his rich frontispiece (Fig. 270) is a Jacobean conception despite its Baroque embellishment, as is the use of tracery in the upper windows. If the latter work was not clearly recorded in his accounts, its date about 1670 would be unacceptable. The inn in the village, a Jacobean building, but not built before 1671, is proof of his conservative tastes.

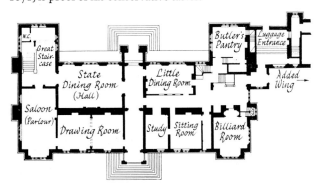

276. The Ground Floor, as in 1935.

A further argument against George Vernon's having merely completed a house begun by his great-grandmother is provided by the family's advance in fortune during the intervening decades. At the beginning of the century they were of little consequence, they possessed no manor house at Sudbury and it is unlikely that Dame Mary could have contemplated building a house no less than 140 feet long. By the reign of Charles II, however, the Vernons had become one of the principal families of the county; George Vernon served as High Sheriff in 1664, and as Member of Parliament for Derby in 1670. He enjoyed the support and friendship of the Cavendishes, for the Earl of Devonshire wrote to his friends requesting them to support him in the election, and in 1680 he was invited to spend Christmas at Hardwick. His new position was enhanced by the 'several mannours' inherited from his mother, a Cheshire Vernon, and which he acknowledged on the tomb (by Edward Pierce) to his father and his first wife. Thereon he stated that his father had held the property 'with much payne and Trouble,' presumably during the Commonwealth. Moreover, his first wife, Margaret Oneley, had been an heiress. In these circumstances it seems reasonable to presume that George Vernon was responsible for the present house.

Each contract and agreement he made is recorded with care, and he clearly enjoyed the process of building. He was probably untutored in architecture (it is not known what books he owned), but learnt as he proceeded. This would explain the slightly more sophisticated treatment of the

277. *The Saloon. Carving by Pierce; plasterwork by Bradbury and Pettifer, 1675; ceiling painting by Laguerre, 1691–4.*

278. *The Drawing Room overmantel. Carved by Grinling Gibbons, 1676. The portrait of Lady Yonge by Vanderbank.*

279. *Portrait of George Vernon, the builder of the house, by Michael Wright, framed by Edward Pierce's carving.*

quoins on the first floor, compared with those below, and again the change to a rich, but archaic pattern in the upper part of the centrepiece of the garden façade. This (Fig. 273) is simpler than the entrance front, but less well proportioned, the frontispiece being too narrow for the length and also too insignificant in comparison with the projecting bays at either end. A puzzling feature of the garden front is a noticeable change in colour of the brickwork ten courses above the stone footings. It could, however, be explained by the employment of different brickmakers, several of whom are mentioned in the accounts.

The end elevations, like those of other early Restoration houses, are less formally treated, that at the east being quite unexpected (Fig. 273). Here the lower cornice rises a foot or so to admit windows lighting a mezzanine floor. The use of a mezzanine at this time is probably unique and makes

the plan particularly interesting. Here again George Vernon seems to have been influenced by a Derbyshire tradition, for the great windows at Hardwick disguise mezzanine floors, while suites of low rooms lie behind the early 18th-century north front of Chatsworth.

Sudbury is divided into halves by a cross corridor running north and south. To the right lie the State Rooms, on the left the family apartments, an arrangement giving the character of a courtier's house. At Eltham, Ramsbury and Longnor there is no such suggestion of division, nor are there similar contrasts of decoration. The first State Room is the Dining Room, occupying three bays to the right of the entrance. Beyond lies the great staircase, filling the west projecting bay on the north front, balanced on the south side by the Parlour. Behind the Dining Room lie two smaller rooms now joined to form a large Drawing Room. The stairs

280. *The Great Staircase. The carved balustrade by Pierce,* 1676; *plasterwork by Bradbury and Pettifer,* 1675; *inset in the ceiling soffit, decorative paintings by Laguerre,* 1691.

281, 282. *Doorcases on the Great Staircase. The Saloon doorcase, possibly carved by Young, and that of the State Bedroom by Pierce.*

lead to the Queen's Room, an ante-room and the Long Gallery, which fills the first floor on the south side of the house, an old-fashioned provision considering the date.

To the left of the cross-passage are three sizeable, but low rooms, with another staircase leading to the mezzanine bedrooms. Above them is another floor of bedrooms and a complete storey lit by the attic dormers. Although more than half the house is occupied by the suite of seven State Rooms, a larger household than one might expect could be accommodated. Partly this is because the fenestration bears so little relationship to the rooms that lie behind. This is characteristic of an amateur designer; perhaps he admired the great windows at Hardwick and wished to emulate them.

The accounts become easier to follow after the years 1664–67, during which time they leave considerable uncertainty on the progress of the work. By the last years of the decade the upper walls were rising fast and work on the porch was in progress. In 1668 the lower part of it was built, and in the following year Blakely and Dick agreed 'to heu mee all my neither cornish att 9d per yd,' and Sam Adams and Thomas Phillips agreed to do 'the over cornish' at 1od. a yard. In 1670 William Wilson, a young local carver who was later to become a successful architect and the

husband of a rich widow, agreed 'to finishe mee ye two frontispieces of my house, on ye top of ye front & backe porch as drawghts for £35. The cutting ye boys over ye porch & ye Ionick heads & frutage hee refers to mee & ye bores heade' (Fig. 270). This carving by Wilson gives a foretaste of the richness of the decorations within.

Most of the interior was decorated in 1675/76, three years after the shell had been completed. Stylistically, the earliest works are the Jacobean-style arches to the entrance door, the cross passage and the Dining Room, to which they give the quality of a great hall, an effect that was surely intentional (Fig. 275). Their consciously archaic character is repeated in the masonry of the entrance arch with a fret pattern playing on the family arms.

The acanthus cornice in the corridor and in the Dining Room is the work of a local plasterer, Samuel Mansfield, to whom several payments were made between 1672 and 75. In 1672 he agreed to do the ceiling of George Vernon's chamber, perhaps the room now joined to the Drawing Room; he also did much plastering of brick walls and lesser apartments such as the nursery closet and the butler's chamber.

Mansfield's most elaborate project was the Queen's Room

283. *Plasterwork beneath the landing of the Great Staircase; part of the main ceiling appears above.*

284. *The Drawing Room ceiling by Bradbury and Pettifer,* 1675. *The painting* Psyche received in Olympus, *by Laguerre,* 1691.

285. *The Long Gallery, looking south; plasterwork by Bradbury, 1676.*

286. *The State Bedroom, also called The Queen's Room; plasterwork by Samuel Mansfield, 1675.*

(Fig. 286), at the head of the Great Stair, the first room to be completed. Since the 19th century it has been used as the State Bedroom, taking its name from Queen Adelaide, who was lent the house by the 5th Lord Vernon. The room has a wonderfully mellow quality, the crimson silk hangings of the bed having faded to a soft brown, harmonising with the broken tones of the alabaster chimneypiece and overmantel (Fig. 287). This is noted by George Vernon as the chimneypiece that 'Mr Wilson agreed to make, axhew, cut, pollish & sett up as p. drawght for £20' in 1670. Unfortunately, the draught is lost and it is not known who made it. Mr Hussey[1] has suggested that it, and the designs for the frontispiece, may have been supplied by a certain Whittricke, a surveyor to whom three small payments were made at the time. Although the design is unusually ambitious, the quality of the work looks provincial when compared with the carving of Gibbons and Pierce elsewhere in the house. The stiffness of the heavy swags and pendants hark back to the generation of Inigo Jones.

Decoration was continued with a new extravagance in 1675, with the engaging of well-known London craftsmen, whose work Vernon may have seen on his visits to the capital.

[1] *Country Life*, LXXVII, p. 652.

The first to appear were the plasterers Bradbury and Pettifer. In that year they completed the ceiling of the Parlour and the decoration of the Stairs Hall, both of which are mentioned in the accounts for November. They were together in 1676, but by the end of the year Bradbury appears to have been left on his own. Possibly he solely was responsible for the ceiling of the Long Gallery (Fig. 285), a task that involved over 337 square yards of plaster, the Gallery being over 138 feet long and 20 feet broad. Both Bradbury and his client measured the work, and the bill came to £101 2s. The design is divided into seven sections. The modelling is at its most inventive in the central three, where horses spring from cornucopiae and dragons and wild boar (perhaps alluding to a Vernon crest) cavort amid the foliage. The cornice is based on a pattern of shells and emperors' heads, and has the necessary breadth and boldness to stand repetition in so long a room. One can wander up and down its length with infinite pleasure, gazing out to the 18th-century lake below the terrace, or quizzing the portraits of George Vernon's friends and relations. The small scale of the panelling admirably suits these half-lengths of the Oneleys, the family of Margaret, his first wife; those of his second wife, Dorothy Shirley from Staunton Harold, just across the Leicestershire border; or of his third, Caroline Vernon, daughter of a London merchant. This company give a feeling of unity to the room, and if their Graces of Cleveland and Portsmouth, or even Nell Gwyn, seem a little out of place, their mellowed faces harmonise with the Vernon sisters, aunts and nieces.

Although the staircase ceiling was put up in 1675, the balustrade (Fig. 280) was not completed until the following year when various payments were made to the carver, Edward Pierce. It would be interesting to know how Vernon induced so active a London craftsman to come to Derbyshire. He was paid £112 15s. 6d. for the balustrade, a dazzling piece of work and without doubt the finest of its type still *in situ*. The massive newels support unattached baskets of fruit which were presumably replaced at night by candelabra. The richness of the carving harmonises with the modelling of the plasterwork in the soffits, the cove and ceiling; the painted panels were an afterthought, the work of Laguerre in the early 1690s. From the foot of the stairs one has an astonishing view of the receding areas of plasterwork (Fig. 283). Set one above another they give an effect of recession and height that is emphasised by the shallow dome. The central oval of this is painted with *A Suppliant Before Juno*.

No less notable are the doorcases, the one at the foot of the stairs leading to the Parlour being worthy of a City Hall (Fig. 281); Mr Hussey has suggested its carver was William Young, who is mentioned in the accounts of 1691 and 92, and later worked at Chatsworth. The doorcases at the head of the stairs are mentioned in Pierce's account (Fig. 282). Of distinguished design, their carved pediments are supported on broken entablatures bearing sprays of olive and palm. The scrolls and demi-pilasters that support the frame, however, seem old-fashioned for their date in contrast with the more assured classicism of the Parlour doorway.

The same combination, plasterwork by Bradbury and Pettifer, painting by Laguerre and carving by Pierce, recurs in the Parlour. The panelling is divided into an unusual system of pedimented bays, with exquisite crossed sprays of carving filling the pediments, and open draperies spilling out swags of flowers below the main panels. Above the doors are garlands tied with white and gold ribbon framing portraits of George Vernon, by Michael Wright, and his third wife. The original effect of the panelling has been altered by the insertion of portraits of the 1st Lord Vernon's family. Clothed in pinks, blues and browns they seem to inhabit this room, so that one is unconscious of the absence of furniture.

The finest of Bradbury and Pettifer's ceilings is perhaps that in the adjoining Drawing Room (Fig. 284), for which Laguerre painted *Psyche received in Olympus*. Yet the eye is drawn from it to Grinling Gibbons' spectacular overmantel (Fig. 278), for which Vernon paid £40 in 1676. As Gibbons was at the time comparatively little known, it would be interesting to learn how Vernon heard of him. In a house so rich in excellent woodwork of the time, the comparisons make the virtuosity of his work more apparent.

The family apartments at the east end of the house come as a comfortable yet interesting contrast to the splendour of the State Rooms. The most attractive is the panelled Sitting Room, which retains its original painted overmantel.

George Vernon's first wife died in 1675, after which he seems to have completed the work in hand, but to have

287. *The State Bedroom chimneypiece. Carved alabaster by William Wilson, 1670.*

undertaken no more. During the years of his marriage to Dorothy Shirley little further was done, but after his third marriage, to Catherine Vernon, he resumed his old interests, calling in Laguerre and Young, as we have seen. He then laid out the formal garden on the south side of the house (Fig. 271), which is shown in John Griffen's painting, but it was all swept away in the 18th century. The house itself has changed little; the steps to the south door have been altered, and the wooden balustrading that crowned the roof removed, its place being taken by one of stone capping the walls.

Succeeding generations of Vernons, and Venables-Vernons, who have lived at Sudbury since George Vernon's death in 1702, have refrained from making alterations to the body of the house, but a long wing was added in 1876. Salvin made a proposal for giving the garden front a Jacobean dress, but fortunately this was not carried out. The house was given to the National Trust in 1965 by the Treasury, who had received it, together with the principal contents, from Lord Vernon in satisfaction of death duties.

LYNDON HALL, RUTLAND

Apparently designed in 1667/68 by John Sturges and built by Sir Abel Barker between 1672 and 1677. The Barker papers give an unusually complete picture of the building of the house. (The home of Lady Conant.)

There are sufficient Restoration houses in existence to give a clear picture of what was desired at that time and what achieved. But this rich visual legacy is for the most part anonymous and a high proportion of the houses described in this book are unsupported by documentary material. In the case of Lyndon, the situation is reversed: the interior was considerably remodelled and redecorated in the 19th century, but what survives is the form of the house, three out of its four façades, and among the Barker papers[1] there are complete notes on the specification and on the architectural literature read by the builder, Sir Abel Barker, a copy of one of the contracts, and annual summaries of its cost. Of these the most valuable are the notes on the sources of the design and the opportunity to relate them to the house as built, a rare, if not unique opportunity of seeing how patrons used

[1] Described in His. MSS Rep. V. Appendix I, p. 398. The architectural material, which is at the end of Volume I of the Barker Correspondence, is not listed and was first noticed by Mr James Lees-Milne. At the time of writing the Conant papers are at the Leicester Record Office, but the *Correspondence* remains at Lyndon.

the architectural writers' theories at the time of the Restoration.

The 17th-century Barkers were an ambitious and successful family, who managed to establish themselves firmly in the ranks of the Rutland gentry. Sir Abel's grandfather, Baldwin, died in 1603 at Hambleton, the next village to Lyndon, but the family had long been in the district; there were yeomen of the name in Lyndon in the reign of Henry VIII. Sir Abel's father, also Abel, acquired considerable property in Hambleton in 1634 and died at the Old Hall there in 1637. Two years later Sir Abel succeeded his elder brother, John, and from then on, with the co-operation of his younger brother, he managed to build up an estate, seemingly out of the profits of agriculture. The Civil War apparently passed him by and, apart from noting paying out £200 in money and supplies in 1644, he appears not to have suffered. He made his peace with the new regime and served as High Sheriff in 1647. However, this did not stop him being made a Deputy Lieutenant of the County at the Restoration, perhaps through the influence of the Noels of Exton, to whom he was related through his second wife, and he was pardoned for any misdeeds he may have committed during the Commonwealth. Later he received more definite recognition of his standing and was granted a baronetcy.

Meanwhile, with his brother Thomas he had bought the

288. *The East Front.*

289. *The South and East Fronts.*

manor of Lyndon, after Sir Geoffrey Palmer of Carleton, sometime Attorney-General to Charles II and a friend of the family, had written to say that Hugh Awdeley was willing to sell it for £9,400. (This price compares with £11,450 in 1634 and £8,890 in 1654: in 1633 it was thought to be worth about £750 a year, and in 1654 there were about 577 acres as opposed to 568 acres offered on lease to the Barkers just before the sale.) Towards the eventual price of £9,200 Sir Abel put up £6,133 and his brother the remainder.

In 1663 the brothers had the property surveyed and the survey still remains in the house. It shows the previous manor house more or less on the same site as the present one, to the south of the church. Presumably Sir Abel continued to live at Hambleton while considering the rebuilding at Lyndon. Plans appear to have been discussed during the winter of 1667/68, and on 10th March, he noted a completely worked out specification for the building (but not its decoration), which corresponds with Lyndon as built in the 1670s. He also gives a list of twelve points and four queries headed *Haec varianda de Modello nuper facto p. Johem Sturges.*

This does not mean that Sturges was the architect in the modern sense of the term, designing and supervising the work. In the annual summary of the accounts for the building there is only one payment of 30s. to Sturges, for advice, in 1672, the first year of building. He was apparently a surveyor, probably a local man, for he is also mentioned in the Belton accounts and later at Milton, Northants.

The evidence points to Sir Abel having built the house himself, and his careful notes on its design suggest that he instructed Sturges of what he wanted and that the latter produced a model. Further evidence of Sir Abel's interest in building appears in some papers relating to the Collin family. He noted the details of contracts made between his widowed sister, Thomasin Collin, and the craftsmen employed on a new house at Medbourne, dated 11th March, 1668.

Sir Abel's notes on architecture are headed *Observacons concerning Architecture taken out of Palladio Gerbier and the Act for rebuilding the City of London.* The Palladio referred to was presumably the first English edition of 1663, although, being a linguist, he could equally well have followed an Italian or French edition. The Gerbier was the *Counsel and Advice to all Builders* of 1663, a work whose influence has usually been discounted. Its full title, *Counsel and Advice to all Builders; For the choice of their Surveyors, Clarks, of their Works, Bricklayers, Masons, Carpenters, and other workmen therein concerned,* perhaps helps to explain its appeal. It is surprising to find him following the Act of 1667, but it contained useful technical details.

Between March of 1667/68 and January of 1671/72 we have no record of work at Lyndon nor any reason for the delay. Perhaps Sir Abel was recovering from his expenditure of over £6,000 on the estate and was saving up funds for his new house. He compressed Palladio's recommendation into: 'The charges wch must be diligently calculated beforehand,

290. (*left*) *The central bay on the South Front.*

291. (*above*) *One of the chimneys.*

& timely provision of money made that the work may not be hindered'.

In January of 1671/72 he made a contract with John Sutton, a mason of Stamford, to build the two middle walls in the house and the chimneys. The work was measured on 27th October, 1673, and costed at £40 9s. Presumably he made separate contracts with the other masons, carpenters and slaters.

The first entry in the specification immediately conjures a picture of Lyndon: 'A house may be built in this manner on all sydes alike,' with the façades 64 feet long and of seven bays. The sixteen flues were to 'come up 4 square in 4 pyles, 4 in each pyle, each pyle 4 ft square, 16 ft from the other and 8 for the railes and ballisters of the roof platform, with a lanthorn in the middle.' The silhouette of the house, with its hipped roof and four chimney-stacks, was clearly influenced by that of Thorpe, but there is no reference to that house in the papers.

The façades of Thorpe are 88 feet × 74 feet and thus Lyndon comes between it and Thorney Abbey, Cambridgeshire, in size. The latter is in the same style and was built

just after the Restoration by John Lovin, a Peterborough builder, but it is only 42 feet × 38 feet.

Apart from a 19th-century porch added to the north front of Lyndon in 1867, three façades survive intact. On the west a long wing was built in 1867, and although this has recently been pulled down, reducing the house almost to its original square, no original detail has been uncovered.

The exterior suggests a conscious attempt to create a work of architecture, as opposed to a piece of country building. This is emphasised by the contrast with Top Hall, another Barker house in the village built in the same generation. Considerable care was taken with the proportions of the windows, of the doorcases with their swan-necked pediments and the windows above framed in Thorpe-like architraves, but a certain lack of confidence gives the impression that the house was built from book knowledge only. It lacks boldness in the handling of mouldings, and there is insufficient contrast of light and shade. The sources of ornamentation are mixed: while the doorcases are characteristic of the 1670s, the windows and the chimney-stacks above are of the 1640s and 50s. The latter are reminiscent of Clare College, Cambridge, built just before the Civil War and copied in the late 1660s and 70s.

The slightly stilted appearance stems from the *Observacons's* concentration on detail: of the quoins Sir Abel noted that 'the angles must be very strong and held with long hard stones: the windows must be as fare from them as the breadth of the Aperture'. The windows 'must be as high again as wyde, the middle transome about 6 ft from the flore'; 'otherwise', as Gerbier said, 'the middle transome would be opposite to a mans eye hindering some to the free discovering of the countrey.' Barker obviously was so struck by Gerbier's comparison that he wrote it as the reason for 'mouldings about windows & dore frontispieces necessary: as the broad brim of a good hat to a travailer in a rainy day'. The details of proportions and precise measurements are given in the specification.

None of the Caroline decoration within the house survives, but with the aid of the specification, it is possible to reconstruct the ground plan. The house was originally approached from the south (the 1663 survey marks a road running through the park in place of the present one to the north of the church) and the first sight of it would have been at the top of a gentle slope.

The south entrance led into a hall, with the Winter Parlour on the left and the Great Hall on the right. In the middle division of the house, between Sutton's two spine walls, was a back hall and a staircase on the left, with the Great Staircase and Drawing Room on the right. The kitchen and its offices were at the north-west corner, with the Summer Parlour opposite. These west and east ranges of rooms were separated by a cross corridor running north and south, making a division resembling that of Thorpe.

Sir Abel was paraphrasing Palladio when he wrote that 'it was graceful, cool in summer and hath many other conveniences' to have doors placed 'to give prospect from one end of the house to another'; he wanted a corridor 'like a Ground Gallery through middle of house long 60 ft wyde 8 ft doore windows at both ends.' The Great Stairs led from this gallery to a corresponding one on the first floor.

Of the living rooms the Great Hall was the largest and loftiest, but it is surprising to find it so described at that time. The Winter Parlour faced south, and the Summer Parlour north and east, the Withdrawing Room east. Upstairs there was a Great Chamber above the Great Hall.

Apart from the Great Chamber, there were three lodgings and two 'pallet chambers' and closets on the first floor and, in the roof, four further lodgings, 'pallet chambers' and closets, as well as a wardrobe and a laundry. Altogether there were forty-four apartments.

The roof as originally projected was hipped and had a crowning balustraded platform, with a central lantern similar to Thorpe. However, point four of the *Varianda* queries this and suggests '2 little roofes on ye top, each 10 ft wide and 24 ft long to crosse each other' and no lanthorne.

In the first season of building, during 1672, £263 was spent; £58 on stone, £103 on timber, £53 to the masons, £5 to a carpenter and £1 10s. to Sturges. In the following year £462 was spent: in 1674 the walls must have been completed and another £300 was spent on plaster, casements, locks, bolts and glass. The Summer Parlour was wainscoted and floored

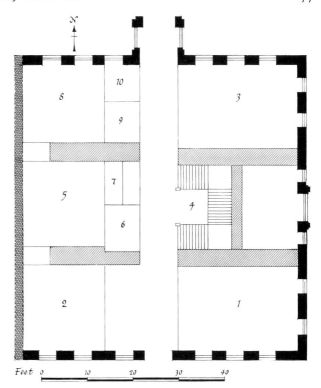

292. *Reconstructed plan of the Ground Floor. 1. Great Hall. 2. Winter Parlour. 3. Summer Parlour. 4. Great Stairs. 5. Back Hall. 6. Pantry. 7. Backstairs. 8. Kitchen. 9. Pastry. 10. Wett larder.*

by a joiner named Richardson at a cost of £20, and the Winter Parlour for £13. The payments for 1675 were £325 and for 1676 £250. In that year 200 yards of wainscotting in the gallery cost £28 and that in Sir Abel's chamber £9. The final sum, paid in 1677, amounted to £90, bringing the total to £1,690, exclusive of the internal painting.

In May, 1670, and again in June, 1677, Sir Abel purchased furniture in London. On the first visit almost £40 was spent on a bed and its upholstery and, at the same time, six turned chairs at two guineas and a large dressing table at 8s. On the second occasion 'a mohayre bed lined, with gilt head bord' and six chairs cost £31, 'a painted paragon bed lined with callico and four chairs' £8, and eighteen turkey work chairs 18s. each. Two years later Sir Abel died. When an inventory was taken, the furniture was valued at £278 18s.; the linen, pewter, plate and brass at £53 6s. 8d., the plate and jewels at £120 and the books at £30. Sir Abel's income must have been considerable, because the stock and crops accounted for about £2,700 (the inventory was taken in September, presumably before the winter slaughtering and after the harvest had been gathered in); of this the grain came to about £268, the 150 cows to about £430, and the 800 sheep to about £908.

As he had no children, Lyndon went to his brother, Thomas, who also died childless. In 1708 Samuel Barker, a cousin, came into the property and it remained with his heirs until 1846, when it was sold, under the will of the last Miss Barker, to a cousin, the Rev. Edward Brown. The latter spent over £5,000 on the house and later left it to his nephew, Mr E. N. Conant.

M

293. *The East, Entrance Front.*

RAMSBURY MANOR, WILTSHIRE

The names of the architect or the craftsmen employed on building the house for Sir William Jones are not known. It was
begun *c.* 1680, but the interior was not completed at Sir William's
death in 1683. (Formerly the home of Lord and Lady Rootes.)

It is typical of the state of country house architecture in the
reign of Charles II that the names of neither the designer
nor the craftsmen who built Ramsbury in the early 1680's
are recorded. Yet it is the most accomplished manor house
of its period to survive and, indeed, is one of the most
beautiful houses in England.

Fifty years ago Avray Tipping wrote of Ramsbury: 'There
is so perfect a sense of proportion, so delicate a feeling of
detail, and so free and personal a touch within the limits of
the prevailing style, that failure to identify its designer is a
matter of regret.' Recently Mr Hussey has suggested that
'the fine but restrained quality of the stonework (replaced by
timber wherever possible) may imply that the designer was
technically a carpenter or joiner rather than a mason.' He
was probably a London man in the Wren atelier, well versed
in the ideas of Pratt and May.

This is suggested not only by the character of the house,
but by the career of its builder, Sir William Jones, an
ambitious barrister. In 1671, when he was thirty-eight, he

was the 2nd Duke of Buckingham's candidate for the
Solicitor-Generalship, but the Duke of York's influence was
more potent, and Francis North was appointed. William
Jones, however, was given a Knighthood and, two years later,
when North was promoted, he succeeded him. Then, in 1675,
he followed North as Attorney-General, an office he held
until his death in 1683, except for a short time after Shaftesbury's fall.

His purchase of Ramsbury was a long-drawn out affair,
apparently hindered by the uncertainties of his career, for he
had Whig sympathies and was in frequent opposition to the
court. In 1676 the Earl of Pembroke had sold the house and
the estate, which the Herberts had owned since 1553, for
£30,155, to three men, Powle, Whitley and Crabford. They
finally conveyed it to Sir William Jones in 1681. Whether
they were acting for him all along or were speculators is not
clear, but it is probable that Sir William began to build the
new house before 1681.

The house, which lies about a mile to the west of Ramsbury
village, beside the Kennet, is carefully sited, so that from the
approach to the east, entrance front, or from the garden on
the west side, the service entrance is hidden by the south-
ward fall of the land towards the river.

The identical east (Fig. 293) and west (Fig. 297) fronts

294. *The central bays of the East Front.*

consist of nine bays divided into three groups of three by the pedimented central feature. The perfect equipoise, the spacing of the windows, the balance of window to wall, and the complementing of mellow red brickwork by stone enrichment give a wonderful feeling of repose. So sensitive is the proportion that the lead down pipes contribute to the harmony of horizontal and vertical, for they strengthen the latter and emphasise the division of the façade into three parts: without them the quoins would lack sufficiently strong emphasis. The simplicity of the façades is subtly brought out by the carving of the pediments (Fig. 294), in the tilting forward of the cartouches and in the curves of their attendant swags, which add a welcome ornament to the chaste design. The swags form a delightfully free swan-necked pediment to the unit formed by the central doorway and the upper window, which are linked together by their stone frames. The doorway entablature is enriched with a stone cartouche between swags, and the keystones of all the windows are carved with strange heads.

All the windows have small panes of late 17th-century type, but it is doubtful whether they were originally of sash form.

Those in the lower storey have an entablature, but this was omitted on the first floor, where its place is taken by the frieze of the main cornice. Surprisingly, this modillioned cornice is of carved wood, painted to simulate stone, as are the cartouches and swags in the tympanums, further confirming that the master builder was a carpenter. The bricks are laid in $2\frac{1}{2}$ inch courses, except in the plinth where $1\frac{1}{2}$ inch courses are used, and the windows are of the earlier mullion type, which continued to be used in such positions in the Restoration period.

The east and west pediments are repeated on a smaller and simpler scale on the other two elevations. But here the designer was confronted by the problem, encountered at Groombridge, of how to emphasise the centre of a façade of an even number of bays. He divided the secondary elevations (Figs. 298 and 299) into three divisions of two bays each. The central pair on the north side is faced with ashlar, further emphasis being given by placing segmental pediments side by side above the lower windows, one of which is a side entrance to the house. On the south elevation no ashlar is used, so that the difficulty is less apparent, and because of the slope of

295. *The house from the north-east.*

the land, the plinth of the main fronts becomes a full storey, so making the elevation more Dutch in its proportions. The formal treatment of these side elevations is an advance on that at Groombridge and is the logical handling of a free-standing rectangular house conceived as a cube rather than in terms of its façades.

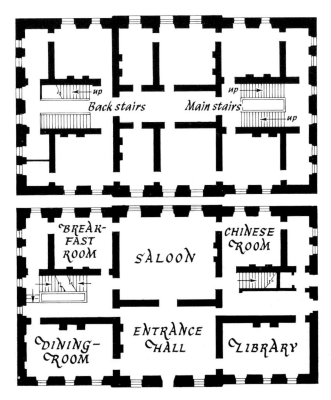

296. *Plan of the First and Ground Floors.*

The deep, steeply-pitched and tiled roof complements the scale of the walls, but does not rise to a leaded and balus-traded prospect platform as at Coleshill or Sudbury. Instead it forms four ranges that surround a sunken lead flat and almost hide the cupola that lights the attic and first-floor corridor. The cupola carries a wrought-iron weather-vane topped with a gilded dolphin, which presides over the house.

The plan (Fig. 296) of both main floors has the same accomplishment as the elevations, for it is a singularly perfect and symmetrical example of the double pile plan, with none of the awkwardness that occurs at Longnor, for in-stance. The Entrance Hall and larger Saloon occupy their normal positions, on the axis filling the centre three bays on both fronts. On either side of the Hall are the Dining Room and Library, both three bays long, and matching them on the west side are smaller rooms, each of two bays, with closets attached. This suggests that these were, or could have been used, if need arose, as bedchambers. The main rooms open out of each other, but the side rooms also have doors onto the two staircase halls, which lie at the north and south ends of the house, so that the family and servants could move through the house out of sight of each other, an advantage recommended by Pratt in his notes.

The similarly ordered plan works equally well on the first floor, where the six bedrooms open on to the central corridor that links the two staircases together. Each bedroom has its own closet.

The early and unexpected death of Sir William Jones in 1683 came before the house was completed, and indeed even before the shell had been quite finished, for the rainwater heads bear the date 1683 and the initials of Richard Jones, Sir William's fourteen-year-old heir. The boy died of fever two years later, and Ramsbury went to his uncle, who died in 1686. The effect of these deaths can be seen in the decoration of the house, which, with the exception of the

297. *The West Front.*

Saloon overmantel, is not particularly remarkable by the standards of its day. There is no elaborate plasterwork of the kind found at Eltham, Sudbury or Eye and little richly carved woodwork.

The Hall, Saloon and Dining Room retain their original oak bolection-moulded panelling, which, as may be seen in the view of the Hall (Fig. 301), is well suited to full length portraits. The double doors lead into the Saloon (Fig. 300), the only room in the house where the woodwork is at all elaborately treated. The doorcase itself is of handsome design with a big broken pediment and well carved detail. The mouldings of the other doorcases in the room and the chief panels are also carved, as is the cornice. The overmantel (Fig. 302) is almost certainly an isolated commission from

298, 299. *The North and (right) South Elevations. The latter is one storey higher on account of the fall in the land.*

300. *The Saloon. The ceiling and chimney-piece date from* c. 1775.

301. *The Enfilade from Hall to Saloon.*

Grinling Gibbons: the virtuosity of his handling of the fruit, flowers, berries and leaves, and his eye for composition, is quite apparent by the contrast with the more pedestrian panel beneath the overmantel painting. It is likely that Sir William Jones would have intended to have a ceiling worthy of the overmantel, but the present one was installed by Sir William Langham Jones about 1775, when the chimneypiece was inserted.

Both staircases are slightly disappointing, and the lack of something more splendid again points to the probable curtailment of Sir William Jones's original ideas. The south staircase is a massive construction with solid newels and turned balusters, typical of a secondary staircase of that date, but on a rather more generous scale. The flying bridge, which connects the first floor landing with the south-east and south-west corner rooms, is unusual. The north staircase is the principal one and more or less follows the Eltham pattern with subsidiary flights from the half landing to the corner rooms, though its balustrade dates from the 18th century.

Between 1685, when Richard Jones died, and 1775, when the Jones heiress married Sir William Langham (who took his wife's name), little was done to the house. Sir William Langham-Jones then inserted the Saloon ceiling, up-to-date chimneypieces and probably the Chinese wallpapers in two ground floor rooms and in the Peacock Bedroom. He also built the south court and may have employed Robert Mitchell to design the orangery and the lodges that flank the splendid late 17th-century gate-piers (Fig. 304), which are reminiscent of some of those at Hamstead Marshall, and may have originally occupied a position at the entrance to the forecourt.

The stables (Fig. 303) are the one survival of the Pembroke period of ownership, and are particularly interesting as bearing a certain resemblance to those at Wilton built about 1635–40. It is tempting to attribute them to de Caus, because it is difficult to think who else would have proposed the row

302. *The Saloon Overmantel; attributed to Grinling Gibbons.*

of *oeil de boeuf* windows or the use of *chaines* to mark the bay scheme.

Lady Langham-Jones died in 1796, leaving Ramsbury to her nephew, Sir Francis Burdett of Foremark, Derbyshire, whose descendants retained the house until 1953. The late Lord Rootes had long hoped to make his home at Ramsbury, but it was bought by the Earl of Wilton, who initiated careful restorations. These were completed by Lord Rootes, who was able to fulfil his intentions in 1958.

303. *The Stables, possibly by Isaac de Caus, 1635–40.*   304. *One of the gate piers at the Main Entrance.*

THE PALACE, LICHFIELD

Built between 1685 and 1689, the Palace is the only building known to have been designed by Edward Pierce. (The Property of The Church Commissioners.)

Civil War and the suppression of episcopacy under the Commonwealth caused havoc to bishops' palaces and castles, the great majority of which dated from the middle ages. When, in 1660, Brian Duppa was appointed to the see of Winchester, he wrote to Sir Justinian Isham: 'I am now for some days gott to my cottage at Richmond, which I look upon as my Chief Palace, the rest which I should enjoy as Bishop of Winchester being most part so demolish'd, that of 4 houses I have not the 4th part of one left to shelter me.'[1]

The Bishop of Lichfield turned to supplying his domestic needs comparatively late, and his new palace is relatively modest, but is the more interesting for showing how little the requirements of a Caroline bishop differed from those of a country gentleman, and having been built all-of-a-piece. Most prelates found sufficient remaining of their castles and palaces to provide a basis for renovation. Bishop Morley of Winchester repaired Farnham Castle and refitted the chapel there before he tackled Wolvesey Palace in Winchester itself; Bishop Fleetwood of Worcester repaired the fabric of Hartlebury Castle about 1675, while the Archbishop of York restored Bishopthorpe and the Bishop of Oxford, Cuddesdon. In the far north, Bishop Cosin of Durham handsomely repaired his two castles at Durham and Bishop Auckland. These undertakings were important in that they introduced the new modes of architecture and decoration to areas often far removed from the influence of the capital.

The old palace of Lichfield, lying at the north-east corner of the close, had been slighted in the Civil War, but Bishop Hacket made no repairs on being appointed to the diocese, devoting his energies to the ruined cathedral. In 1671 he was succeeded by Thomas Wood, who was said to have been 'an idle, wasteful and corrupt man'. He was later suspended,

[1] *Correspondence of Bishop Brian Duppa and Sir Justinian Isham,* Letter CXXIII, 9th October, 1660, Northants. Record Society, XVII, 1955.

305. *The Entrance Front from within the Forecourt.*

Archbishop Sancroft ordering him to pay £4,000 towards the cost of building a new palace. The Archbishop himself undertook the direction of its building and presumably chose Edward Pierce as architect. A sculptor, carver and mason well known in the Wren circle, Pierce's appointment is surprising because, as far as we know, this was the sole occasion in which he acted as architect; it shows the elasticity ruling in the profession at the time. It is also evidence of the versatility and competency of some of Wren's leading craftsmen. Sancroft had close connections with Wren; after being Master of Emmanuel College from 1662 to 1664, he was appointed to the Deanery of St Paul's, where he found Wren a member of the commission investigating the reparation of the old Cathedral. In 1668 he prevailed on Wren to design the new Chapel and Gallery for his old college at Cambridge, in which enterprise he took particular interest. Edward Pierce and John Oliver had been entrusted with the design of some of the fittings for the Chapel, and this would appear to have led to Pierce's commission at Lichfield.

The foundation stone was laid in May, 1685, and shortly afterwards Lancelot Addison, the Dean, wrote to the Archbishop[1] that Pierce was 'signally diligent about the work here, and will not leave it.' Progress was rapid. By October the carpenters were working on the roof, and on 11th December the Dean wrote: 'The outside of the Bishop's house is now ready, and in all likelihood is strong enough for generations and for comeliness and convenience fit to receive a person of quality.'

There is an account, initialled by Sancroft and dated 1st March, 1689, giving the total cost of the house as £3,972 3s.,

¹ Bodleian Library MS Tanner, 131.

306. *The central bays of the Entrance Front framed by the gate piers of the forecourt.*

307. *Preliminary scheme for a house of eleven bays.*

308. *The Garden Front. To the right appears the central spire of the cathedral.*

309. *Plan of a house of seven bays.*

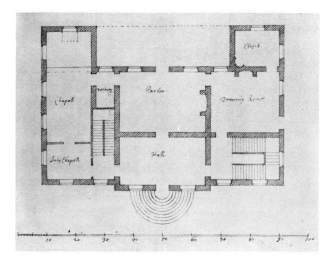

of which Pierce received £113 3s. The accounts, which are among the muniments of the Church Commissioners, show that the carpenter was one Russell, and the painter apparently an Italian named Bessono, Besano or Bassan. In spite of the comparative simplicity of the house, the plasterer's name is given as the celebrated Henry Doogood, one of the foremost craftsmen of the day.

The Palace is approached from the Close between massive stone piers, from which hang white painted wooden gates, framing a view of the centre bays of the house, seen across a small forecourt (Fig. 306). It conforms to the usual Restoration type in the Eltham tradition, of which it is almost a textbook example. Supported on a basement, the two principal storeys of seven bays are divided by a projecting centrepiece surmounted by a pediment containing the only decorative feature of the exterior — a cartouche bearing the arms of the diocese. This is flanked by swags and the date 1687, all presumably from the hand of Pierce. The plain façade (Fig. 305) is relieved with quoins, string courses, doorcase and window architraves, surmounted by a white painted cornice. The original windows, with their wooden mullions and transomes and leaded casements, have fortunately survived. On the garden front (Fig. 308) the central bays are recessed behind projecting wings of two bays width and one bay depth; some of the windows here have been altered, drawing attention by contrast to the significance and importance of fenestration at this period.

The first project (Fig. 307) for the Palace had been on more ambitious scale, judging by the drawings in the

Bodleian Library: eleven bays with a projecting centre and concave roofs terminating in finials on the wings. The plan (Fig. 309) shows a house of seven bays, with a hall and parlour on the central axis, but adapted to episcopal needs by the provision of a Chapel in the left-hand wing.

In spite of both Pierce and Sancroft's care, the Palace did not become the Bishop's residence, because succeeding Bishops preferred to occupy Eccleshall Castle, only returning to Lichfield in 1868. Bishop Selwyn then added wings on the forecourt side and a Chapel on the other, but leaving Pierce's façade intact. The Palace is now occupied by a boys' school.

310. *The East Front*, c. 1687–93.

DUNSLAND HOUSE, DEVON

The East Front was added to an earlier manor house, probably in the 1680s or 90s, by Arscott Bickford. (A Property of the National Trust.)

Dunsland is one of the most isolated of country houses. To approach it today is an experience surely not unlike one of Celia Fiennes during her rides through England. Its remoteness — six miles from Holsworthy and standing far off the nearest paved road — brings home the isolation of the West Country in the 17th century, and partly explains its architectural conservatism.

The small 15th- or early 16th-century manor house of Dunsland was extended twice during the Restoration period by the Arscott family. It came to them when Philippa, wife of John Arscott the younger, inherited it from her father, Humphrey Battyn, in 1522. Her son died in 1580, and her grandson, John, who married Mary Monk, of Potheridge, died in 1623. He was succeeded by his son, Arthur, who died in 1662. The house then passed to Arthur's daughter, Grace Bickford, whose son, Arscott, inherited it in 1687.

The first signs of Caroline work date from the end of Arthur Arscott's life, but whether he himself was responsible, or his daughter and son-in-law, Grace and William Bickford,

is not clear. William died in 1659 and in the following year the ceiling of the so-called Chapel Room (Fig. 319) was completed, displaying the date 1660 and on the overmantel the Bickford arms impaling Arscott. This is puzzling because there is no record of the house having been assigned to Arthur's heirs. The plasterwork is still Jacobean in style with the usual ribbed pattern and strapwork in the lunettes. Similar work exists in a number of West Country houses, notably at Rashleigh Barton, Ford, Newton Abbot and Nettlecombe Court, and is probably the work of the Abbott family, of Barnstaple.

When part of the south front (Fig. 311) was rebuilt after the Restoration, the end bay was left untouched, save for a new window on the first floor, but the adjacent three bays and the front of the porch were rebuilt, and the mullioned and transomed windows inserted. The work is commemorated by a heraldic panel bearing the arms of Arscott Bickford and Mary Parker, his first wife, whom he married in 1660. The room behind the former Great Hall is entered from the screens passage through spiked gates set in a Caroline arch. The design of its ceiling represents a modest revolution in taste from that in the Chapel Room of 1660.

Arscott's first wife died in 1675, and Honor Prideaux, his

311. *The South Front. The three bays west of the porch rebuilt* c. 1670.

312. *The South and East Fronts.*

313. *Doorway and steps on the East Front.*

314. *Plan of the Ground Floor.*

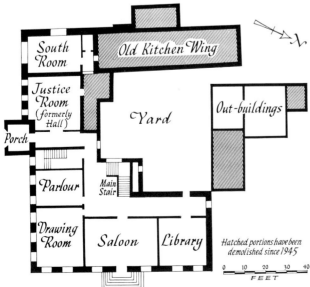

South Room

Justice Room (*formerly Hall*)

Porch

Parlour

Main Stair

Drawing Room

Saloon

Library

Old Kitchen Wing

Yard

Out-buildings

Hatched portions have been demolished since 1945

0 10 20 30 40
FEET

second, died before 1680. In 1683 he married Bridget Prideaux, a daughter of Edmund Prideaux, of Place, Padstow, and a sister of the Dean of Norwich; it is presumably their arms that appear on the leadwork on the new east front. Mr Arthur Oswald[1] has suggested that this was added after Grace Bickford's death in 1687, and before that of Arscott in 1693, on the hypothesis that 'it was only when she was no longer at hand to exercise maternal restraint that Arscott let himself go.'

Arscott Bickford, who was responsible for the new addition, does not appear to have been a wealthy man, or to have taken part in public affairs, and one can only surmise that he wished to express himself by a grander environment. This might be deduced from his apparently rapid change of taste between erecting the 1660 ceiling and rebuilding the south front. The revolution in Caroline architecture and decoration is thus illustrated in the work of one generation.

The east front (Fig. 310), which almost comprises a

[1] *Country Life*, CXXVIII, pp. 18 and 78.

315. *Detail of the Drawing Room ceiling.*

316. *The Drawing Room chimneypiece.*   317. *The Saloon doorway, showing the 19th-century staircase beyond.*

318. *The Drawing Room ceiling, c. 1687–93.*

319. *Ceiling of the Chapel Room, c. 1660.*

320. A Panelled Bedroom. The wainscot is grained to represent burr-walnut.   *321. Painting in a bedroom overmantel copied from the engraved frontispiece to* Eikon Basilike.

separate house by itself, is well sited. It stands proudly above falling ground and looks across a small valley to a ridge, so that a good view of it is gained from the approach road. At first sight the house has the appearance of a characteristic Charles II façade, but closer inspection shows a number of provincial mannerisms. It is built of finely dressed and laid local stone and consists of two storeys, divided into three parts by a giant order of doric pilasters. These, however, are not directly related to the pediment-gable above, which is itself an odd compromise that recurs at Longnor. The feature of this front is the noble doorcase (Fig. 313) with its broken pediment surmounted by *putti* and a cartouche bearing the Bickford-Arscott arms. Standing at the head of a flight of stone steps, it admirably expresses the felicity of Caroline design.

The door leads directly to the Saloon, the walls of which are lined with large-size bolection-moulded panelling. Behind it is the Stairs Hall, giving access to two other rooms on the east front, as well as those on the south. The staircase, seen through the double doors of the Saloon (Fig. 317), is not the original however, but a 19th-century reproduction.

The Drawing Room, which is on the left of the Hall, is lined with panels similar to those in the Saloon. The chimney-piece (Fig. 316) is surprisingly richly carved and strongly reveals the Grinling Gibbons influence on some provincial craftsman. The lower section is a 19th-century rearrangement that destroys something of the original smooth-fronted character. Nothing does this more completely than the insertion of a widely-projecting shelf. The outstanding feature of the room is its plasterwork. This is of exceptional

character, and Mr Oswald has hazarded the name of Henry Doogood as the craftsman responsible, one of the most eminent plasterers of the day. The ceiling (Fig. 318), with its deep cove embellished with floral swags, is an astonishing achievement and exhibits the new manner of the Restoration period when the wreaths and garlands, with their fruits and flowers, were individually modelled and mounted on wire. There are several ceilings of the type in the far west; examples occur at Bowringsleigh, at Youlston Park and in the Customs House at Exeter, which was executed by John Abbott in 1680/81. He would appear to be a likely candidate for the Dunsland ceiling.

Both the Parlour and some of the rooms on the first floor contain interesting examples of graining. The panelling in the former simulates walnut veneer with the panels bordered in black, and the cornice is decorated with plaster acanthus leaves. One of the bedrooms is grained in imitation of burr-walnut and has a painted cornice (Fig. 320); that in the south-east corner has a painted overmantel derived from the engraved frontispiece to *Eikon Basilike* (Fig. 321).

The descendants of Arscott Bickford retained the house until 1945; four years later the late Philip Tilden, the architect, saw it when it was in an advanced state of decay, shorn of the surrounding woods and likely to be demolished. He acquired the property, rescued some of the doomed trees near the house and, with his wife, heroically set about restoration. Five years later ill-health brought his work to an end and he sold it to the National Trust, who have since completed the restoration and furnished some of the rooms.

325. *The East Front.*

326. *The West Front,*
facing the stable range.

327. *The Marble Hall. The ceiling is 19th century.*

fortunate. At the time he was one of the chief mason-contractors in the country, a position he inherited from his uncle, Thomas Stanton, in 1675. He served as Warden of the Masons Company in 1681 and again in 1684, and as Master of the Company in 1683. Like other London master-masons, he was occupied with the rebuilding of the city churches, in 1684 contracting with Edward Pierce to rebuild St Andrew's, Holborn. His connection with Pierce is of interest because the latter frequently worked for William Winde, but it is unlikely that Winde recommended him as contractor for the new house because in 1679 Stanton had already carved the striking monument to Old Sir John and Lady Brownlow in Belton church.

There are two approaches to the house from Grantham, either along the elm avenue by way of the Lion Gates, or through Belton village. The former reveals the house a mile or so distant from the end of the avenue. On closer approach (Fig. 323) one sees the broadly welcoming centrepiece crowned by its cupola, and appreciates the fine quality of the stonework, the crisply-cut mouldings, architraves and quoins, and the chimney-stacks. This pleasing precision is subtly emphasised by the contrast of the office range on the west, which has a self-effacing squatness, a dominating roof and slightly over-size cupola, but it admirably sets off the house itself. As may be seen from Henry Bug's delightfully naïve

view (Fig. 322), the house was originally set behind a screen between stone piers enclosing a forecourt, which was taken down by Lord Tyrconnel, Young Sir John's nephew and successor. Another change is that the entrance door has a new architrave, introduced by James Wyatt in 1776, when he removed the cupola and roof balustrade, but these were replaced by the 3rd Earl in 1879. The *oeil de boeuf* windows and the swags supporting the cartouche in the tympanum shown in the painting have disappeared. The picture also shows that the windows were always of sash form, but originally were four, instead of three panes wide. The north front is identical (Fig. 324), but because of a slight fall in the ground, the rather longer wings appear to stand out more prominently.

Approaching from the village, past the stable building, the hipped roof of the house is seen rising above the office range, its pitch repeating that of the house, and the cupola echoing that on the higher roof. From this point the buildings make a pleasing composition, inviting the visitor to pass through the archway framing the west elevation (Fig. 326). Simple as this façade is, monotony is avoided by the slight recession and by a narrower spacing of the four central bays; the projecting porch is a 19th-century innovation. This front corresponds with the more rarely seen east elevation (Fig. 325), facing up the long avenue to Bellmont tower, a

328. *The Saloon, looking west.*

329. *The Saloon, looking east. The ceiling is* 19th *century.*

330, 331. *Overmantels in the Marble Hall. Portrait of Sir John Brownlow, with carving possibly by Grinling Gibbons, and (right) Lady Brownlow, with carving by Edmund Carpenter.*

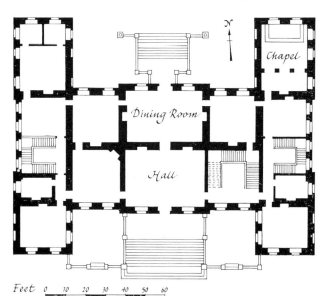

332. *Plan of the Main Floor.*

mid-18th-century ruin half-way up the ridge. On this side the house is framed by trees and it is easy to imagine its original setting of parterres.

The plan of the house (Fig. 332) is symmetrical, clear, and as logical as the elevations. There are six rooms on the main floor of the centre block, with the Hall and Saloon on the central axis. In the corners to left and right of the Hall are the Parlour, now the Tapestry Room, and the main staircase, leading to the Great Parlour above the Hall. These are balanced on the north side by the Red Drawing Room and the Tyrconnel Room, originally the State Bedroom, all of them inter-communicating. Both east and west wings have central staircases. The east wing contains the Chapel at its northern end and at its south the Blue Bedroom. Similar suites occupy the south end of the west wing. The original kitchen, in the north end, was converted into a Dining Room by the 1st Lord Brownlow in about 1776 and has since been used as a reception room.

The Marble Hall (Fig. 327) derives its name from Stanton's black and white floor. On its bolection-panelled walls hang portraits of Charles II and members of the Brownlow, Cust and Hume families. The portraits of Old Sir John and Lady

333. *The West Over-mantel in the Saloon, with carving possibly by Gibbons. The portrait is of Margaret Brownlow.*

Brownlow are framed by splendid naturalistic carvings. The position of these two portraits appears to be appropriate, but it is doubtful whether they were originally hung here because, in the 1688 inventory, the only pictures mentioned in the Hall are those of the Kings and Queens of England.

The design and execution of the two surrounds (Figs. 330 and 331) are not identical, the carving surrounding Sir John's portrait being far richer, fuller and freer than that around Lady Brownlow's portrait. The latter may be the work of Edmund Carpenter, a hitherto unknown carver, whose account for 1688 has been discovered by Mr Rupert Gunnis among the Brownlow papers. This lists three overmantels, one of which, costing £25, is described as 'for a very rich chimneypiece in the withdrawing roome at the Great Parlour, done with a variete of fish and shells with birds, fouliage, fruit and flowers.' This may be the one framing Lady Brownlow's portrait in the Marble Hall; if so, it was placed there at an unknown date, perhaps when the original ceiling and the

doors and doorcases were replaced in the late 18th or early 19th century.

There is more remarkable carving in the Saloon (Fig. 329), over the elegant marble chimneypiece, above the doors, and between the four full-length portraits, by Riley, of Young Sir John and his wife, and his brother and sister-in-law, Sir William and Lady Brownlow of Great Humby. The third of the overmantels in Carpenter's account, one costing £18, described as a 'chimneypiece in the Great Parlor with fruit and flowers', is probably that surrounding the portrait of Sir John's daughter, who became Duchess of Ancaster, at the east of the room, and does not refer to the much more elaborate surround to Margaret Brownlow's portrait (Fig. 333), which is the richest in the house and presumably cost more than £25, at the west end.

No payments to Grinling Gibbons have come to light, but his name has always been linked with the carving at Belton and it would be no surprise if it were discovered that

334. *The West End of the
Chapel. The household pews
below, and the family gallery
above.*

he was responsible for both the carving round Old Sir John's portrait in the Marble Hall and round Margaret Brownlow's in the Saloon. The carving is so striking that it inevitably overshadows the bolection-moulded panelling and the boldly pedimented doorcases.

The ceiling is 19th century, but is a good reproduction. The crimson velvet chairs here have always been in the house, while the pair of buhl bureaux and the large Chinese jars, although a little later in date, are typical of late 17th-century taste. According to the inventory taken soon after the house was completed, in 1688, this room was furnished with a set of eighteen rush chairs, two Japan tables, 'two verie large Seeing Glasses' and with crimson sarsnet curtains.

The Red Drawing Room, which is to the west of the Saloon, was redecorated in the early 19th century in a modified Caroline style, but the Tyrconnel Room has remained more or less untouched. It contains portraits on its panelled

and damask-hung walls, mainly of its namesake's generation. The Chapel Drawing Room, although redecorated since Sir John's day, reveals the taste of his generation. The simple panelling is painted to simulate green marble and set in the big panels are two large chinoiserie tapestries by Vanderbank; acquired either by Sir John or his successor, their gay colouring and exotic figures would have appealed to the cognoscenti of the day. That the Brownlows shared such taste is evidenced by the quantity of japanned furniture they amassed. Much of it still remains in the house, although it is impossible to identify any of the pieces mentioned in the inventory.

From the gay heathen world of the tapestries one steps into the well-upholstered Squire's Gallery overlooking the Chapel. This is made to appear smaller than it is by the immense size of the creamy-white marbled reredos (Fig. 336) which rises from the basement level of the house. Here the

335. *The Chapel Ceiling, plasterwork by Goudge.*

336. *The marbled reredos.*

337. *The Staircase Ceiling, plasterwork by Goudge.*   338. *A late 17th-century State Bed, upholstered in pale blue damask.*

household sat below in box-pews while the master and mistress sat at their ease on velvet chairs, warmed by a fire and separated from the preacher behind the richly carved screen, which consists of a triple arcade, the insets of the pilasters being filled with carving (Fig. 334).

The ceilings in both Chapel (Fig. 335) and Gallery are distinguished, and presumably the work of Edward Goudge; the former has its enrichment well contrasted by a plain central field. The ornament employed has little of religious derivation, and indeed the air of the Chapel is one of social conformity rather than of stirring piety.

Another contemporary ceiling is that above the main staircase (Fig. 337), again presumably Goudge's work, an attribution resting on Mr Geoffrey Beard's discovery of letters from William Winde to Lady Bridgeman. One of these, written in 1689, refers to Goudge who, he says, 'is now looked on as ye beste master in England in his profession as his works atte Combe, Hampstead & Sir John Brownlowe's will Evidence'.

The balustrade of the staircase is not the original, but probably an early 19th-century replacement. Although competently executed, it somewhat disturbs the unity of the Hall,

which, with its black and white marble floor, and good panelling, provides a fitting approach to the Great Parlour above.

Less than ten years after the house was completed, Young Sir John died (according to Narcissus Luttrell, he shot himself), but his widow ruled the house until her death in 1721. Belton then descended to their nephew, John Brownlow of Great Humby, who had married their daughter, Eleanor. He was created Viscount Tyrconnel, a title that lapsed on his death without children. His heir was his sister Anne, Lady Cust, who outlived her son, Sir John Cust, the Speaker. When she died in 1779 she was succeeded by her grandson Brownlow Cust, who had been created Baron Brownlow in 1776. He employed James Wyatt to restore and also to redecorate part of the house. His son, the 1st Earl Brownlow, employed Wyatville, as Jeffry Wyatt had by then become, to make further minor alterations; his great grandson, the 3rd Earl, carried out a remarkably sympathetic restoration in 1879, replacing external features removed by Wyatt, and redecorating some of the rooms in an excellent version of the Caroline manner. Thorough repairs have recently been completed with the aid of a grant from the Historic Buildings Council.

339. *The East, now the Entrance Front.*

DENHAM PLACE, BUCKINGHAMSHIRE

The house was built between 1688 and 1701 by Sir Roger Hill. The details of its construction and the names of many of the craftsmen employed have recently come to light. (The home of Lady Vansittart.)

The 1680s saw the divergence between grand houses of the aristocracy and those of the gentry; side by side with the perfection of the Restoration type in Ramsbury and Belton, the Baroque first appeared at Thoresby and Chatsworth. The Pratt-May model remained the common form of house of the 'middling sort' until the Palladian idiom was established in

the first quarter of the 18th century. To illustrate this continuity of tradition, we include Denham Place and Nether Lypiatt, although both houses were built slightly after the period to which this book is devoted.

Since Denham was built, the layout has been considerably altered, but it remains one of the most interesting examples of its epoch, more especially since recent research has revealed details of its building. When, in 1925, Mr Christopher Hussey[1] described the house, the document recording Sir Roger Hill's expenditure had been mislaid, but this has since

[1] *Country Life*, Vol. LVII, p. 602.

340. *The West, originally the Entrance Front.*

341. *The Entrance Doorway, now on the East Front.*

342. *Detail of the cornice and quoins at the south-west corner of the house.*

343. *The original layout, from a painting in the house.*

344. *The Tapestry Room; the tapestries depict the Legend of the Golden Fleece.*

345. *Sir Roger Hill, the builder of the house.*

346. (*below*) *The Drawing Room ceiling.*

come to light and has been published by Mr John Harris.[1] It is inscribed in Sir Roger's hand: 'An account of the money layd out in Building my new house in Denham', and concluded in the hand of an 18th-century owner, Benjamin Way; 'commencing in 1688 & continued to 1701, Total £5591. 16. 9 as per enclosed particulars all of Sir Roger Hill's own handwriting B.W. Septr 3 1765.'

Sir Roger Hill (Fig. 345), who came of Puritan Somerset stock, eventually inheriting the family seat, Poundisford Park, from his half-brother in 1680. His father had been Member of Parliament for Bridport and one of Cromwell's Barons of the Exchequer; it was on his account that Sir Roger was knighted at the age of twenty-six. He himself sat as Member for Wendover and served as High Sheriff of Buckinghamshire in 1673. In that year he bought the west half of the manor of Denham, including the older house, but did not begin rebuilding for some fifteen years. In 1688, when the Revolution evidently reassured him, the work was put in hand with the assistance of the mason-contractor, William Stanton.

[1] Records of Buckinghamshire, Vol. XVI, Part III, 1957–58, p. 193.

347–350. *Details of the Drawing Room frieze, partly taken from engravings by Francis Barlow. Fishing, otter-hunting and shooting, a deer-hunt, rabbiting and fox-hunting are among the subjects illustrated.*

Between 24th August, 1689, and 13th October, 1694, Stanton received £214 4s. 2d., as compared with the £5,000 he obtained as contractor at Belton, which points to his probably acting at Denham only as designer. A bird's eye view of the house and the original layout appears in an old painting (Fig. 343), and the house itself has not greatly changed; it is still a two storey block on the H plan with a hipped roof, a descendant of the Clarendon House type. The balustrade that formerly crowned the roof has disappeared, as has the cupola, which was removed by Benjamin Way. The windows have been altered, probably more than once, for according to the painting they were originally taller. Benjamin Way II removed the glazing bars, which Lady Vansittart has now replaced, reproducing their profile from some at Hampton Court. Benjamin Way I turned the house about, bringing the main entrance from the west to the east front (Fig. 339). He also substituted the elaborate garden layout, of parterres and formal canal, by a free landscape setting, and removed the stables elsewhere.

The shifting of the main entrance affected the internal arrangement of the house. The Hall and staircase now fill the east side of the centre part, while the Dining Room occupies the position of the former Hall on the west front. The normal arrangement of Hall and Saloon on the central axis can never have prevailed here, because the former Hall (now the Dining Room) would have led, as it does now, into the Drawing and Tapestry Rooms in the northern arm of the H. The original staircase was replaced by an 18th-century one, but it appears to occupy the same position as its predecessor.

The payments to craftsmen are recorded from a year or so after work had started; between September, 1691, and August, 1694, 'Mr Taylor, Mr Stanton's man,' received £98 12s. 8d. The glazier, Price, presumably the Joshua Price who worked at St Andrew's, Holborn, was paid

351. (above) The Drawing Room.

352. (left) The Library.

353. (below) Detail of doorcase in the Library.

354. *The Principal Bedroom.*

355. *Detail of the cornice in one of the bedrooms.*

356. Love on the Wing, *the central panel of the Tapestry Room ceiling.*

£150 0s. 6d. between September, 1691, and November, 1695. The name of the plumber, Hiorn, appears between 1691 and 1697, and those of the carpenter, William Woodhouse, and the joiner, Ball, from 1689 to 1697.

Progress seems to have been slow, because the final payment was not made until 1701, although internal decoration had been begun ten years earlier. In June, 1692, the carver, Lord, was paid £26 5s., which, Mr Harris suggests, was for work on the Chapel Gallery, dated 1692, and also the cartouche above the east window in the Chapel. Apart from Stanton's name, perhaps the most interesting is that of Parker, the plasterer, which occurs in the accounts from 1691 until 1695. William Parker appears in the Plaisterers Company List from 1677 until 1696, probably the year of his decease. Here he was probably responsible for the unique friezes in the Drawing and Tapestry Rooms, the latter carrying the date 1693. The ceiling (Fig. 356) in the Tapestry Room has a spirited figure of Cupid leaping across the clouds in the central oval, and in the frieze above the chimneypiece he appears with a tortoise, an emblem of impatient love. The frieze displays a delightfully naïve panorama of country scenes. The room still retains its original decoration, with a painted overmantel set in a carved frame above a black

marble chimneypiece, and overdoor paintings. The fine set of Flemish tapestries, depicting the legend of the Golden Fleece, have always hung in the house.

The main feature of the Drawing Room (Fig. 351) is again the plasterwork in the coving (Figs. 347–50) and on the ceiling (Fig. 346). The latter has medallions of the seasons with sprays of olive, palm and flowers decorating the smaller spaces, while a spectacular trophy of musical instruments, partly carved in wood, forms the central feature. The mouldings and enrichments are painted white and the ground a light brown. The scenes in the frieze, displaying field sports, are taken from Francis Barlow's *Several Wayes in Hunting*, a set of engravings published twenty years or so previously. In its way this frieze is perhaps the most original of all plasterworker's performances of the period.

At the end of the house is the Library (Fig. 352), where the bookshelves, which are set back into the wall, constitute one of the earliest instances of this practice. The woodwork, both in design and execution, is of the first order; the arrangement of the mouldings, architraves and entablature are all competently disposed and the carving is crisply cut. Altogether, this room achieves a distinction that anticipates 18th-century work.

The upper floor retains its original layout almost unchanged, with the principal bedrooms, each with three closets, filling three wings of the H plan. Many of the rooms are panelled and display finely modelled cornices and painted overmantels, the most elaborate bedroom being at the south-east corner. This has low relief carving in the panels surrounding the overmantel above the fireplace, and a distinguished geometrical plasterwork ceiling.

Sir Roger's endeavour over many years to establish a seat for his family came to nought, for his son died within a few hours of him in 1729. Sodden with drink, his heir died of apoplexy while reading the will stolen from his father, then dying in another room. Realising her husband's condition, his wife tried to make him sign everything over to her, but the scrap of paper was not accepted and Denham never became her property. Instead, it passed to Sir Roger's eldest daughter, Hester, who died in 1742, from whom it went to a niece, the daughter of Abigail, her younger sister, who married Lewis Way, as his third wife. The property remained in that family until 1920, when it was sold to Mr and Mrs Fothergill, from whom the late Lord Vansittart acquired it in 1930.

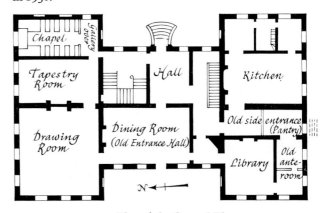

357. *Plan of the Ground Floor.*

358. *The West Front, seen through the forecourt gates.*

NETHER LYPIATT, GLOUCESTERSHIRE

Though built about 1700-5 by an unknown mason, this beautiful building exhibits so clearly the influence of the Restoration country house that it is included to show the continuity of that tradition. (The home of Mr and Mrs F. Nettlefold.)

Nether Lypiatt has been compared to Ashdown. Both stand high, Ashdown on the now-open downs above Lambourn, and Nether Lypiatt on a ridge-top, some 700 feet above Stroud. Both have a marked vertical emphasis strange to the English tradition. At Nether Lypiatt, however, there is no sense of isolation as there is on the downs: the setting is good farming land, with a country lane leading past comfortable farm buildings adjoining the house, which is beautifully revealed behind its forecourt. The stone piers and iron grilles come first into view, as they are seen in perspective from the lane (Fig. 362), and then the house, framed by its gate piers (Fig. 358), a serene and restrained composition, with a captivating contrast of warm grey stone, rich ochre roof and green velvet of the grass.

The house itself is an exact cube on plan (Fig. 364), with four storeys and five bays to each face. The low wings, of which two of the three are visible on the west, or entrance front (Fig. 359), form pavilions at its base and provide an admirable foil to its upward thrust. Originally there was

no direct communication between house and wings, and as they only just touch at the corners, it has been suggested they were afterthoughts, but it is difficult to imagine that the house could have been conceived without them, so important are they to the composition. (The roof of the left hand pavilion is new, having been added in 1931.) The bold chimney-stacks that encircle and crown the house recall those at Coleshill, and possibly the unknown local builder had that house in mind when he designed Nether Lypiatt.

Ashdown and Coleshill are two of the houses that come to mind when one looks across the forecourt. A third and fourth might be Thorney and Lyndon, both in the eastern half of England, and again considerably earlier. Both have the same clear-cut cubic feeling about them, which was a new element in the smaller English country house in the 1660s and 70s. Inigo Jones was initially responsible for this, but by 1700 it had become absorbed in the practice of country masons. For this reason Nether Lypiatt has strong bonds with the Caroline idea, only here made more sophisticated, and perhaps a little disguised by the pavilions, which create an un-Caroline architectural excitement.

Nothing is known of the builder or the exact date when the house was built, but it probably was erected about 1700–5,

359. *The West Front seen through the clairvoyée.*

360. *The East Front.*

361. *The Porch and one of the pavilions.*

when Judge John Coxe was the owner. From 1699 until his death in 1728, he was Clerk of the Patent Office and also represented Circencester and Gloucester in the House of Commons. He had inherited Nether Lypiatt from his father-in-law, Thomas Chamberlain, to whom it had come through marriage to the heiress of the Freme family, the ancient possessors of the place.

Apart from these bare facts of his life, little is known about him, except for what can be gathered from the legend about the forecourt gates. According to this, the smith who made them was sentenced to death for some crime before they were finished, and Coxe reprieved him only long enough to enable him to complete the job.

The gates are also of interest in that their design relies solely on a linear patterning of voluted scrolls, with none of the usual embossed foliage and scrollage in the manner of Tijou or his followers. But they came from the hand of a skilled smith working on traditional lines.

A wide flagged walk leads across the greensward of the forecourt to a raised terrace between the flanking pavilions. Thence a flight of straight steps rises to the entrance door in

front of which stands a colonnaded and pedimented porch of slightly later date (Fig. 361).

The principal floor of the house is raised fourteen steps above ground level. Roger Pratt as early as 1664 advocated the main floor of a house being raised upon 'a very good storey — for by this means,' he said, 'is place sufficient to keep the servants, to avoid the digging of cellars and the rising of springs; it is much easier ascending 12 steps on the outside of your house than 22 within; an ascent is most graceful with such a basement for it looks like a thing complete in itself, and this adds to the height and majesty of a building; and a prospect is more pleasant to a house than where none, as must necessarily fall out where we cannot see over the top of our out-walls'. These arguments favouring a *piano-nobile* evidently influenced the Judge.

The first floor windows are of the same height as those below, and both have elaborate architraves. So symmetrical are the four sides of the house that it resembles a Dutch doll's house in its formality. At the time of its building the windows were of the early stone mullioned and transomed type, with casements and leaded lights. Several of these remain on the

363. *The South Front.*

364. *Plan of the House in* 1934.

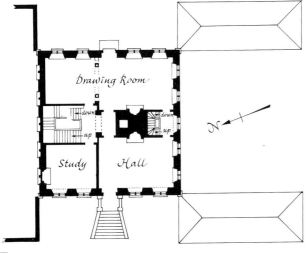

north side and in the centre of the south front, but the introduction of sashes adds to the serenity and charm of the façades.

The cornice conceals a lead gutter which, until recently, had been covered by the lower courses of the roof slates, while a new gutter had been fixed to the extremity of the cornice. During recent repairs the original concealed guttering has been reinstated.

On the south side of the house a small enclosed forecourt lies between the east and west pavilions, and on the far side of the screen wall lies the formal garden. On the east side a raised terrace and flight of steps leads up to a central doorway on the principal floor. This has long remained blocked, but the present owner has inserted glazed dummy-doors, which are at least satisfying to the eye. These minor variations in the designs of the façades add greatly to the visual interest of the house.

The effects created by the relationship of the central pile and the pavilions are not repeated within, and indeed would not be expected in a house of that date built on a 45 foot square. There is no elaborate decoration in the form of carving, painting or plasterwork, but most of the rooms retain pleasing panelling. The Entrance Hall (Fig. 365) is lined with bolection-moulded wainscot of chestnut, now waxed to a warm glowing tone. The fine chimneypiece of richly carved local stone on a background of grey 'touch' must have been inserted about 1730. The Study (Fig. 366) has similar wainscot, but made of beech. The photograph was taken when the house was the home of that exquisite

365. *The Entrance Hall.*

366. *The Sitting Room.*
The photographs on this
page were taken in 1934.

367. *The Staircase, looking down the central well.*

musician, Violet Gordon Woodhouse, of whom Sir Osbert Sitwell gives so enchanting a description in *Noble Essences*. The long Drawing Room across the stairs landing has been formed by throwing two smaller rooms together, one of which was probably the Dining Room. The panelling and the fireplace appear to have been installed in about 1720. It is an elegant room extending the whole width of the house and its windows afford charming glimpses of the clipped yews in the garden. The main staircase (Fig. 367), which continues the entire height of the house, is of oak and elm with a wainscoted dado of mahogany. The lower flights are slightly wider than the remainder to facilitate the service of food from kitchen to dining room. Dignified arches on each landing form imposing entrances to the principal rooms.

An ingeniously contrived service stairs, on the south side, gives directly into the rooms of the upper floors, from whose windows extend views to the west across the Severn estuary to the Welsh mountains.

The house remained the property of the Judge's descen-

dants until the death of his great-great-great grand-daughter, Miss Gordon, in 1884, but for much of this time they did not use it, so that it survived the extravagances of Victorian enlargement. The first restoration was begun by Mr A. W. Stanton, and completed after the 1914–18 war by the next owner, Mr Corbett Woodall. He had bought the property in about 1914, but only called in Mr Morley Horder to restore the house after 1918. In 1923 it was bought by Mr and Mrs Gordon Woodhouse, who completed the restoration. The present owners acquired it in 1955.

As with so many houses, 19th-century neglect was its salvation, but fortunately this did not develop into ruin. Nor did the Judge's monument to his horse disappear. On this obelisk in a deep and thickly wooded ravine to the east of the house is inscribed:

> *My name is Wag that rolled the green*
> *The oldest horse that ever was seen*
> *My years they number forty-two*
> *I served my master just and true.*

NOTES ON THE PRINCIPAL CAROLINE HOUSES

This list of 125 houses, which makes no claim to be complete, gives brief particulars of the more important built or altered during the period, more especially those referred to in the Introduction. It does not include those described in the main text. Where known information is given of the builders, the architect and craftsmen employed and the nature of the work. Where a house has been described in *Country Life*, reference is given to the date of publication.

ABBREVIATIONS

C.L.: *Country Life*
Tipping: Period III, Vol. I: *English Homes: Late Tudor and Early Stuart*, 1558–1649
Period IV, Vol. I: *English Homes: Late Stuart, 1649–1714*
Period IV, Vol. II: *Sir John Vanbrugh and his School, 1699–1736*
Hussey I: *English Country Houses. Early Georgian*, 1720–60

Hussey II: *English Country Houses. Mid-Georgian, 1760–1800*
III: *English Country Houses. Late Georgian, 1800–60*
Kip: *Nouveau Théâtre de la Grande Bretagne* (1716)
V.C.H.: Victoria County History
R.C.H.M.: Royal Commission on Historical Monuments

Abbotstone, Hampshire   (*Demolished*)
Built about 1680 by the 1st Duke of Bolton (created 1689), son of the 5th Marquess of Winchester, whose seat, Basing House, had been destroyed in the Civil War. (See also Hackwood.)
Description of house by Povey (B.M. Add. MSS 14296. f. 62): 'A large noble Brick house edged with stone built by Duke of Bolton A⁰ Dni I for a convenient Hawking Seat of which Sport he was a great admirer, in allusion whereof he caused two vast large hawks to be fixed on ye top of two Banquetting Houses just before ye Entrance into ye House; It is built after ye Italian manner opening a Vista from one End of ye House to ye other, The Wings are rather of ye largest, darkening ye Body too much; . . . there are above 100 Rooms in ye house in one of which adorned wt curious ffret-work ye Duke of Bolton had ye honour to entertain Q Ann; in ye ceilings are figured several keys, in memory of his being the Chamberlain when he built it. It is little regarded and left unfinished since Hackwood has been built a much pleasanter seat, not far distant from this.'

Acklam Hall, Yorkshire
William Hustler bought the property in 1637. His grandson, Sir William, married Anne, widow of Sir Matthew Wentworth of Bretton, in 1680, and built the house about that time.
A brick and stone house of 7 bays and 2 storeys. The windows are capped with broken pediments alternately bearing balls or busts. The attic storey is much altered. There is some elaborate plasterwork in the house, including the staircase ceiling dated 1683–84. (The late Walter Brierley made alterations in the Caroline manner.)
Plate in Kip, Vol. I, pl. 64.
C.L. Vol. xxxv, p. 342.

Acrise Place, Kent
Thomas Papillon (died 1703) bought the house in 1666 for £5,000. He was a mercer and a director of the East India Co., anti-court in sympathy. He served as M.P. for Dover and London. About 1677 he added a new front of 12 bays and 2 storeys to the old house. Mr Woodstock, the designer (?), Nevett, the builder (?).
C.L. Vol. cxxii, p. 258 and p. 300.

Albyns, Essex   (*Dismantled in 1920s, bombed 1945, remains demolished 1954*)
Acquired by John Wood in 1587. His daughter (died 1614) married Sir Thomas Edmunds (died 1636).

The latter remodelled the house about 1620. Built on a courtyard plan, it had regular façades, a hipped roof with dormers capped by Holborn gables. Interior was mostly Jacobean. Walpole commented on an 18th-century attribution to Inigo Jones: 'If he had any hand in it, it must have been during his first profession and before he had seen any good buildings,' and of the interior, 'all entirely of the King James's Gothic'.
V.C.H. *Essex* Vol. 4, p. 225 (with a view dated 1654).
R.C.H.M. *Essex* Vol. 2, p. 222.

Aldenham House, Hertfordshire
Supposedly built by Henry Coghill, the elder, who married Faith Sutton in 1620. He served as High Sheriff 1632 and died 1672.
Date uncertain, probably 1640–60. Originally a 2 storey hipped roof house of 5 bays. Hall panelling (rearranged) influenced by Dietterlin designs.
C.L. Vol. lv, p. 282. Corres. lxxi, p. 189.

Aldermaston Court, Berkshire   (*Burnt 1843*)
Inherited by Sir Humphrey Forster (created a baronet 1630). His property, which was heavily mortgaged to support the King, was sequestered in the Civil War.
A 2 storeyed house with a hipped roof, built of brick with stone quoins. Inscribed: 'Humph:⎱
Ann⎰Forster/Vivimus et Aedificamus uno animo/utrumque: Deo, et Fato consecramus: Anno Dom 1636'.
There was a fine staircase with balustraded pierced panels; based on 'boys' supporting shields, the newels crowned with Jacobean-like figures.
Engraving of exterior from J. P. Neale's *Views of Seats* reproduced in Lees-Milne *Age of Inigo Jones*, pl. 88, p. 200. Staircase in Nash *Mansions of Old England* 3rd Series.
C.L. Vols. vi, p. 240 and xxii, p. 54.

Althorp, Northamptonshire   (*Remodelled*)
Inherited by 2nd Earl of Sunderland, ambassador to Madrid and Paris, a great traveller, politician and collector of pictures (many of which remain in the house). Brother-in-law of 5th Earl, later created 1st Duke of Bedford, the builder of Thorney.
He devoted about 20 years to altering the Elizabethan house from c. 1665–66. In 1669, Duke Cosimo visited the house and left a flattering account of it, describing the refacing as 'after the Italian manner, to which country the Earl was indebted for the model of the design'. The Staircase and Gallery are the main

368. *(right) Albyns, Essex. The South and West Elevations (demolished).*

369. *(below) Amesbury Abbey, Wiltshire. Measured drawing of the house designed by Webb (rebuilt).*

survivors of this period. It is now possible to see how the house was planned at that time, with the Hall separated from the Great Parlour (now part of the Marlborough Room) by the Staircase, which filled the courtyard. On the first floor above the Great Parlour was another great chamber whose proportions have recently been restored. Anthony Ellis paid bills (Clerk of Works?), Joshua Marshall supplied stone and marble work. (Information from Earl Spencer.)

Painting at Althorp. Plate in Kip, Vol I, pl. 27.

C.L. Vols. xlix, p. 714, p. 764, p. 721, p. 771, p. 792; l, p. 14; lxxxiii, p. 293; cxxvii, p. 1122, p. 1186.

Amesbury Abbey, Wiltshire   *(Rebuilt)*

Built about 1661, during the time of William Seymour, Duke of Somerset (1652/54–1670/71), son of Mary Capell, sister of Earl of Essex, and later Duchess of Beaufort. (The dukedom was revived in 1660, but the holder died a few months later and was succeeded by his young grandson.)

370. *Althorp, Northamptonshire: part of a painting showing the house as altered in the 1660s (refaced).*

371. *Arbury Hall, Warwickshire, showing the doorway on the stable range designed by Wren, c. 1674.*

Designed by John Webb, perhaps derived from a design of Inigo Jones.
Plate in *Vitruvius Britannicus*.
Plates and plans in Kent's *Designs of Inigo Jones*.
Measured drawings in R.I.B.A.
Drawing of staircase detail V. & A. 3436–124.
C.L. Vol. xi, p. 272 (present house).

Arbury Hall, Warwickshire   (*Altered*)

Inherited by Sir Richard Newdigate, Bt. (created 1677), who was an M.P., a lawyer with an official practice during the Commonwealth and a private one after; died 1678. He made Arbury over to his son, who carried out the work.

The Chapel was refitted about 1678. This is the date of its ceiling by Edward Martin, who charged £39 for it. The stables, with Dutch gables, built a few years earlier, have a central doorcase designed by Wren, who was a friend of Newdigate. The builder was Martin Bond (family appears at Chesterton).
Wren drawings: *Wren Society*, Vol. XII, pl. xlix.
C.L. Vols. xxi, p. 522; xxxiv, p. 356; cxiv, p. 1126, p. 1210, p. 1414.

Ashburnham Place, Sussex   (*Rebuilt*)

Inherited by John and William Ashburnham. The property had suffered during the Civil War, and at the Restoration the brothers began to restore it. John served as Groom of the Bedchamber to Charles II and was M.P.; he died in 1671. William, the builder of Ashburnham House, Westminster, was also M.P. and Cofferer to the household of Charles II; he died 1679. Succeeded by his great-nephew, John's grandson, born 1655.

As well as building the church, William rebuilt the house 1675–76. Building was superintended by John Plummer, a godson, who was told: 'Remember I care not a pin how it looks from the top of the hill, whether bocht or uniforme.' A brick house with a hipped roof resting on a white wooden cornice.
C.L. Vol. cxiii, p. 1158, p. 1246, p. 1334 (mainly devoted to the later house).

Astley Hall, Lancashire

In 1665, Richard Brooke married Margaret Charnocke, heiress of Astley.

In 1666 they added the south range containing a Great Hall and Long Gallery in a conservative style. A staircase with crude acanthus carving and sumptuous plasterwork, presumably English, leads from the Hall to Drawing Room. A remarkable example of the impact of classicism on so remote a house.
C.L. Vol. lii, p. 14, p. 50, p. 82.

Aston Hall, Warwickshire

Inherited by Sir Thomas Holte (born 1571).
He began the new house in 1618 and completed it in 1635. Very

372. *Aynhoe, Northamptonshire. Drawing dated 1683 showing the Charles II façade.*

ambitious, but conservative in style. A progressive plan with a central entrance hall and no screens passage.
C.L. Vol. cxiv, p. 552, p. 620, p. 694.

Avington Park, Hampshire *(House altered internally)*
Probably acquired by George Brydges about 1680. He came of a West Country family of squires and was a gentleman of the Bedchamber to Charles II.
Brydges may have designed the 13 bay house himself, under the influence of Wren's schemes for Winchester Palace. Imposing doric portico; roof partly disguised by a parapet.
C.L. Vol. lii, p. 882.

Aylesford, The Fryers, Kent *(Partly burnt since C.L. articles and now again a Carthusian priory)*
Acquired by Sir John Banks in 1657. He was an M.P., and amassed a fortune from his financial operations, commerce and landowning. Unusually full records have been quoted in D. C. Coleman's *Sir John Banks, Baronet and Business Man,* 1963.
In 1670s he made considerable alterations to the Carthusian monastic buildings, including a great room, latterly the ballroom. In 1677–79 spent £4,500 on improvements.
C.L. Vol. lv, p. 570, p. 606.

Aynhoe Park, Northamptonshire *(Altered)*
Inherited by John Cartwright from his father, who had acquired it. A man of Parliamentarian sympathy, he married Catherine Noy, daughter of Charles I's Attorney-General. The house was damaged in Civil War. In 1644 Cartwright was discharged by the Committee for the Advance of Money, having already contributed property worth £800 and 'suffered much by the King's forces' — and later obtained compensation from the Earl of Northampton, who was responsible for the damage.
House repaired to the design of Edward Marshall.
Drawing dated 1683 by Fish shows façade. Another dated about 1720 in B.M. Add. MSS 32467.
C.L. Vol. cxiv, p. 42, p. 122, p. 202.

Badminton, Gloucestershire *(Altered)*
Acquired by the Somerset family in 1608. The house was altered by Henry Somerset, Marquess of Worcester (created 1st Duke of Beaufort in 1682). He claimed to have lost £700,000 or £800,000 in Civil War. He married a sister of the Earl of Essex, builder of Cassiobury.

373. *Badminton, Gloucestershire. A detail of Kip's view showing the 1st Duke's façade, c. 1660.*

He rebuilt the centre of the main front soon after the Restoration, copying the Jones-Webb gallery at Somerset House, London. Mr Geoffrey Beard has found payments in the Duke's bank account to craftsmen from 1666 to 1684. These include sums to Grinling Gibbons in 1684.
Kip I, pls. IX, X, XI, XII.
C.L. Vol. lxxxvi, p. 550, p. 574, p. 600, p. 626, p. 630 and Hussey I, p. 161.

Balls Park, Hertfordshire
John Harrison, M.P., knighted in 1640 for advancing £50,000 on account of the subsidies, farmer of sugar customs from 1626 bought the estate in 1637, and built the house about 1640. Visited by Evelyn 1643. Harrison suffered in Civil War, with heavy

374. *Balls Park, Hertfordshire. The Entrance Front, c. 1640.*

375. *Bayhall, Kent. Detail of a painting by Siberechts (demolished).*

fines for delinquency, followed by outlawry for debt, so reducing his wife to destitution. Balls was later sequestered.

A 2 storey brick house with rich stone and ornamental brick details. The overhanging hipped roof is supported on big paired consoles. Dietterlinesque detail on central porch. The interior contains some interesting plasterwork.

C.L. Vol. xxxi, p. 578.

Balmes House, Hackney, Middlesex (Demolished 1852)

Acquired about 1634 by Sir George Whitmore, Lord Mayor of London 1631–32. His sister was Lord Craven's mother. The house probably built about 1635.

An artisan house of a 5 bay cube form, with a huge hipped roof and, most unusual, 2 storeys of dormers. The elevation was faced with a giant order of paired pilasters.

Views by Toussaint in Hackney Public Library, and in B.M. by J. W. Archer. Also *Illustrated London News*, 5 June, 1852.

Priscilla Metcalf, *Architectural Review*, June, 1957.

Bayhall, Kent (Demolished)

Property acquired by Richard Amherst early in the 17th century. His son built the house during the Commonwealth, and completed it about 1664.

An ambitious artisan house with a giant order of pilasters on the entrance front. Perhaps an earlier house was incorporated.

Paintings. One by Siberrechts reproduced C.L. lxi, p. 726; another in Mellon Collection, U.S.A. (Fig. 375).

An 18th-century engraving and photographs taken in 1908 in *Archaeologia Cantiana*, xlii, p. 173.

Bell Hall, Yorkshire

Built *c*. 1680 by Sir John Hewley, Puritan, Royalist, lawyer and M.P. for York.

A 5 bay brick house of 2 storeys with a basement and hipped roof. Some carving by Etty (?) and painted panels in the drawing room.

C.L. Vol. li, p. 820.

Belvoir Castle, Leicestershire (Rebuilt)

Old castle stormed in 1643 and 1645, and in early 1650s the 10th Earl of Rutland considered rebuilding it.

Webb prepared ambitious designs based on the Grand Wilton schemes and visited the site in 1654. His designs were not executed. Engraved in Kent's *Designs of Inigo Jones*. House eventually repaired 1662–68, perhaps to the design of Samuel Marsh.

C.L. Vol. cxx, p. 1284, p. 1402, p. 1456, p. 1500.

Blickling Hall, Norfolk

Acquired in 1616 by Sir Henry Hobart, Lord Chief Justice under James I.

House designed by Robert Lyminge, 1616–28, in a late Jacobean style, with some artisan detail. Like Aston a grand example of the survival of the old manner. One of office wings dated 1624. Gallery ceiling based on plates in Peacham's *Minerva Britannia*. Prideaux Drawings, see *Architectural History*, VII, pls. 6–9.

C.L. Vols. xviii, p. 822; xxvii, p. 673; lxvii, p. 814, p. 902, p. 936; Corres. p. 23, p. 58, p. 157.

Bolsover Castle, Derbyshire (Terrace buildings in ruins)

Little Castle begun in 1613 by Sir Charles Cavendish, brother of the Earl of Devonshire and uncle by marriage of the Earl of Arundel's wife. His son, later Viscount Mansfield and 1st Duke of Newcastle, continued work on the Terrace buildings 1617–20 on a revised plan prepared by John Smythson. He completed the Little Castle between 1620–30 with details altered in the light of John Smythson's visit to London in 1618. Between 1630–34 he added the Riding School range, perhaps to Huntingdon Smythson's design. After the royal entertainment of 1634 he remodelled the Gallery range, of which the double pile axial plan can still be made out, although it is in ruins. The Castle was damaged in the Civil War and repaired between 1662–66. (It will be fully described and illustrated in the volume covering the preceding period.)

C.L. Vols. xvi, p. 198; xlii, p. 132, 156. Tipping: Period III, Vol. I. *Archaeological Journal*, 1961, p. 199.

Boston Manor, Ealing, Middlesex

Inherited in 1598 by Sir William Reade, who died 1621. The house was rebuilt in 1622–23 by his widow, who married as her 2nd husband Sir Edward Spencer. In 1670 the house was acquired by James Clitherow.

An early double pile plan with a cross corridor. A coarse screen of the 1620s survives, but not in its original position. The staircase walls are painted in *trompe l'oeil* to match the balustrade. The Great Chamber on the first floor has a rich ceiling with emblems taken from Galle engravings after Marc Gheeraets. In 1671 Clitherow altered the house, perhaps refacing the front and side elevations, and redecorating some of the rooms.

Two 18th-century views in a grangerised Lysons' *Environs of London* in Guildhall Library.

C.L. Vol. xv, p. 272; cxxxvii, p. 603.

Boughton, Northamptonshire

Inherited in 1683 by Ralph Montagu, the 4th Baron, later created an Earl by William III and Duke of Montagu by Anne. He married firstly Elizabeth Percy, Countess of Northumberland and the heiress of the Earl of Southampton, and secondly Elizabeth, Duchess of Albemarle, daughter of 2nd Duke of Newcastle. He was ambassador to France in 1669–72 and 1678–79. Builder of Montagu House, London.

He began to rebuild old Boughton soon after he inherited, but the exact dates of the work are unknown, as is the designer. The new north front is influenced by French fashion and copied from the engraving of *Profil d'une maison particuliere de Paris* in *Le Petit Marot*: the elevation is of 13 bays, with the centre nine recessed, the ground floor being arcaded. The roof is of mansard form. (Most of the interior decoration dates from the years after 1685 and will be illustrated in the next volume in the series.)

C.L. Vols. xxv, p. 162, p. 198; lxxii, p. 596, p. 626, p. 649; lxxviii, p. 246.

Bradenham Manor, Buckinghamshire

Bought by Sir Edmund Pye in 1642. His daughter, who married Lord Lovelace, probably built the house *c.* 1670.

A 2 storey brick house of 9 bays with a hipped roof. The elevation was extended later, and the interior altered and redecorated.

C.L. Vol. lxxii, p. 154.

Bretby Park, Derbyshire   (*Rebuilt*)

2nd Earl of Chesterfield built the house. Born 1633, inherited the earldom 1656 and died 1714.

Celia Fiennes comments in 1698: 'None of the windows are sashes which in my opinion is the only thing it wants to render it a compleate building.'

Plate in Kip I, pl. XXVI. Painting at Highclere Castle, Hants.

Bridge Place, Kent   (*Destroyed*)

Property acquired in 1638 by Sir Arnold Braems, who built the house. His daughter-in-law sold it in 1704 and the next owner demolished most of it.

A 9 bay house with hipped roof, pilasters, and a central porch with balcony over.

Drawings by Schellink, who stayed there in 1661, in Van den Hem atlas. National Library of Vienna, reproduced in *Walpole Society*, Vol. XXXV, No. 20, 21, Intro.

Broadfield, Hertfordshire   (*Rebuilt* 1882)

Inherited by Arthur Pulter, sometime High Sheriff, who 'shortly after the breaking forth of the late Civil War declin'd all publicke Imployment, liv'd a retir'd life, and thro' the importunity of his wife [a daughter of James, Earl of Marlborough] began to build a very fair house of Brick upon theis Mannor, but dying [1689] he never finished it.' (Chauncey). Completed after his death.

Plate in Chauncey's *History of Hertfordshire*.

Broome Park, Kent

Acquired by Sir Basil Dixwell, M.P., a younger son, who inherited property from an uncle in 1626. He served as Sheriff, was created a baronet in 1637, and died unmarried 1642.

He built the house, 1635–1638, at a cost of £8,000, one of the more ambitious of Charles I's reign. It has elaborate Flemish gables and is an excellent example of early Caroline brick technique.

C.L. Vols. xxii, p. 18; lxxxvi, p. 494.

Brympton D'Evercy, Somerset

Inherited by Sir John Posthumous Sydenham, who married a Poullet of Hinton St George.

The long façade of 10 bays copied from Hinton St George was

376. Brympton D'Evercy, Somerset. The Garden Front, c. 1670.

377. Burford Priory, Oxfordshire. Speaker Lenthall's Chapel, c. 1660.

probably built in the 1670s. Provincial in handling, e.g. the mismanagement of the pediments to the windows, but traditionally attributed to Inigo Jones.

Plate in Kip I, pl. 66.

C.L. Vol. lxi, p. 718, p. 762.

Burford Priory, Oxfordshire

Acquired in 1637 by William Lenthall, M.P. and later Speaker during the Commonwealth.

Soon after 1660, he built the Chapel, partly gothic and partly classical, similar in character to John Jackson's work at Brasenose Chapel 1656–59. It is linked to the house by a gallery.

C.L. Vol. lxxxv, p. 586, p. 616.

Burghley House, Northamptonshire

Inherited by the 5th Earl of Exeter in 1678; died 1700. He married a sister of the 1st Duke of Devonshire, the rebuilder of Chatsworth, and was also a brother-in-law of Viscount Scudamore, the builder of Holme Lacy. He formed a large collection of Italian pictures.

He redecorated much of the Elizabethan house, beginning with the lower rooms in 1680–85 and continuing with the State Rooms from 1687. The decorations were inspired by Charles II's State Rooms at Windsor Castle. Like Boughton, they mostly belong to the succeeding period. The architect employed was Talman. Two payments to Grinling Gibbons in 1683–84, but most of the carving by Jonathan Maine and Thomas Young between 1682 and 1687. Edward Martin, possibly the plasterer. Verrio painted the State Rooms 1689 — .

C.L. Vol. cxiv, p. 1828, p. 1962, p. 2038, p. 2104, p. 2164.

C.L. Annual, 1965.

Callaly Castle, Cumberland

The old seat of the Claverings, probably altered by Robert Trollope about 1675, who applied the crude classical detail. An interesting example of the late advance of classicism in the North.

C.L. Vol. cxxv, p. 304, p. 358.

Cassiobury, Hertfordshire (*Altered in the 19th century and demolished in* 1922)

Inherited by Arthur Capel, son of the 1st Lord Capel, who had inherited it from his mother. The 2nd Lord Capel was created Earl of Essex in 1661 and served as Lord Deputy of Ireland in 1672–76. His sister married the Duke of Beaufort. Involved in the Rye House plot, he was found with his throat cut in 1683.

Hugh May, a kinsman, remodelled the house in 1674–75, retaining one wing of the Elizabethan house to form one side of the H plan. It was remarkable for its oval Entrance Hall, a splendid staircase, now in the Metropolitan Museum, New York, and fine carved woodwork by Gibbons divided between Luton Hoo, the Untermayer Collection, New York and Chicago Art Gallery. The house also contained fine plasterwork admired by Horace Walpole: 'Bagotti's [Bagutti, the 18th-century stuccadore] stucco ceiling bad, & very inferior to several in the house of the time of Charles 2nd.'

Kip I, XXVIII, Britton's *Description of Cassiobury*, 1838.

The Connoisseur, April, 1958.

C.L. Vol. xxviii, p. 392.

Castle Ashby, Northamptonshire

Containing work undertaken by three generations of the Compton family in the 17th century. The remodelling of the Elizabethan house was begun by the 1st Earl of Northampton (created an Earl in 1618). This included the inscription round the parapet. Either

378. Burford Priory. The Chapel doorway. The carvings show The Burning Bush and two angels, and beneath the latter are Latin inscriptions: 'Take off thy shoes, for the ground is holy and 'We shall be saved as by fire'.

379. *Castle Ashby, Northampton-shire. The Forecourt Screen.*

380. *Castle Ashby. The central bay of the Screen.*

381. *Castle Bromwich, Warwickshire. The Porch.*

he or the 2nd Earl, who inherited in 1630 and was killed fighting for the King at Hopton Heath in 1643, was responsible for the West Staircase, carved with hunting scenes and panels of pierced strapwork carving, and the Painted Bower. The gallery front, formerly attributed to Inigo Jones, is almost certainly not by him and may date from after 1660, when the East Staircase with its acanthus balustrade was fitted and some rooms redecorated.
C.L. Vols. lx, p. 422, p. 462, p. 901; lxi, p. 925.

Castle Bromwich Hall, Warwickshire
House bought in 1657 by Sir John Bridgeman, the eldest son of Sir Orlando Bridgeman, the Lord Keeper. He built the rich porch in a style akin to that of St Mary's Church, Oxford. Main work done by his son, also Sir John, who was related to William Winde, and his wife.
A series of 80 letters, discovered by Mr Geoffrey Beard at Weston Park, describe alterations and the furnishing of the house 1685–1700 supervised by Winde. Among the craftsmen employed were Wilcox, who surveyed the house before work began, a joiner named Ayscough, Pierce, who provided chimneypieces, Edward Goudge, who executed plasterwork in 1689, and ten years later Laguerre, who was employed on some decorative painting.
C.L. Vols. xxxii, p. 228; cxi, p. 1408.

Charborough Park, Dorset *(Greatly altered)*
Inherited by Sir Walter Erle, M.P. (died 1665). He rebuilt the house after its predecessor was destroyed in the Civil War.

382. *Chirk Castle, Denbighshire. The Long Gallery, 1677–78.*

383. *Chirk Castle. The end wall of the Long Gallery.*

A cube-like house with a hipped roof, judging by paintings preserved in the house. (One illustrated in John Steegman *The Artist and the Country House.*) Celia Fiennes gives a description, p. 14. C.L. Vol. lxxvii, p. 322.

Chesterton, Warwickshire (*Demolished* 1801)
House begun about 1655 by Edward Peyto, who died in 1658. House completed about 1662.
An ambitious house of 11 bays, 2 storeys, hipped roof, the centre-piece faced with a double order of pilasters or demi-columns and capped with odd arcading (an idea taken from Whitehall Banqueting House).
Thomas Bonde, father and son, were the masons. (Martin Bonde at Arbury in Warwickshire.) Long family connection of Peytos with the Stones, and John Stone and his foreman, Cibber, involved here, so John Stone was perhaps the designer. All that remains is a brick gateway and, also on the property, a windmill and water-mill attributed in the past to Jones.
Drawing B.M. Add. MSS 29264 ff. 189–90, also one in Aylesford collection, Birmingham Central Library, Vol. I, p. 118.
H. M. Colvin, *Architectural Review*, August, 1955.

Chevening, Kent (*Altered*)
Inherited by 13th Lord Dacre in 1616. According to Colin Campbell in *Vitruvius Britannicus*, he built the house which is 'said to have been designed by Inigo Jones.' This would mean it was built before 1630, when Lord Dacre died. In the 1650s John Webb was consulted and in the Chatsworth *Book of Capitals*

there are details of Chevening, presumably for interior decoration, and he mentions 'making ornaments of wainscot' in 1655. A 4 storey house of cube-like form, with a hipped roof and a platform, appears on an estate map of 1679 (Fig. 19). This shows the house with a modillioned cornice in keeping with Inigo Jones's style, while the *Vitruvius Britannicus* plate shows a full entablature. There is no evidence to show that the 1679 house is the 13th Lord Dacre's, but it probably is perhaps he did not finish it and Webb completed it, or perhaps Webb was redecorating part of it. The splendid pine-panelled Saloon is surely his (Fig. 20).
C.L. Vols. xlvii, p. 512, p. 548, p. 586; cxxv, p. 1312; cxxxvi, p. 776.

Chirk Castle, Denbighshire (*Redecorated*)
Purchased in 1595 by Thomas Myddleton, who was Lord Mayor of London 1613–14. The 2nd Bart., Sir Thomas, inherited in 1663, but did not come of age until 1677 and died in 1683. He married first a daughter of Sir Thomas Wilbraham of Weston, and then a daughter of Sir Orlando Bridgeman.
From the *Chirk Castle Accounts*, 1666–1753, by W. M. Myddleton, the restoration of the castle can be followed in some detail from 1668–80. The most important survival of this work is the Long Gallery of 1677–78. The joiner was Jonathan Hooke, who charged £100 15s. for 403 yards of wainscot, and the carver was Dugdale, who also must have worked at Weston, for there is a reference to work done 'in pursuance of agreement made at Weston.' Lady Wilbraham gave her advice about the work: 'a trip

to Weston to get my Lady Wilbraham's direccons about the wainscott in the great room in the bell tower.'
C.L. Vol. cx, p. 896, p. 980, p. 1064, p. 1148, p. 1641.

Chiswick, Sir Stephen Fox's House   (*Demolished*)

Built by Stephen Fox, Paymaster-General to All the Forces, and in 1678 one of the Lords of the Treasury. Rebuilt the church at Fawley in Wiltshire and one of those responsible for the foundation of Chelsea Hospital.
The house was designed by Hugh May in 1685. According to a late 18th-century drawing in a grangerised Lysons' *Environs of London* (in the Guildhall Library), it was a 7 bay house with a 5 bay centrepiece capped by a pediment.

Clifton Hall, Nottinghamshire

House inherited by Sir Gervase Clifton, brother-in-law of Strafford and friend of Wotton.
Apart from a drawing room *c.* 1630, and a fine Restoration ceiling in another room, the most interesting interior is the Pages Room, where the panels are decorated with paintings after Jacob de Gheyn engravings, *c.* 1630.
A plan in Thorpe's book in the Soane Museum; 2 Smythson drawings dated 1632 in R.I.B.A.; an etching by Hollar of the house.
C.L. Vol. liv, p. 246.

384. *Clifton Hall, Nottinghamshire. The Pages Room, c. 1630.*

Cliveden, Buckinghamshire   (*Rebuilt*)

Acquired after 1660 by the 2nd Duke of Buckingham, a member of the Cabal and a prominent courtier. His estates supposed to have been worth £26,000 a year. He died 1687.
A 3 storey house of 9 bays, built about 1670 by William Winde. It was set on a great terrace and, later, colonnades and flanking wings were added. The house appeared to have a low pitched roof set behind a balustrade, and in its outline, looked forward to Thoresby built in the 1680s.
C.L. Vols. xxxii, p. 808, p. 854; lxx, p. 38, p. 68.

Cobham Hall, Kent   (*Altered*)

James, 4th Duke of Lennox, married Lady Mary Villiers, the widow of Lord Charles Herbert. Webb prepared a grand design for the completion of the house, but it was not carried out and the Duke died in 1655. Work was resumed after 1660 by Charles, 6th Duke, who died in 1673 aged 33.
From surviving papers and letters it appears considerable expenditure was made in 1660–62, and work was still continuing in 1667, 1669 and 1672. The ceiling of the Gilt Hall bears the monogram CRL and the date 1662 appears on the building.
Plate of the 6th Duke's house is included in *Vitruvius Britannicus*; Webb's design of 1648 is at Worcester College, Oxford.
Archaeologia Cantiana Vols. XI and XVII.
C.L. Vols. xv, p. 906; xciv, p. 1124; lxxv, p. 619.

Colyton House, Devon   (*Demolished* 1800)

Built for Sir Walter Young, M.P. and Commissioner for Customs, who inherited in 1670 and died in 1731. The house was begun to Hooke's design in 1677 and completed in 1690.
Plate in *Vitruvius Britannicus* and *Walpole Society*, Vol. XXV, pl. 39.

Compton Park, Wiltshire

Seat of the Penruddocks. Work was probably carried out by Thomas Penruddock, aged about 30 in 1660; served as M.P. for Wilton 1688.
House fitted with panelling and carving.
C.L. Vol. xxviii, p. 228; Tipping: Period IV, Vol. I.

Cottestock Manor, Northamptonshire

Built by a Mr Norton. Initials FN and date 1658 appear on the house.
A gabled house with Dutch gable for centrepiece. Not at all advanced for the period.
Gotch, *Old Halls and Manor Houses of Northamptonshire*.

Court of Hill, Shropshire

Inherited by Andrew Hill.
In 1683 he built a 2 storey brick house of 7 bays with a hipped roof. It has a big hall similar to Longnor, but otherwise a simpler house.
C.L. Vol. c, p. 716.

Cranborne Manor, Dorset

Acquired by William Cecil about 1600. He altered the medieval house in 1610–11. There is more work about 1647, when the west wing was rebuilt after damage in the Civil War. This was designed by Captain Ryder, whose name appears at Wilton and is found in the City of London after 1660. Fort was the mason in charge.
C.L. Vol. lv, p. 910, p. 964.

Cromwell House, Highgate, London

Built about 1637–38 by Sir Richard Springnell, Bt. (created in 1641), a Captain of the Trained Bands.
Dietterlinesque detail to centre window of the 7 bay brick front. Interior contains an elaborate staircase with strapwork and carved trophies and figures on the newels, coarser than Ham.
Survey of London Monograph 12.

385. *Eaton Hall, Cheshire. The Charles II house (demolished).*

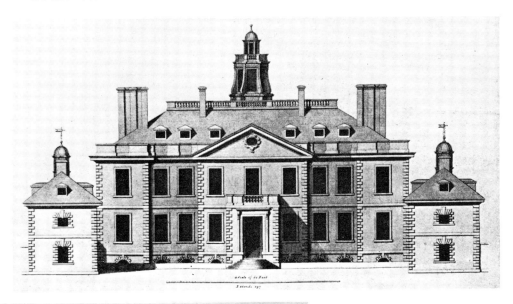

386. *Euston Hall, Suffolk. Detail of a painting showing the house remodelled c. 1666–70 (altered).*

Dingley Hall, Northamptonshire
Sir Edward Griffin inherited in 1680, married a daughter of the Earl of Suffolk, created a baron in 1688. Treasurer of the Chamber to Charles II.
Sir Gyles Isham has suggested that May might have designed the 1684 wing (the year of his death), for May and Griffin were kinsmen. Little decoration of the period survives.
C.L. Vol. xlix, p. 462, p. 494.

Dunster Castle, Somerset
Francis Luttrell inherited in 1670 (probably aged about 12, as he was baptised in 1659). He later served as M.P. and died 1690.
His restoration of the old castle include a fine staircase with an acanthus balustrade and some elaborate ceilings, one dated 1681.
C.L. Vol. xiv, p. 686.

Eaton Hall, Cheshire (*Rebuilt twice in the 19th century. Demolished in 1962*)
Inherited by Sir Thomas Grosvenor, 2nd Bart., who married a London property heiress. M.P. Related to the Myddletons of Chirk.
House designed by Samwell and built 1675–83. According to the plate in *Vitruvius Britannicus* it was a rectangular house, 9 bays by 7, with a Hall and Saloon on axis. The balustraded roof was surmounted by a cupola. The main block was flanked by straight wings forming a deep forecourt.
Kip I, pl. 62.
C.L. Vols. ii, p. 182; ix, p. 496; xlvii, p. 724 (later house).

Elton Hall, Huntingdonshire
House probably acquired by Sir Thomas Proby, M.P. (created a baronet 1661–62) about 1664, perhaps from his wife. His father had been Lord Mayor of London in 1622.
About 1664–66 he added a new wing to the Tudor house. A craftsman of the name of Roe employed for 'drawing a chymny-peice', perhaps the Isaac Rowe known at Lamport and Drayton. Christopher Chapman, mason; Fisher, carpenter.
C.L. Vol. cxxi, p. 334, p. 380, p. 426.

Erthig Park, Denbighshire
Bought by John Edisbury in 1657; the house built by his son, Sir Joshua Edisbury, who was Sheriff in 1682.
Designer was Thomas Webb of Middlewich, who agreed in November, 1683, to 'entertake and perform the care & oversight of the contriving building & finishing of a case or body of a new house . . . according to the designes, compass, manner & methode of draughts already given by the said Thomas Webb.' The house, 85 feet long and 50 feet deep, was originally of 9 bays, and was to cost £678. William Carter, bricklayer; Edward Price, mason; Phillipp Rogers, carpenter. The house was finished about 1686.
C.L. Vols. xxvi, p. 742; lxvii, p. 441, p. 623; lxviii, p. 206, p. 234, p. 718.
Tipping: Period IV, Vol. I.

Euston Hall, Suffolk (*Altered in 18th century, partly burnt in 1902 and since reduced in size*)
Lord Arlington (created a baron, 1665, and an earl, 1672) acquired

the estate in 1666. Secretary of State from 1662. He built Arlington House, London, and also Euston Church in 1675, one of the best country churches of its period.

The house altered between 1666 and 1670, but nothing known of the architect employed, or the craftsmen. Evelyn described it as 'a very noble pile consisting of 4 pavilions after the French.' The low dormers could have been copied from Salomon de Brosse's Château de Blerancourt. Celia Fiennes saw the house in 1698: 'The house is a Roman H of brick, 4 towers with balls on them, the windows are low and not sarshes else the roomes are of a good size and height . . .' Verrio decorated some of the rooms.

A late 17th-century painting at Euston. Prideaux Drawings see *Architectural History*, VII, pls. 28–32.
C.L. Vol. cxxi, p. 58, p. 102, p. 148.

Eye Manor, Herefordshire
Bought in 1673 by Ferdinando Gorges, a Barbados merchant.

He built the house about 1680 (the date appears above the central window on the upper floor of the entrance front). A small 5 bay house, almost square on plan, but remarkable for its interior decoration, which includes decorated ceilings of the highest quality, perhaps by Halbert and Dunsterfield, similar to those at Holme Lacy.
C.L. Vol. cxviii, p. 546.

Fawley Court, Buckinghamshire
Built in 1684–85 for William Freeman, a merchant in the sugar trade. One of the few country houses designed by Wren: a 2 storey house of red brick with stone quoins, and a hipped roof, built on an H plan. It has been much altered internally, but a splendid ceiling remains in the Saloon.
Wren Society, Vol. XVII, pl. 51, plan plate LII.

Felbrigg Hall, Norfolk
Inherited by William Windham, born 1647, died 1689. He stood for Parliament 1679, but was not elected.

A long drawn out scheme to add a new wing to the Elizabethan house. This was designed by Samwell and drawings dated 1674 and 1675 survive. Some fine plasterwork dated 1687 similar to that at Melton Constable survives.
C.L. Vol. lxxvi, p. 666.
Felbrigg, by R. W. Ketton-Cremer (1962).

Forty Hall, Enfield, Middlesex
Built by Sir Nicholas Raynton, 1629–33. Lord Mayor of London, 1632–33. The house was repaired and altered by the Wolstenholmes about 1700 (Fig. 15).

A 3 storey house of advanced character with broad surrounds to windows typical of 1630. Hipped roof probably put on about 1700. Early double pile plan.
See R.C.H.M. *Middlesex*, p. 23 (includes plan).

387 *and* 388. *Eye Manor, Herefordshire. Details of the Drawing Room ceiling.*

389. *Fawley Court, Buckinghamshire. By Wren, 1684–5.*

Four Oaks Hall, Warwickshire (*Demolished* 1936)
Built by William Wilson for Lord Folliott *c*. 1680.
A U shaped house, with L shaped buildings flanking the fore-court, leading up to the entrance front. A 2 storey house with a basement, the front 9 bays wide and side elevations of 7 bays. Dutch gables on both house and stables.
Wren Society: XI, Pl. LXI. Dugdale's *History of Warwickshire*.

The Grange, Alresford, Hampshire (*Altered*)
Acquired by Sir Robert Henley about 1662. At an unknown date and possibly with William Samwell as his architect, he built the house described by Povey, C.B.M. Add. MSS 14296. (.62): 'Neat brick House pleasantly situated ye Seat of being all surrounded with Trees, so yt it cannot be seen till you come close to it, it is so pleasant ye Marquess of Winton preferred it to Abbotstone, it has 11 windows in front 5 garret windows, 2 plain Wings, 3 stories high, no sashes'. It appears that it is encased in Wilkins's neo-classical skin and that the north front was the entrance front. The normal plan of a big hall and saloon on axis appears to have existed. Traces of Caroline decoration remain on the ceiling of the main staircase and in the spinal corridor on the first floor.

Grimsthorpe Castle, Lincolnshire (*Caroline work rebuilt by Vanbrugh*)
Inherited in 1666 by Robert, 3rd Earl of Lindsey. The new north front shown in Kip built in 1685. The Earl's grandmother was daughter of Lord Montagu of Boughton. His wife, Miss Massing-berd, an East India co-heiress (father Treasurer of East India

Co.), died 1655. 2nd wife, Elizabeth Wharton, died 1669; 3rd wife, Elizabeth, Lady Lee.
The Caroline work consisted of 2 wings 2 bays wide and with a recessed centre of 9 bays, divided into three sections 3, 3, 3, central one having a pediment and pilasters.
Kip I, pls. xx, xxi, xxii, xxiii.
C.L. Vols. xiv, p. 272; lv, p. 572, p. 614, p. 650.
Tipping: Period IV, Vol. II.

390. *Felbrigg Hall, Norfolk. Samwell's design for the West Wing, 1674.*

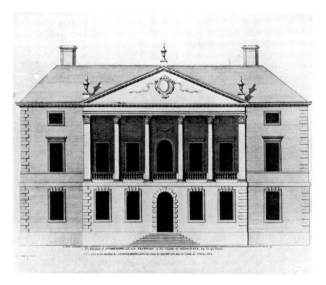

391. *Gunnersbury Park, Middlesex. By Webb, 1658–63 (rebuilt).*

Gunnersbury Park, Middlesex   (*Demolished* 1800)

Built 1658–63 for Sir John Maynard, a successful money-maker in office before and after the Restoration, M.P. and Judge (died 1690).
Designed by Webb; Marshall worked there. Main front was of 7 bays, with a 5 bay centrepiece consisting of a recessed portico on the first floor. Much of the house devoted to a central columned hall off which all the rooms opened, and a similar arrangement on the upper floor. Pratt very critical of the house: [We] 'must by no means proceed to a rash and foolish imitation (of Italian models) without first maturely weighing the conditions of several climes, the different manners of living etc., and the exact dimensions and other circumstances of the building, especially the lights, in all which things the hall and portico at Gunnersbury are very dificient.'
A drawing in Webb's *Book of Capitals* at Chatsworth. One overmantel now at Milton Manor, Berkshire. Plates in *Vitruvius Britannicus.*
C.L. Vol. viii, p. 656 (present house).

Hackwood Park, Hampshire   (*Altered*)

One of the houses of the 1st Duke of Bolton (created 1689).
House begun about 1683. Rainwater heads dated 1687. A Palladian layout of central block, curved links to flanking wings, but the exterior now much altered. Some rich carving in the house, partly from Abbotstone, but now partly removed to Bolton Hall, Yorkshire.
Plan in Bodleian Library, Gough A/34.
C.L. Vol. xxiii, p. 706, p. 742.
Tipping: Period IV, Vol. I.

Hall Barn, Buckinghamshire   (*Altered internally*)

Bought by Waller family in 1624. House probably built in the 1650s to Edmund Waller's own design. He travelled extensively, went to Vicenza with Evelyn, returned 1651. Was an M.P.
A tall brick house of 5 bays, hipped roof, platform and cupola, influenced by Rubens's *Palazzi di Genova*. The 3 storeys are divided by superimposed paired pilasters.
C.L. Vol. xci, p. 564, p. 612, p. 663.

Halnaby Hall, Yorkshire   (*Demolished* 1952)

Bought in 1649 by Mark Milbanke, a Durham alderman. He, or his son, built the house.
A brick and stone house of 3 storeys and 7 bays with stone mullions and a balustraded roof. Not a typical silhouette for such an early date. Extended in the 18th century.
C.L. Vol. lxxiii, p. 334, p. 362.

Highnam Court, Gloucestershire   (*Redecorated*)

Inherited by Colonel William Cooke, M.P. and Sheriff (1663).
The house is supposed to have been built in the late 1650s to replace one burnt in 1642–43 in the Civil War. A 2 storey hipped roofed house with a slightly recessed centre — a design of unusual quality for its date.
C.L. Vol. cvii, p. 1377, p. 1462.

Hinchingbrooke, Huntingdonshire   (*Altered*)

Bought from the Cromwells in 1627 by Sir Sydney Montagu, brother of 1st Lord Montagu of Kimbolton and of 1st Lord Montagu of Boughton. His son, created 1st Earl of Sandwich, helped to bring Charles II back in 1660; was a cousin of Pepys and F.R.S.
Sandwich began to alter house in 1661. All that remains of the work is part of the staircase carved by Kennard, the King's master-joiner, in 1663.
C.L. Vol. lxv, p. 482, p. 514.

Holme Lacey, Herefordshire   (*Exterior altered about* 1820, *interior largely despoiled of its rich decoration*)

Inherited by 2nd Viscount Scudamore in 1671. Died 1694. In 1672 he married Frances, daughter of 4th Earl of Exeter, and so was a brother-in-law of the remodeller of Burghley.
An ambitious house on an H plan (?), perhaps by May. In 1673–74 the mason was Anthony Deane, who also worked at Horseheath. He was told that the principal windows and chimney-stacks 'to be done as Sir John Duncombe's are at Battlesden.' He undertook 'to do all Mason's Carpenters and Bricklayers work, tyling and paving only excepted' for £1,645 14s. 10d. In case of a dispute, Hugh May was to arbitrate. The interior had splendid plasterwork and woodwork, much of it now removed. Some of the

392. *Hall Barn, Buckinghamshire, c.* 1655.

393. *Halnaby Hall, Yorkshire (demolished).*

Gibbons carving now at Kentchurch Court; some in Metropolitan Museum, New York.

C.L. Vol. xxv, p. 870, p. 906.

Plan in R.C.H.M. *Herefordshire*, Vol. 2, shows ceiling patterns.

Honington Hall, Warwickshire

House bought by Sir Henry Parker, an M.P. in 1679 and died 1713. His father died about 1670, but the baronetcy came from his uncle, who died in 1697.

The house, built about 1670, is externally one of the best Charles II manor houses. Of 7 bays with a recessed centre, and hipped roof. The ground floor windows surmounted by busts. Contemporary panelling in one room and another decorated with panels of leather imitating oriental lacquer. Much 18th-century work within and without the house (see Hussey I).

C.L. Vol. xlvii, p. 630, p. 666, p. 694.

394. *Holme Lacy, Herefordshire. The Saloon ceiling.*   395. *Honington Hall, Warwickshire. Leather panels painted to resemble oriental lacquer, late 17th century.*

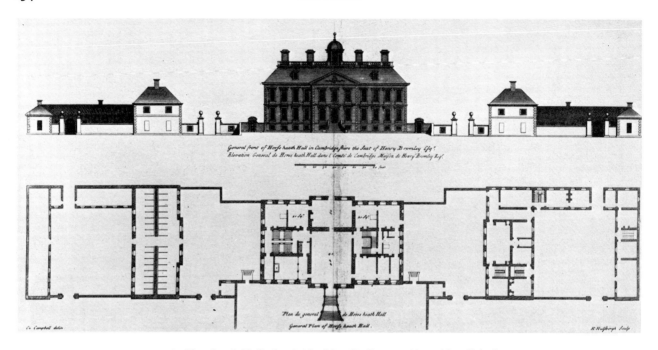

396. Horseheath Hall, Cambridgeshire. By Pratt, 1663–5 (demolished).

Horseheath Hall, Cambridgeshire   (*Demolished*)
Inherited by 3rd Lord Alington, M.P., Lord Lieutenant. House
sold 1687.
House built in 1663–65 to Pratt's design. An ambitious plan
140 × 76 feet and 44 feet high.
Plates and plan in *Vitruvius Britannicus* (where it is attributed to
Webb and dated 1669).
See Gunther, *Architecture of Sir Roger Pratt*.
Cambridge Antiquarian Society, XLI, 1941.

Houghton Conquest House, Bedfordshire   (*In ruins*)
In 1615, James I granted it to Mary, Dowager Countess of
Pembroke, a sister of Philip Sidney and mother of the 3rd and 4th
Earls of Pembroke. She built the house 1615–21.
A house of late Jacobean type, but possessing advanced features
that might be attributed to Jones, particularly a double-storeyed
loggia. According to Aubrey: 'The architects were sent for from
Italy. It is built according to the description of Basileus's house
in the first booke of the *Arcadia*.' Horace Walpole said that some
say 'that the two best fronts were improved by Inigo Jones.' A
panelled room believed to have come from the house (Figs. 8A and
8B) is now at The Victoria and Albert (see *The Haynes Grange
Room*, 1935) and the staircase is at the Swan Inn, Bedford.
Drawing of house *c*. 1785 at Woburn Abbey, reproduced in *The
Haynes Grange Room*.

Huntercombe Manor, Buckinghamshire
George Evelyn bought the medieval house in 1656–57 and died a
year later. His son and namesake, a kinsman of the diarist, altered
it in the 1670s. Died 1699.
The Caroline interest mainly lies in the interiors, where some of
the panelled rooms have painted ceilings set in rich plaster surrounds. Some of the painting perhaps by Verrio.
C.L. Vol. cv, p. 1310, p. 1374, p. 1438.

Hutton-in-the-Forest, Cumberland
In 1606, pele tower with additions bought by Richard Fletcher,
son of a Cockermouth merchant. His son, Sir Henry, added the
Long Gallery about 1640. His grandson, Sir George Fletcher,

High Sheriff and M.P. erected a new front *c*. 1675, designed by
Edward Addison. An interesting northern stone-built version of
a town-house façade of 5 bays and 3 storeys. Little remains of this
period inside the house, except for richly carved panels of Sir
George's staircase re-used in the 19th century.
Kip I.
C.L. Vols. xxi, p. 18; cxxxvii, p. 232, p. 286, p. 352.

Kew, The Dutch House, Surrey
Built by Samuel Fortrey, a Flemish merchant, in 1631.
A 3 storeyed cube of 70 feet by 50 feet, with a 7 bay front rising
to elaborate gables. Crowning range of chimneys as at St Clere.
Transitional plan with a cross corridor. An early example of
Flemish bond, with interesting use of cut and rubbed brick. Simple
panelling within (Fig. 12).
John Charlton, *Kew Palace*. Ministry of Works Guide.
C.L. Vol. lxvii, p. 532.

Kingston Lacy, Dorset   (*Altered*)
Sir John Bankes, Chief Justice of Common Pleas, acquired Corfe
Castle. After its destruction in the Civil War, his son, Sir Ralph,
built Kingston Lacy. It was designed by Pratt in 1663 (Fig. 27).
Originally a brick house with stone quoins, etc., it was cased in
Caen stone by Barry. Interior also altered in 19th century.
Notes on house in Gunther's *Architecture of Sir Roger Pratt*.
C.L. Vol. xv, p. 558.

Kirby Hall, Northamptonshire   (*In ruins*)
Sir Christopher Hatton purchased the incomplete house in 1575.
His namesake, Christopher Hatton III, son of his godson, a man
of letters, altered the house about 1638. Controller of the Household to the court in exile. Died 1670.
Alterations carried out by Nicholas Stone and probably designed
by Inigo Jones. The north front was remodelled, and the fenestration on the inside of the range altered. The window above the
hall door inserted and the hall redecorated. House decayed in the
19th century.
C.L. Vol. xx, p. 558.
Ministry of Works Guide to Kirby Hall by C. H. Chettler (1955).

397. *Hutton-in-the-Forest, Cumberland. The East Front by Edward Addison, c. 1675.*   398. *A detail of the staircase, c. 1675.*

Ledston Hall, Yorkshire

Acquired by Thomas Wentworth, Earl of Strafford, about 1617. Sold by his son in 1653 to Sir John Lewis, an East India merchant. Strafford began to alter the medieval and Tudor quadrangular house by adding the south-west wing to one side as a start to forming a new entrance front. It is uncertain whether he or Lewis built the balancing wing, but he was probably responsible for the Dutch gables. Lewis extended the façade. The result is an unusually ambitious façade for its date. The best interior is the Dining Room.

C.L. Vols. xxi, p. 942; lxxxiv, p. 556, p. 580.

Lees Court, Kent   (*Interior burnt* 1910 *and rebuilt*)

Acquired about 1600 by the Sondes family. Sir George Sondes, the builder of the house, a supporter of Charles I, a K.B., M.P., married a daughter of a rich London merchant and Lord Mayor of London. Heavily fined and lost much property in the Civil War. Created Earl of Feversham 1676. Despite these losses he is supposed to have built the house c. 1650, perhaps about 1655–56, when he married Mary, daughter of Sir William Villiers.

It is not by Jones, as Hastead would have it, and is more likely to be by a London artisan builder. An unusual big façade with giant pilasters and far overhanging roof. Badeslade, c. 1719, shows a balustrade roof. Possibly the intended design never carried out because of the war. The centre of house, filled by a 2 storey hall modelled on Queen's House, with some joinery, apparently similar to details at Thorpe, was destroyed by the fire (Figs. 21 and 22).

C.L. Vol. lii, p. 178, p. 210.

Lindridge, Devon

House probably rebuilt about 1673 for Sir Peter Lear (created 1660), who bought the house after the Restoration. He may have been a Barbados merchant. Died 1684.

The main room is a 2 storey saloon. In other rooms overmantels and doorcases of artisan type. The good plasterwork is probably by local men, perhaps by the Abbotts of Barnstaple.

C.L. Vol. lxxxiv, p. 356, p. 378.

399. *Ledston Hall, Yorkshire. A marble niche in the Dining Room.*

400. *Lodge Park, Gloucestershire*, c. 1655.

401. *Milton Manor, Berkshire. The central block*, c. 1680.

Lodge Park, Gloucestershire

Built for a member of the Dutton family about 1655, as a hunting box for Sherborne, Glos.

A 2 storey pavilion of 5 bays, with a 3 bay projecting portico with big balcony above. Richly detailed façade. Perhaps by Valentine Strong.

Plate in C.L. Vol. cxxxiv, p. 739.

Melton Constable, Norfolk

Old house, partly destroyed in the Civil War, inherited by Jacob Astley, aged 19. He served for 44 years as M.P. and died in 1728.

New house built 1664–70 (?) and designed by Astley (?). Nothing definite known about this fine house. A model of the house, not quite as executed, survives. The interior was altered later, but there is some elaborate plasterwork dated 1683 and some 1687, similar to that at Felbrigg and Hintlesham (Fig. 34).

Kip I, pl. 51.

Prideaux Drawings, *Architectural History* VII, pl. 58.

C.L. Vol. lxiv, p. 364, p. 402.

Milton Manor, Berkshire   (*Extended in 18th century*)

Inherited by Paul Calton, who held it from 1664–88, and built the house about 1680.

A 3 storeyed, hipped roofed house of Dutch or Rubens-like outline. The front has odd giant pilasters with brooches, unusual at that late date, but similar to those at the College of Heralds. A screens passage and hall off it. A joiner's version of an Italian staircase. Best piece of contemporary decoration is an overmantel from Gunnersbury.

C.L. Vol. civ, p. 1274, p. 1330.

Moresby Hall, Cumberland

Belonged to a younger branch of Fletchers of Hutton-in-the-Forest.

402. *Moulton Hall,*
Yorkshire, c. 1654–60.

An interesting provincial building of about 1675. A heavily rusticated façade of 7 bays and 2½ storeys, with alternating pediments to first floor in windows and solid parapet to the ridge roof. Plate in Belcher and Macartney, *Later Renaissance Architecture in England*, 1901.

Moulton Manor and Moulton Hall, Yorkshire
Two houses in the same village, which belonged to the same family in the 17th century. The Elizabethan Manor, built by Leonard Smithson about 1575, was altered by a later Smithson about 1650. Crude classical detail, including pediments to the windows and a roof balustrade applied to the Elizabethan fabric. Moulton Hall was probably built by George Smithson about 1654–60 on a double pile plan with a spine wall carrying the chimneys. The façades are richly treated with Dutch gables (of no structural purpose on the principal front), pediments to the windows, and unusual fish-scale masonry formed by alternate courses of rusticated and plain masonry. Internally the main feature is a richly carved acanthus staircase. These two houses illustrate the coming of classicism to the remote north.
C.L. Vol. lxxix, p. 250.

Moyles Court, Hampshire
Built by John Lisle or his widow in the 1650s or 1660s.
A hipped roofed manor house. According to a plate in the *Gentleman's Magazine* 1828, p. 17, the present front had gables and a long range at the back, demolished in 1818–28.
C.L. Vols. xi, p. 232; xxvi, p. 876.
Tipping: Period IV, Vol. 1.

New Hall, Boreham, Essex (*Mostly demolished* 1737. *Only Tudor remains*)
The 1st Duke of Buckingham bought the vast Tudor mansion from the Earl of Sussex. In 1622–23, alterations were carried out

by Inigo Jones, but he was superseded by Gerbier, who was the Duke's man. The house later belonged to Monck and he was visited by Grand Duke Cosimo of Tuscany.
Three Jones drawings for features in the R.I.B.A.

Nottingham Castle (*Destroyed by fire in* 1831 *and rebuilt as a museum in* 1868)
In 1674 the 1st Duke of Newcastle (*see* Bolsover) acquired the site. Built 1674–79 by Samuel Marsh, but its unusual design probably by the Duke himself under the influence of the Capitoline Palace, Rome, and the plates in *Palazzi di Genova*. The result is a curious mixture of a progressive silhouette anticipating Thoresby and Chatsworth, with ponderous outdated detail. The total cost was about £14,000. The Duke died before it was finished, but he left funds for its completion according to the model in his will.
The model kept at the Castle may be this original model, but adapted and painted after the fire of 1831 to show the damage done by rioters. As well as this, there is a Hawksmoor sketch at the R.I.B.A. and a 19th-century drawing in the V. & A. (Fig. 32).

Powis Castle, Montgomeryshire
Bought by the Herberts in 1587. Stormed in 1644 by Sir Thomas Myddleton of Chirk. Restored by 3rd Lord Powis, later created Earl and Marquess, who inherited in 1667. Suspected of being involved in Oates Plot and sent to the Tower in 1678, but returned to favour under James II. He went into exile in 1688, leaving castle empty till it was regranted in 1696 to Lord Rochford. Lord Powis was the son of Lord Craven's sister, and married to the Duke of Beaufort's sister (Fig. 39).
The most important parts of his restoration of the castle are the State Bedroom, c. 1668–70, and the Grand Staircase. The detail of the bedroom is distinctly provincial, but the staircase is of fine quality, with a ceiling attributed to Verrio (after 1674 as it bears

the Earl's coronet) based on the *Triumph of Venice* by Veronese. (Walls painted *c.* 1705 for Lord Rochford.)
C.L. Vols. xli, p. 108, p. 132; lxxix, p. 564, p. 598, p. 624, p. 652.

Ragley Hall, Warwickshire *(Decorated in the 18th century and exterior altered by James Wyatt)*
Bought by the Conways in 1591, a family rising through office in the 17th century. The 1st Viscount considered rebuilding it in 1628, but nothing was done till 3rd Viscount (and 1st Earl), who served as a Secretary of State to Charles II, began work in 1677.
He had advice from Robert Hooke, who refers to it in diary in 1678, 79 and 80. The building supervised by Mr Holbert (probably William Hurlbut or Hulbert), a local man, according to Hooke 'a carpenter but a Pap.' The house is one of the most ambitious of the reign, consisting of a central block with 4 pavilions. Axial plan with a 2 storeyed hall on the *piano nobile*. The house was unfinished when Conway died in 1683 and remained a shell till 1750s (Fig. 29).
Kip I, pl. 71.
Hooke drawings B.M. Add. MSS 5238 no. 60 (elevation): 31323 W.3. plan by Gibbs.
C.L. Vols. lv, p. 438, p. 476, p. 505; cxxiii, p. 938, p. 1006.

Ribston Hall, Yorkshire
The Goodrickes acquired the house 1545. Sir Henry, a supporter of William III, built it in 1674.

Kip shows a 2 storey front of 15 bays. The interior was redecorated and only one overmantel of the period survives.
Kip I, pl. 61.
C.L. Vol. xix, p. 198.

Ryston Hall, Norfolk *(Altered beyond recognition by Soane)*
Inherited in 1667 by Roger Pratt, the first architectural knight, from his cousin, Edward Pratt.
He rebuilt the house in 1668–72 as a 3 storey pavilion capped with a semi-circular pediment and cupola, flanked by lower wings of 3 bays, with dormers in their hipped roofs. He used a double pile plan with hall and saloon on axis.
Full details, plan and painting (Fig. 24) in Gunther *The Architecture of Sir Roger Pratt*.

Shavington Hall, Shropshire *(Demolished 1959)*
Inherited 1668 by 6th Viscount Kilmorey (1659–87).
A large plain house, finished 1685. Contained a big hall 70 feet long and 30 feet high, with a narrow gallery behind. Not usual plan for the date. Little of the original decoration survived at the time of demolition.
C.L. Vol. xliv, p. 92, p. 112.
Tipping: Period IV, Vol. I.

Sprotborough Hall, Yorkshire *(Demolished 1925)*
Inherited by Sir Godfrey Copley, 2nd Bart. who married an heiress in 1681. An M.P., travelled abroad 1685, F.R.S. 1691.

403. *Powis Castle, Montgomeryshire. The State Bedroom,* c. 1668–70.

404. *St Giles's House, Dorset*, 1650–1.

405. *St Clere, Kent*, c. 1630.

The house built 1685–90. Copley's travels account for French look of the house. Painted decorations by Henry Cooke, but only one ceiling left in the 1920s.

Kip I, pl. 56.
C.L. Vol. li, p. 174.

Squerries Court, Kent

Built in 1681 by Sir Nicholas Crisp, a grandson of a Guinea merchant who had financed Charles I and Charles II. Squerries came to him from his mother. He married in 1674, died 1698. The house was sold 1700.

A 7 bay, 2 storey house, with a central pediment and hipped roof, in the Eltham tradition. Interior redecorated.

St Clere, Kent   (*Redecorated*)

Bought and built by Sir John Sidley, Bt.

An early double pile house, c. 1630. Of 3 storeys and 5 bays, originally with a hipped roof. At the corners of the house polygonal turrets. The roof is crowned with a central range of chimneys as at Kew. Broad window surrounds as at Forty Hall.

C.L. Vol. cxxxi, p. 450, p. 518.

St Giles's House, Dorset   (*Redecorated*)

Inherited by Anthony Ashley-Cooper, when a minor. Created a baron at the Restoration and Earl of Shaftesbury, 1672. His 2nd wife, whom he married in 1650, was a daughter of the 3rd Earl of Exeter.

The house dates from about this time, for the foundation stone was laid 19th March, 1650/51. The first classical house in Dorset, but built on the foundations of the old quadrangular house. Designer not known. Within, all that remains are a few chimney-pieces and a couple of ceilings.

C.L. Vol. xciv, p. 464, p. 508, p. 552.

Stapleford Park, Leicestershire

Two periods of work in the 17th century. First was the restoration of Lady Abigail Sherard's 15th-century wing in 1633 by the 1st Lord Sherard of Leitrim. He gave it Holborn gables.

About 1670, the 2nd Lord, who was also an M.P., made considerable additions to form an H shaped house, building 3 new ranges and also the centre block. The interior contains some interesting panelling (perhaps indebted to French engravings) and good carving, some of it similar to that at Thrumpton and other parts to work at Belton.

C.L. Vols. xxiii, p. 270; lvi, p. 228.

Staunton Harold Hall, Leicestershire   (*Greatly altered*)

Inherited in 1669 by the second son of Sir Robert Shirley, who built the church 1653, later created Earl Ferrers.

He began to rebuild the old house. Saloon of his time, corresponding to right hand half of entrance front, has a fine ceiling, plasterwork and inset paintings. A garden gate (1681) copied from a plate in Vignola of a gate by Michelangelo for the Duke of Sforza.

Kip I, pl. 43.
C.L. Vols. xxxiii, p. 490, p. 526; cvii, p. 516.

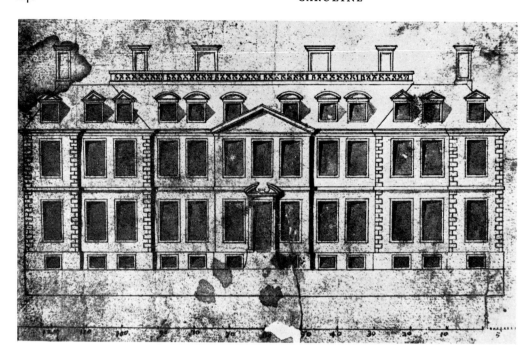

406. *Stowe, Buckinghamshire. Design for the North Elevation, c. 1680 (altered).*

Stowe, Buckinghamshire (*Altered beyond recognition*)
Acquired by John Temple about 1591. His grandson, Sir Richard Temple, began the house about 1672; was M.P., died 1697. In 1683 consulted Wren about gardens (see Mr John Harris's letter C.L. Vol. cxxx, p. 254). For the original appearance of 13 bays see C.L. Vol. cxxii, p. 68.

Stowe, Cornwall (*Demolished c. 1720*)
Inherited by John Grenville, 1st Earl of Bath, Lord Lieutenant of Cornwall and office holder.
Built house about 1680, an ambitious building copied from Clarendon House with a façade of 11 bays and wings 7 bays deep. Fragments are scattered; carvings by Michael Clarke from the chapel now in Stowe School chapel; the staircase supposed to be at Cross near Great Torrington in Devon; a room in the town hall at South Molton, and other fragments at Prideaux Place, Cornwall. *Architectural History*, VII, pls. 101 and 102.

Stratfield Saye, Hampshire
Property acquired in lieu of debts between 1620 and 1629 by Sir William Pitt, Comptroller of James I's Household.
About 1630 he rebuilt house with an ambitious 15 bay façade that

407. *Stowe, Cornwall. Drawing of the house c. 1720 by Edmund Prideaux (demolished).*

has gables on the end wings. Above bay windows (now removed) on first floor there are niches flanked by pilasters. House now stuccoed. Original plan was a double pile house with a corridor, but little remains of the period except for two staircases and fragments of wall painting.

C.L. Vol. civ, p. 1050, p. 1106, p. 1162, p. 1218.

Swakeleys, Middlesex

Bought in 1629 by Edmund Wright, an alderman of London, who was Lord Mayor in 1640. Died 1643.

He built the house 1629–38 on an H shaped plan with double pile centre, but with a great hall and screens passage. The exterior has elaborate gables and coarse ornamental brickwork. During the Commonwealth Sir James Harrington made alterations and, according to Pepys, added the screen. In 1665, Sir Robert Vyner bought the house and had the staircase ceiling and walls painted, probably by a follower of Verrio (Fig. 14).

Survey of London 13th Monograph. R.C.H.M., *Middlesex.*

C.L. Vol. lxi, p. 61.

Thoresby Hall, Nottinghamshire (*Rebuilt*)

William, 4th Earl of Kingston, born 1662, succeeded his brother in 1682, married 1684 and died 1690. Lord Lieutenant.

House began about 1683 to Talman's design and in progress 1686–87 as Cibber and Laguerre mentioned in the accounts. One of the first baroque houses with a silhouette based on the Capitoline Palace, Rome, but with a courtyard plan. Typical of a Talman plan. Exciting use of internal space. Early use of sash windows. Drawing of ½ façade at All Souls College, Oxford.

Plate in *Vitruvius Britannicus.*

Painting now in the possession of the Ministry of Works.

Architectural History, Vol. 4 (1961) and Vol. 6 (1963), by John Harris.

Thorney Abbey House, Cambridgeshire

The house was added to an older one by the 5th Earl (later 1st Duke) of Bedford. Built for use in connection with the Thorney estate and not as a family seat. He knew Thurloe of Wisbech Castle through fen drainage schemes.

The new work built by William Lovin of Peterborough under the influence of Thorpe. The contract, dated 1660, is published in

409. *Thorney Abbey House, Cambridgeshire, 1660–62.*

408. *Thrumpton Hall, Nottinghamshire. The Staircase.*

Family Background, by Gladys Scott-Thomson. It was agreed that a house 42 feet × 38 feet was to be finished by 1662 for £420, Lovin 'to make and perform all such carpenters' masons' slaters' smiths' plumbers' and Glaziers' work as shall in any way be necessary.'

C.L. Vol. xlvi, p. 392.

Tipping: Period IV, Vol. I.

Thrumpton Hall, Nottinghamshire

Begun by Gervase Pigot, 1609 and completed 1616–17. Gervase Pigot II altered house soon after the Restoration. Served as High Sheriff 1669, but died that year.

Elaborate grand staircase with pierced acanthus carving and finer woodwork in Saloon and Oak Room, where the carving could be by the carver who worked at Stapleford and in the chapel at Belton.

C.L. Vol. cxxv, p. 1138, p. 1194, p. 1254.

Tredegar, Monmouthshire

Inherited by Sir Thomas Morgan, and house probably built by his son, Sir William, who inherited 1664. He married an heiress and was an M.P.

Elaborate 2 storey house retaining original glazing and stone mullions. The interior, which may have been completed by 1674, contains rich, but un-refined carved woodwork. A complete house of the day, now a convent.

C.L. Vol. xxiv, p. 792, p. 838.

Tregothnan, Cornwall (*Greatly altered*)

Inherited by Hugh Boscawen, Sheriff of Cornwall, 1635, and M.P., who built a 5 bay, hipped roof house *c*. 1650.

Celia Fiennes described the house 1698: 'A large high hall and so to a passage that leads you right up a good staircase; on the right side is a large common parlour for constant eating in, from whence goes a little roome for smoking that was a back way into the roome wainscoted all very well, but plaine, the great parlour is

410. *Tring Manor House, Hertfordshire. By Wren, 1669–71 (rebuilt).*

Cedar, out of that is the drawing roome, which is hung with pictures of the family . . . .'
18th-century drawing and plan, Hussey: Vol. III.
C.L. Vol. cxix, p. 1051, p. 1112.

Tring Manor House, Hertfordshire (Rebuilt)

Built by Henry Guy, M.P., a lawyer and close companion of Charles II. His first office was Cupbearer to Queen Catherine. Later Groom of the Bedchamber to Charles and from 1679 Secretary of the Treasury. Died 1710. Tring was granted to him in 1669 on the death of Henrietta Maria. He sold the house in 1702.
Built 1669–71 to designs of Wren. A front of 9 bays with niches and awkward central window.
Plan of a similar house at All Souls. Plate by John Oliver in Chauncey's *Hertfordshire* and in Wren Society, XIX, pl. LXXIII.

Tythrop House, Buckinghamshire

House probably built by James Herbert, 6th son of the 4th Earl of Pembroke, and Jane Spiller, grand-daughter of Henry Spiller. The Spillers had acquired the property in 1619. Herbert died 1676. (A Henry Spiller [Jane's grandfather?] had served with Jones on the commission of New Buildings for London.)
House apparently of 9 bays and 2 storeys, with a hipped roof and a projecting central bay on garden side. Mr John Harris has suggested it may be a Webb house. Best internal feature is a superb carved acanthus balustrade to the main staircase.
C.L. Vol. xv, p. 306.

Uffington House, Lincolnshire (Burnt 1904)

Built for Charles Bertie, 5th son of the 2nd Earl of Lindsey. He bought Uffington 1673.
An oblong house of 9 bays and 2 storeys, with a high hipped roof crowned by a balustrade, in design somewhat similar to Walcot Hall. The staircase was decorated by Verrio. House designed in 1675 by a Mr Grant: 'Paid to Mr Grant, Surveyor, for making a plan of Uffington House and surveying several parcels of land adjoining to it £4. 2s. 6d.'. Preparations for building begun in 1681 and work largely done in 1686 and 87. In August '87 Bertie wrote: 'The house which I am now building "in the after-

noon of my age" you must not call a fine house: but I hope it will be big enough for a younger brother's family.'
A History of the Parish of Uffington with Casewick by F. E. d'A. Willis.
C.L. Vol. xvi, p. 992.

The Vyne, Hampshire

Bought 1653 by Chaloner Chute, M.P. (died 1659) from the Sandys family. In 1649 he had married the widow of the 13th Lord Dacre of Chevening. A successful lawyer and Speaker of the Commons in interval before Charles II's return.
His alterations probably designed by Webb. They include the portico with stone columns and wooden pediment, erected by Edward Marshall. Contract for portico, battlements and other alterations 4th March, 1654/55, survives. Memoranda and receipts of payments, 1655–57. Some chimneypieces and a garden house are the main survivals. Much altered by John Chute in the 18th century (Fig. 17).
C.L. Vols. xlix, p. 582, p. 612, p. 642, p. 619, p. 649; cxxi, p. 16

Walcot Hall, Northamptonshire

Bought about 1674 by Sir Hugh Cholmley, former Governor of Tangier and builder of the Mole there. He married in 1666 Lady Anne Compton, daughter of the Earl of Northampton.
He built the 2 storeyed house, 9 bays by 5. Dated 1678 on two rainwater heads.

Warwick Castle

Granted in 1604 by James I to Fulke Greville, a cousin of Philip Sidney, who spent £20,000 on it. He was succeeded by a cousin, Robert Greville, who married a daughter of Francis, Earl of Bedford, and was killed 1643. His younger son, who died 1676, restored the castle and created the range of state rooms.
Red Room, Cedar Room (with later gilded enrichments), Green Room, State Bedroom and Boudoir decorated at this period. Cedar Room and Boudoir have good ceilings.
C.L. Vols. i, p. 112, p. 126; xxx, p. 792, p. 842.

Weston Park, Staffordshire (Redecorated)

Belonged to Elizabeth Mytton, who married in 1651 at the age of 20, Sir Thomas Wilbraham of Woodhey, Cheshire. She owned a

411. *Tythrop House, Buckinghamshire. The Staircase.*

412. *Walcot Hall, Northamptonshire, c. 1678.*

413. *Uffington House, Lincolnshire. Designed 1675 and built 1681-7 (burnt).*

414. *Weston Park, Staffordshire*, c. 1671.

copy of the 1st English translation of Palladio and also a 2nd
edition of Le Muet. More references to Woodhey's costs than to
Weston. (Woodhey demolished 1730, views in Rylands Library,
Manchester, Roundell MSS 1288/28.)
She built the present garden front c. 1671, an ambitious stone and
brick elevation of 11 bays and 3 storeys. Like Raynham and
Sudbury, the work of an amateur.
C.L. Vol. xcviii, p. 818, p. 864, p. 910.

Westwood Park, Worcestershire
About 1660, Sir John Packington (died 1680) added the diagonal
wings to the Jacobean hunting lodge in the same style. He paid
for work probably out of £4,000 compensation from the King for
the destruction of his Buckinghamshire seat in the Civil War. The
interior contains some rich plasterwork.
Kip I, pl. 65.
C.L. Vols. lxiii, p. 166; lxiv, p. 50, p. 94.

West Woodhay, Berkshire   (*Altered* 1881)
Bought in 1634 by Sir Benjamin Rudyerd, surveyor of the Court
of Wards, 1618–47; M.P. He died in 1658 and his son in 1661.
House built in 1635. Of H form, of 2 storeys and 7 bays, with
rubbed quoins, and a hipped roof.

Whitmore Hall, Staffordshire
Inherited by Edward Mainwaring III, who built the stables c.
1640 (died 1647). His son and namesake (1603–75), M.P., re-
fronted the house c. 1670. (The porch altered in the 19th century,
but still bears the date 1676.) The design is an interesting reaction
to an imposing new house like Weston.
C.L. Vol. cxxi, p. 1144.

Wimpole Hall, Cambridge   (*Altered*)
Inherited by Thomas Chicheley, M.P., Royalist and Master of the
Ordnance after the Restoration.
At the centre of the long front still stands Chicheley's house of
about 1632, of 7 bays, with a hipped roof. An early double pile plan.
Kip I, XXXII.
C.L. Vols. xxiii, p. 234; lxi, p. 806, p. 844.

Wisbech Castle, Cambridge   (*Demolished* 1816)
Built about 1658 for John Thurloe, who acquired it in the Civil
War and lost it at the Restoration, when it reverted to the Bishop
of Ely. He was Cromwell's Secretary of State and had been to
Holland with Oliver St John as his Secretary.
Colvin (C.L., cxi, p. 1732) suggested that it was so close in
design to Thorpe that it might be by Mills. One of the houses
influenced by *Palazzi di Genova*.
Drawing in the Wisbech Museum. (See Fig. 16.)

Woburn Abbey, Bedfordshire
Inherited by 4th Earl of Bedford in 1626, died 1641.
He did a certain amount of rebuilding, of which the chief remnant
is his grotto-hall, perhaps by de Caus, a unique survival. There is
also some post-Restoration plasterwork, probably done in the 5th
Earl's time (Fig. 10).
G. Scott-Thomson, *Life in a Noble Household*.
C.L. Vols. cxvii, p. 854, p. 866, p. 977; cxviii, p. 434, p. 488.

Wolseley Hall, Staffordshire   (*Rebuilt and derelict*)
Inherited in 1646 by Sir Charles Wolseley, 2nd Bart., a Cromwellian supporter and M.P. Married Anne Fiennes, and so a
connection of Celia Fiennes, the diarist. He restored the house in
the Restoration period. The staircase and panelled parlour by
Pierce from his house, incorporated in a later building.
According to Celia Fiennes (p. 165) . . . 'the house is old timber
building only a large parlour and noble staircase with handsome
chambers Sir Charles has new built'.
C.L. Vol. xxvii, p. 234.

Yotes Court, Kent
Bought in 1650–51 by James Master, son of a London merchant.
He built the house in 1658, adding 3 wings round part of a Tudor
house to form an H shaped plan, with a double pile spine. The
new wings have hipped roofs, broad quoins and surrounds to the
windows, a number of them of the original casement design. The
interior has been redecorated, and all that survives is the original
staircase.
C.L. Vol. cxxxv, 1580, 1648.

THE PRINCIPAL ARCHITECTS

Inigo Jones (?1573–1652). Masque designer and architect. Little is known of his youth and upbringing, except that his father was a clothworker in the parish of St Bartholomew the Great, London. Webb and Vertue say that his first patron was William, 3rd Earl of Pembroke, who succeeded in 1601. There is some uncertainty about his early travels, but he may have gone to Italy about 1597, and later to Denmark with the Earl of Rutland. In 1605 he staged his first masque (others not listed here) the *Queen's Masque of Blacknesse* at Oxford. He possibly visited Rome that year and in 1607.

1606 earliest reference to his work as an architect in the dedication of a book
1609 sent to France as a King's Messenger
1610 earliest known, but unidentified, work at Hatfield House
1611 appointed Surveyor to Prince of Wales, who died in November, 1612
1612–13 left on his final European journey with the Earl and Countess of Arundel
1615 returned and was soon appointed Surveyor-General of the King's Works and Buildings in succession to Simon Basill
1615–17 work on Lord Arundel's houses at Greenwich and the Strand
1616 earliest dated architectural drawing
1616–23 engaged on the Prince's Lodging at Newmarket
1616–17 engaged on Oatlands Palace
1616 began the Queen's House at Greenwich (halted in 1618)
1617 some connection with Holyrood
1618 worked for the Duke of Buckingham at Whitehall
1619 designed the Queen's hearse
1619–22 designed the Banqueting House, Whitehall
1621 designed a gateway at Chelsea House for Lionel Cranfield
1622 worked for the Duke of Buckingham at New Hall, Essex
1623–24 worked at Theobalds for the King
1623–26 designed and built the Queen's Chapel (Marlborough House)
1625 designed James I's hearse
1629–35 resumed work on and completed the Queen's House and about the same time probably designed the pavilions at Stoke Park
1631–38 concerned with the layout of Covent Garden and designed St Paul's Church
1632–38 worked at Somerset House
1634–38 employed at St Paul's Cathedral and designed the portico
1636 designed the Barber Surgeons Hall
c. 1636 concerned with the rebuilding of Wilton
1638 probably designed alterations to Kirby Hall
1647 or 1648 onward consulted over the restoration of Wilton
c. 1649 advised Pratt about building of Coleshill.

Nicholas Stone (1586–1647). Master mason and statuary. Founder of a dynasty of mason-statuaries, which included Nicholas Stone the younger, died 1647, John, another son who died in 1667, and had worked at Windsor; William de Keyser, his brother-in-law, who came over in 1621 and after 1653 and was still here in 1674, with Hendrik de Keyser the younger.

1606 met Hendrik de Keyser, the leading Flemish sculptor, in London, and returned with him to Antwerp
1613 married Hendrik's daughter and returned to England
1616 received first royal commission and in following years worked at Holyrood, St James's, Theobalds, Nonesuch, Somerset House, Greenwich, St Paul's Cathedral, Queen's Chapel, Windsor Castle
1619 appointed master mason at Banqueting Hall at Whitehall
1619 active as a monumental mason
1627 and 1630 Warden of the Company of Masons of the City of London
1633 and 1634 Master of the Masons' Company
designed the three gateways for the Oxford Botanic Garden and wing at Cornbury Park; also did unspecified work at Wilton
1638–39 worked for Christopher Hatton III, presumably at Kirby.

Balthasar Gerbier (1591/92–1667). Miniaturist, diplomat, art dealer and architect.

1616 came to England in the suite of the Dutch ambassador to James I and entered Buckingham's service, working as a miniaturist and assisting him with his collection, buildings and entertainments
1623 went to Spain with Prince Charles and Buckingham
1625 visited Paris and met Rubens
1626 designed the York House watergate
1628 entered Charles I's service after Buckingham's assassination
1631–41 acted as royal agent in Brussels
1638 knighted
1641 appointed Master of Ceremonies at Court
1643–49 out of England
1649 instituted the Bethnal Green Academy
1658–60 abroad
1660 (December) dismissed from Mastership of Ceremonies
1661 designed triumphal arches for Charles II's coronation
1662–65 designed Hamstead Marshall
1662 published *A Brief Discourse concerning the three chief principles of Magnificent Building*
1663 *Counsel and Advice to all Builders.*

Peter Mills (*c.* 1600–70). Builder and architect.

1613 apprenticed
1629 engaged his first apprentice
1639 designed and built terrace of houses in Great Queen Street, London
1643 appointed Bricklayer to the City of London
1649–50 and 1659–60 Master of the Tylers' and Bricklayers' Company
1653 or 1654 designed Thorpe Hall
1659 designed Hitcham Building at Pembroke College, Cambridge
1666 one of the Surveyors appointed by the City to supervise the rebuilding after the great fire.

John Webb (1611–72). Architect. Born in London of a Somerset family.

1628 became a pupil of Inigo Jones, by whom he was trained (there is no evidence of his having travelled abroad)
1636 earliest surviving drawings are of the theatre of the Barber Surgeons Hall. Probably prepared his first designs for Whitehall Palace about this time
1642 end of royal employment
1649 designs for Durham House, London, and for Wilton, where he was in charge of redecorations
1649 supplied details for Coleshill
1653 drawings for interior details at Drayton
1654–57 drawings and correspondence about work at Lamport

415. Sir Charles Cottrell, William Dobson, and Balthasar Gerbier, *by Dobson*.

416. Sir Roger Pratt, *by Lely*.

417. Sir Peter
Lely and Hugh
May *by Lely*.

418. Sir Christopher Wren *by Kneller*.

1654 made unexecuted designs for Belvoir and altered The Vyne
1655 published *The Most notable Antiquity called Stone-Heng* and worked at Chevening, probably designing interior decorations
1657–60 carried out decorations at Northumberland House
1658 designed Gunnersbury House
1661 probably designed Amesbury and made alterations to Queen's House, Greenwich
1663–68 designed and built King Charles II block at Greenwich.

Sir Roger Pratt (1620–85). Gentleman and architect. Grandson of a Norfolk squire.

1637 matriculated at Oxford
1639 entered Inner Temple
1640 his father died
1643–49 his inheritance enabled him to spend these years abroad, in France, Low Countries and Italy; studied architecture and met Evelyn in Rome
1649–50 designed Coleshill for his cousin, Sir George Pratt (completed in 1662)
1663–65 designed Kingston Lacy, Dorset, and Horseheath Hall, Cambridgeshire
1664–67 designed Clarendon House, London; consulted on repair of Old St Paul's Cathedral before the fire and after it appointed one of the Commissioners for the rebuilding
1667 inherited Ryston, in Norfolk, which he rebuilt 1669–72
1668 created the first architectural knight.

Hugh May (1622–84). Architect. Little is known of his early years, except that he was in the service of the 2nd Duke of Buckingham, probably in connection with his picture collection. Knew Lely and lived with him in Covent Garden in the early 1650s.

1650–51 visited Holland and again in 1656 with Lely
1660 appointed Paymaster of the Works at 2s. a day
1663–68 built the stables, and east front (completed 1677) and designed chapel (built 1677) at Cornbury
1664 designed Eltham Lodge
1665 designed Berkeley House, London; consulted about repair of Old St Paul's Cathedral
1666 appointed one of three royal Commissioners for the rebuilding of the City and acted as Surveyor of the Works during Denham's illness
1668 appointed Comptroller of the Royal Works, but passed over in 1669 when Surveyorship fell vacant, and Wren was appointed
1673 involved in building of Holme Lacy; Comptroller at Windsor Castle, which he restored and remodelled 1675–83
c. 1677–80 remodelled Cassiobury
1682–83 designed a house for Sir Stephen Fox at Chiswick.

William Samwell (1628–76). Gentleman and architect. Eldest son of Anthony Samwell of Dean's Yard, Westminster, and grandson of Sir William Samwell of Upton Hall, Northamptonshire. He may have designed Ashburnham House about 1660.

After 1660 purchased Manor of Watton, in Norfolk, where he lived till his death.
1668–70 worked on the King's House at Newmarket
1674 designed the west wing of Felbrigg Hall, Norfolk
1675–83 designed Eaton Hall, Cheshire. Also Grange Park, Hampshire.

Sir Christopher Wren (1632–1723). Scientist and architect. (A list of his chief works before 1685.) Born at East Knoyle, Wiltshire, son of a future Dean of Windsor, whose brother was successively Bishop of Hereford, Norwich and Ely; educated at Wadham College, Oxford, where he came in contact with the circle of scientists who were to form the Royal Society, of which he became a foundation member.

1650–51 took his B.A. degree
1653 became a Fellow of All Souls
1657 Professor of Astronomy at Gresham College, London
By 1660 displaying an interest in architecture
1661 Professor of Astronomy at Oxford
1663 designed chapel of Pembroke College, Cambridge; appointed to Commission for the repair of Old St Paul's Cathedral
1664 designed the Sheldonian Theatre, Oxford
1665 visited Paris, where he met Bernini (his sole journey abroad)
1666 appointed one of the Surveyors for rebuilding the City
1668 designed Chapel and Gallery of Emmanuel College, Cambridge; worked at Trinity College, Oxford
1669 appointed Surveyor of the King's Works
1671 designed St Stephen Walbrook
1673 knighted
1675 began work on St Paul's Cathedral
1676 designed Library, Trinity College, Cambridge
1682 designed Chelsea Hospital
1683 designed Winchester Palace.

William Winde (?–1722). Soldier and architect. (A list of his works before 1690.) Of Norfolk descent, but apparently born in Holland during his father's exile during the Civil War.

1660 returned to England and became a Gentleman Usher to Elizabeth of Bohemia
1662 elected an F.R.S.
1665–88 took over from Gerbier at Hamstead Marshall
1667 bought a cornet's commission in the King's Troop of the Royal Regiment of Horse
1676 became a lieutenant
1678 promoted captain
1680–91 designed alterations to Combe Abbey
1684–89 designed Powis House, Lincoln's Inn Fields
1684–85 possibly supplied the design for Belton
1685–90 altered Castle Bromwich Hall
Before 1687 designed Cliveden House, Buckinghamshire.

BIBLIOGRAPHY

A list of books and articles, except for those on specific houses and families, which appear in Part II.

G. P. V. Akrigg	*Jacobean Pageant* (1962).
Maurice Ashley	*England in the 17th Century* (1952).
J. Aubrey	*Brief Lives and Other Selected Writings* (Edited by Anthony Powell, 1949).
M. I. Batten	*The Architecture of Dr Robert Hooke, F.R.S.* Walpole Society, XXV (1937), p. 83.
G. W. Beard	*The Golden Age of English Craftsmen.* C.L. cxxxi, p. 650.
Sir Reginald Blomfield	*A History of Renaissance Architecture in England 1500–1800* (1897).
Anthony Blunt	*Art and Architecture in France 1500–1700* (1953).
	Calendar of State Papers Domestic.
	Calendar of Proceedings of the Committee for the Advance of Money.
	Calendar of Proceedings of the Committee for Compounding.
Colin Campbell	*Vitruvius Britannicus* (Vol. I, 1715; Vol. II, 1717; Vol. III, 1725).
E. F. Carritt	*A Calendar of British Taste 1600–1800.*
H. M. Colvin	*Biographical Dictionary of English Architects 1660–1840* (1954).
Edward Croft-Murray	*Decorative Painting in England.* Vol. I (1962).
Ralph Dutton	*The Age of Wren* (1951).
Ralph Edwards and L. G. G. Ramsey	*The Connoisseur Period Guides. The Stuart Period 1603–1714* (1957).
John Evelyn	*The Diary of John Evelyn.*
Celia Fiennes	*The Journeys of Celia Fiennes.* Ed. Christopher Morris (1947).
Prunella Fraser and John Harris	*Burlington-Devonshire Collection. Part I The Drawings of Inigo Jones, John Webb and Lord Burlington* (1960).
Katharine Fremantle	*The Baroque Town Hall of Amsterdam* (1959).
K. and C. French	*Devonshire Plasterwork.* Devon Assoc., Vol. 89, p. 124 (1957).
Mark Girouard	*The Smythson Collection.* Architectural History Vol. 5 (1962).
J. A. Gotch	*Early Renaissance Architecture in England* (1901).
	Inigo Jones (1928).
	The Old Halls and Manor Houses of Northamptonshire (1936).
Colonel Grant	*Old Houses by Old Painters.* C.L. cxi, p. 726.
David Green	*Grinling Gibbons: His Work as Carver and Statuary* (1964).
	Versatility of Grinling Gibbons. C.L. Annual 1962, p. 74.
Rupert Gunnis	*Dictionary of British Sculptors 1660–1851* (1953).
R. T. Gunther	*The Architecture of Sir Roger Pratt* (1928).
John Harris	*Inigo Jones and His French Sources* (Metropolitan Museum Bulletin, May, 1961).
	The Prideaux Collection of Topographical Drawings. (Architectural History, 7, 1964.)
Frank Jenkins	*Architect and Patron* (1961).
Margaret Jourdain	*English Decoration and Furniture of the Early Renaissance.*
	English Decorative Plasterwork of the Renaissance (1927).
J. Kip	*Britannia Illustrata* (1707).
	Nouveau Théâtre de la Grande Bretagne (1716).
Edith L. Klotz and Godfrey Davies	*The Wealth of Royalist Peers and Baronets During the Puritan Revolution.* English Historical Rev. Vol. 58, 1943, p. 217.
D. Knoop and G. P. Jones	*The London Mason in the 17th Century* (1935).
James Lees-Milne	*The Age of Inigo Jones* (1953).
Francis Lenygon	*Decoration in England From 1660 to 1770* (1914).
	Furniture in England 1660 to 1760.
Nathaniel Lloyd	*A History of English Brickwork* (1925).
P. Macquoid and R. Edwards	*Dictionary of English Furniture* (revised 1954).
David Mathew	*The Social Structure in Caroline England* (1948).
Eric Mercer	*English Art 1553–1625* (1962).
	Houses of the Gentry. Past and Present, V, 1954, ii.
W. Notestein	*The English People on the Eve of Colonization, 1603–1630* (1954).
Arthur Oswald	*Country Houses of Dorset* (2nd Edition, 1959).
	Country Houses of Kent (1933).
Nikolas Pevsner	*Buildings of England.* Various vols.
Rachel Poole	*Edward Pierce, The Sculptor.* Walpole Society, XI, 1923.
Albert Richardson	*17th-Century Buildings in Search of an Architect.* R.I.B.A., Vol. XL, 3rd series, p. 624, June 17, 1933.
Sacheverell Sitwell	*British Architects and Craftsmen* (1945).
W. L. Spiers	*The Note-Book and Account Book of Nicholas Stone.* Walpole Society, Vol. 7 (1919).
John Steegman	*The Artist and The Country House* (1949).
L. Stone	*The Inflation of Honours 1558–1641.* Past and Present, XIV, November, 1958, p. 45.
J. W. Stoye	*English Travellers Abroad 1604–67* (1952).
Arthur Stratton	*The English Interior* (1920).
Sir John Summerson	*Architecture in Britain 1530–1830* (1953 and 1963).
Joan Sumner-Smith	*The Italian Sources of Inigo Jones's Style.* Burlington Mag., XCIV, 1952, p. 200.

A. A. Tait — *Architecture of Robert Trollope*, C.L. cxxxviii, 390.

R. H. Tawney — *The Rise of The Gentry*. Econ. Hist. Rev., Vol. XI, No. 1, p. 1, 1941.

Avray Tipping — *English Homes*: Period III, Vol. I (1922, 2nd ed. 1928).
English Homes: Period IV, Vol. I (1920, 2nd ed. 1929).
Grinling Gibbons and The Woodwork of His Age 1648–1720 (1914).

George Vertue — *Notebooks*. Walpole Society, Vols. XVIII, XX, XXII, XXIV, XXVI, XXIX (index), XXX.

Geoffrey Webb — *Inigo Jones Tercentenary*. C.L. cxi, p. 1904.
Baroque Art. Proceedings of the British Academy, Vol. XXXIII (1947).

Margaret Whinney — *William Talman*. Journal of Warburg and Courtauld Institutes XVIII (1955) 121.
John Webb's Drawings for Whitehall Palace. Walpole Society, Vol. XXXI, p. 45.

Margaret Whinney and Oliver Millar — *English Art 1625–1714* (1957).

Hugh Ross Williamson — *Four Stuart Portraits* (1949).

Rudolph Wittkower — *Inigo Jones, Architect and Man of Letters*. R.I.B.A., LX (1953), p. 83.

Wren Society — *Volumes* (1924–43).

List of books and articles on individual houses and families described in the book, in alphabetical order of the houses. References to other houses will be found under the entries referring to them in the Appendix.

Ashdown House — C.L. xxxiii, 454.

Belton House — *Connoisseur*, April, 1963, by G. W. Beard.
See Tipping: Period IV. Vol. I.
C.L. iv, 368, 400; xiv, 614, 677; xxx, 308; cxxxvi, 562, 620, 700.

Coleshill — See Tipping: Period IV. Vol. I.
C.L. xv, 666; xlvi, 108, 138.

Combe Abbey — C.L. xxvi, 794, 840.

Cornbury — *Cornbury & The Forest of Wychwood*, by Vernon J. Watney (1910).
C.L. cviii, 922.

Denham Place — By John Harris. *Records of Bucks.*, XVI, Part III, 1957/58.
C.L. xviii, 702; lvii, 602, 642.

Dunsland — C.L. cxxviii, 18, 78.

Eltham Lodge — See Tipping: Period IV. Vol. I.
C.L. xix, 498, 882; xlvi, 168, 210.

Forde Abbey — C.L. vii, 368; xxvi, 18, 54; cxxxiii, 540, 596, 656, 714.

Groombridge Place — C.L. ii, 350; xii, 625, 656; xiv, 400; cxviii, 1376, 1480, 1524.

Ham House — *Ham House*, by Ralph Edwards & Peter Ward-Jackson (1951).
See Tipping: Period IV. Vol. I.
C.L. vi, 144; xlvii, 372, 404, 410, 440, 447; lxviii, 598, 754; ciii, 226.

Hamstead Marshall — C.L. xxxiii, 454.

Lamport Hall — See *Some Newly Found Drawings and Letters of John Webb*, by J. A. Gotch. R.I.B.A., XXVIII, 565 (1921).
Sir Gyles Isham. *Northants. Past & Present*, 1948.
See *Sir Thomas Isham: An English Collector in Rome*, by Gerald Burdon. *Italian Studies* XV. 1960.
Sir Gyles Isham. Northants. Archit. and Arch. Society, LVII, 13.
See *Isham-Duppa Correspondence*, by Sir Gyles Isham. Northants. Record Society, XVII.
C.L. iii, 518; xlix, 672; cxii, 932, 1022, 1106.

The Old Bishop's Palace, Lichfield — C.L. cxvi, 2312.

Longnor Hall — See Tipping: Period IV. Vol. I.
C.L. xli, 156; cxxv, 328, 392.

Nether Lypiatt — C.L. lxxv, 512, 540.

Queen's House — By C. H. Chettle. *Survey of London*, 14th monograph.
C.L. lxxxi, 458, 484.

Ramsbury — C.L. xxii, 198; xlvii, 432, 468; cxxx, 1376, 1526, 1580.

Raynham Hall — *The Building of Raynham Hall* by H. L. Bradfer-Lawrence. *Norfolk Archaeology*, XXIV, 1929, p. 93.
R. Charles Lines. *Connoisseur Year Book* 1955.
John Harris. *Archaeological Journal* CXVIII.
C.L. xxiv, 90; lviii, 742, 782.

Stoke Park — C.L. cxiv, 280.

Sudbury — C.L. xvii, 486; lxxvii, 622, 650, 682.

Thorpe Hall — A. W. Hakewill, 1852.
Sir Gyles Isham. *Northants. Antiquarian Society*. Vol. LXII, p. 37.
See Tipping: Period IV. Vol. I.
The Architect of Thorpe Hall, by H. M. Colvin. C.L. cxi, 1732.
C.L. xvi, 234; xlvi, 300, 330, 364.

Tyttenhanger — See Tipping: Period IV. Vol. I.
C.L. xviii, 594; xlvi, 424, 454.

Wilton — *The South Front of Wilton House*, by H. M. Colvin. *Arch. Journal*, CXI, 181 (1954).
Isaac de Caux & the South Front of Wilton House, by A. A. Tait. *Burlington Mag.*, February, 1964.
Aubrey. Notes for *Natural History of Wiltshire*.
C.L. iv, 304; xi, 464; xv, 774; xcv, 112, 156; cxxxiii, 1044, 1109, 1176; cxxxiv, 206, 264, 314.

A list of principal architectural books published before 1685 and probably known in England.

Alberti, L. B. — *De re aedificatoria* (Florence, 1550); French, 1512, 1553.

Barbet — *Livre d'Architecture, d'Autels, et de Cheminées* (1633).

Blume, Hans — *Quinque Columnarum* (Zurich, 1550).

Campen, Jacob van — *Afbeelding van't Stadt-Huys van Amsterdam* (1664–68).

Du Cerceau, J. Androuet — *Livre d'architectura* (1559). *Le Premier Volume Des plus excellents Bastiments de France* (1576).

Collot, Pierre — *Pièces d'Architectura ou sont comprises plusieurs sortes de cheminées, portes* etc. (Paris, 1633).

Dietterlin, Wendel — *Architectura von Ausstheilung Symmetrie und Proportion der fünff seulen,* etc. (1598).

Francart, Jacques — *Premier Livre d'architecture* (Brussels, 1616).

Francine, A. — *A New Book of Architecture Wherein is Represented Forty Figures of Gates and Arches Triumphant* (English Edition, 1669).

Freart, R. — *Parallele de l'architecture antique et de la moderne* (1650) (Evelyn's translation 1664).

Gerbier, B. — *A Brief discourse concerning the three chief principles of magnificent building* (1662). *Counsel and advise to all builders . . .* (1663).

Hendrik de Keyser and Cornelis Danckerts — *Architectura Moderna* (1631).

Marot, Jean — (Le Grand Marot): *L'Architecture francoise ou recueil des plans, . . . batis dans Paris et ses environs* (Paris, c. 1670). (Le Petit Marot): *Recueil des plans, profils et élévations* (1660–70).

Le Muet, P. — *Manière de bien bâtir pour touttes sortes de personnes* (1623). *Augmentations de nouveaux Bastimens* (1647) (Translated into English, 1670, as *The Art of Fair Building*).

de l'Orme, Philibert — *Le Premier Tome de l'Architecture* (1567).

Palladio, Andrea — *I Quattro Libri dell'Architettura* (Venice, 1570).

Post, P. — *Les Ouvrages d'architecture ordonnez par Peter Post* (1715).

Quellin, Hubertus — *Van de voornaermste statven ende ciraten, vant Konstryck Stadhuys van Amsterredam* (Amsterdam, 1665–69).

Rubens, P. P. — *Palazzi di Genova* (Antwerp, 1622).

Scamozzi, V. — *L'Idea della architettura universale di V-S* (Venice, 1615).

Serlio, S. — *Tutte l'Opere d'Architettura et Prospetiva* (Venice, 1584) (Peake, 1611).

Shute, John — *The First and Chief Grounds of Architecture* (1563).

Vignola — *La Regola delli Cinque Ordini d'Architettura* (Venice, 1562).

Vingboons, P. — *Afbeedsels der voornamste Gebouwen* (Amsterdam, Vol. I, 1648; Vol. II, 1674).

Vitruvius — Barbaro's edition *Dieci libri dell' architettura di M. Vitruvio* (Venice, 1567).

Wotton, H. — *The Elements of Architecture* (1624).

INDEX

The figures in italics are plate numbers